TOWARD INSTRUCTIONAL ACCOUNTABILITY

A PRACTICAL GUIDE TO EDUCATIONAL CHANGE

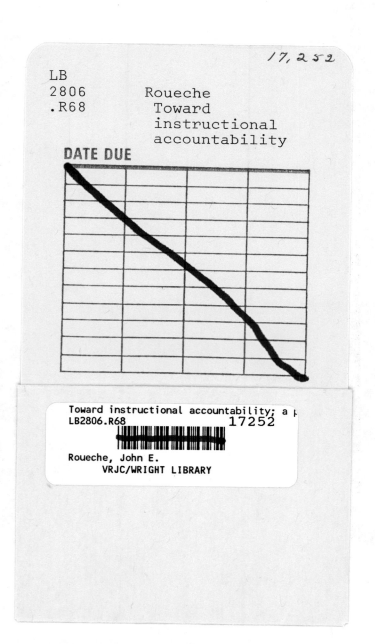

TOWARD INSTRUCTIONAL ACCOUNTABILITY

A PRACTICAL GUIDE TO EDUCATIONAL CHANGE

John E. Roueche
The University of Texas at Austin
Austin, Texas

Barton R. Herrscher
Mitchell College
Statesville, North Carolina

Westinghouse Learning Press
Division of Westinghouse Learning Corporation

Toward Instructional Accountability
A Practical Guide to Educational Change

Text set in 10 point Times Roman, with
display lines in Helvetica by Holmes
Composition Service, San Jose,
California

Design and cover by Joseph di Chiarro,
Palo Alto, California

Cover photo: Jim Goldberg,
San Francisco, California

Development and production by
Westinghouse Learning Press,
Palo Alto, California

Printed and bound by R. R. Donnelley
& Sons

Library of Congress
Catalog Card Number: 73-5256

Westinghouse Learning Press
Palo Alto, California 94304

Division of Westinghouse Learning Corporation
New York, New York 10017

Printed in the United States of America

1 2 3 4 5 6 7 8 9 10 77 76 75 74 73

1 "The Future of Learning: Into the Twenty-first Century," by John I. Goodlad. Excerpted from a paper prepared for the White House Conference on Children, 1970.

2 "A Systematic Approach to Instruction," by Barton R. Herrscher. Reprinted from a revised version of Chapter 2 of *Implementing Innovative Instruction,* by permission of the author and the publisher, ArChem Company.

3 "Minicourses—The Style of the Future?" by S. N. Postlethwait and James D. Russell. Reprinted by permission of the authors and the Commission on Undergraduate Education in the Biological Sciences.

"Practical Approaches to Individualizing Instruction," by Philip G. Kapfer. Reprinted from *Educational Screen and Audiovisual Guide* (now *Audiovisual Guide: The Learning Media Magazine*), vol. 47, no. 5, 1968, pp. 1–3, by permission of the author and Trade Periodicals, Inc.

4 "Ten Untenable Assumptions of College Instruction," by Robert Glaser. Reprinted from *Educational Record,* vol. 49, Spring 1968, by permission of the author and the publisher.

"Alternatives to the Invalid Assumptions of Current Educational Practice," by Barton R. Herrscher. Reprinted from *Revista/Review Interamericana,* vol. 2, no. 1, Spring 1972, by permission of the author and the publisher.

5 "Defining Instructional Objectives," by Arthur M. Cohen. Reprinted from *Systems Approaches to Curriculum and Instruction in the Open Door College,* Occasional Report No. 9 from the UCLA Junior College Leadership Program, 1967, pp. 1–9, by permission of the author and the Graduate School of Education, UCLA.

"The Meaning of a College Education," by Paul Dressel. Reprinted from the *Journal of Higher Education,* vol. 39, December 1968, pp. 481–489. Copyright © 1968 by the Ohio State University Press and reprinted with its permission.

6 "Are Children Born Unequal?" by William H. Boyer and Paul Walsh. Reprinted from *Saturday Review,* 19 October 1968, pp. 61–63, 77–79, by permission of the authors and the publisher.

"The Teacher As Pygmalion: Comments on the Psychology of Expectation," by Peter Gumpert and Carol Milligan. Reprinted from *The Urban Review* (a publication of the Center for Urban Education), vol. 3, no. 3, September 1968, pp. 21–25, by permission of the authors and the publisher.

7 "Learning for Mastery," by Benjamin S. Bloom. Reprinted from *Evaluation Comment* (a publication of the Center for the Study of Education, UCLA), vol. 1, no. 2, May 1968, pp. 1–11.

8 "The Evaluation of Instruction: Cause-and-Effect Relations in Naturalistic Data," by M. C. Wittrock. Reprinted from *Evaluation Comment,* vol. 1, no. 4, May 1969, pp. 1–7.

"Implications of Criterion-Referenced Measurement," by W. James Popham and T. R. Husek. Reprinted from *Journal of Educational Measurement,* vol. 6, no. 1, 1969, pp. 1–9, by permission of W. James Popham and the publisher.

"Evaluating Tests in Terms of the Information They Provide," by Stephen Klein. Reprinted from *Evaluation Comment,* vol. 2, no. 2, June 1970, pp. 1–6.

"Different Kinds of Evaluation and Their Implications for Test Development," by T. R. Husek. Reprinted from *Evaluation Comment,* vol. 2, no. 1, October 1969, pp. 1–3.

Source Notes

9 "Evaluation for the Improvement of Instructional Programs: Some Practical Steps," by Garth Sorenson. Reprinted from *Evaluation Comment*, vol. 2, no. 4, January 1971, pp. 1–5.

"Antidote to a School Scandal," by John D. McNeil. Reprinted from *The Educational Forum*, vol. 31, no. 1, November 1966, pp. 69–77, by permission of Kappa Delta Pi, an Honor Society in Education, the author and the publisher.

"A New Role in Education: The Evaluator," by Garth Sorenson. Reprinted from *Evaluation Comment*, vol. 1, no. 1, January 1968, pp. 1–4.

"Teacher Evaluation: Toward Improving Instruction," by Marcia A. Boyer. Reprinted from *Junior College Research Review*, vol. 4, no. 5, January 1970, pp. 1–3, by permission of the author and the American Association of Junior Colleges.

10 "Accountability Defined," by Marvin C. Alkin. Reprinted from *Evaluation Comment*, vol. 3, no. 3, May 1972, pp. 1–5.

"Accountability for Student Learning," by John E. Roueche. Reprinted from *Revista/ Review Interamericana*, vol. 2, no. 1, Spring 1972, pp. 6–13, by permission of the author and the publisher.

Preservice training and in-service development of teachers in an age of scientific acceleration and technological advance presents complex problems for educators. In higher education particularly, the obsolescence of skills, knowledge, and competencies in teaching dictates the need for continuous staff development. Recent technological advancements have sharpened the awareness of and the need for educational innovations that contribute to effective teaching.

The underlying theme of *Toward Instructional Accountability: A Practical Guide to Educational Change* is that superior and innovative instruction that motivates student learning can shape institutional identity. The editors have selected readings that advocate a systematic approach to instruction that allows instructors to meet the diverse needs of student bodies that are becoming increasingly heterogeneous at the upper levels. The salient feature of such an approach is the emphasis placed on validated means of promoting teaching effectiveness in terms of predictable and measurable evidence of student learning. Responsibility for successful learning is placed on both the teacher and the student.

The purpose of this book is to generate the development of an instructional approach that is adaptable to a broad spectrum of subject matter. This approach should demonstrably improve teacher–student interaction by providing a sense of direction, location, and progress on the learning continuum. The approach also emphasizes the need for maximum flexibility in relating instructional media to the diverse learning capabilities of college students.

This book is designed to assist the reader in developing the skills, attitudes, and knowledge that are necessary for functioning effectively as teacher, counselor, or administrator. Whether the reader is currently in one of these positions or expects to be, this book can serve as a self-contained course in instructional improvement. The reader needs no prerequisites to profit from *Toward Instructional Accountability;* ample introduction to the subject and an integrated overview are provided.

Each unit of the book contains a rationale or introductory statement, a set of objectives specifying the competencies that can be derived from thoughtful study of the topic, and carefully selected readings that represent incisive and definitive treatment of the area being considered. Such organization helps the reader to become aware of precisely what he is expected to learn and permits him to proceed at his own pace in the process of learning. When the reader has achieved the objectives, he has completed the unit and can move on.

Although objectives specify both cognitive or affective learning to be attained, the actual behavior or performance for demonstrating mastery is

Preface

not specified. The conditions of the learning situation must be taken into consideration in determining the behavioral options. The learner might write, verbalize in a group, think about, or demonstrate in actual practice what the objective calls for. For example, to show attainment of an objective calling for the formulation of a case for or against a certain educational practice, a student might demonstrate his learning in an essay, a formal debate, or a group discussion—or he might simply process the information by careful thought. Participants in any learning situation where this book is used should be encouraged to suggest alternate forms of assessment that demonstrate that learning has taken place.

John E. Roueche

University of Texas at Austin
Austin, Texas

Barton R. Herrscher

Mitchell College
Statesville, North Carolina

Contents

Author

"The Future of Learning: Into the Twenty-first Century" has been excerpted from a paper prepared for the White House Conference on Children by a group headed by Dr. John I. Goodlad, Dean of the Graduate School of Education at the University of California, Los Angeles.

1 A Rationale for Educational Change

Educational change is desperately needed because so many people in this country have been denied the right to learn. Among the many reasons for this denial, one stands out—our mindless adherence to unproductive teaching concepts and practices. Change is absolutely essential.

After completing this unit, you should be able to

1 develop a case in support of the need for educational change

2 defend the viewpoint that education of the future will feature learning, not as a means to some end, but rather as an end in itself

3 outline the role of instructional technology in realizing the goals of education in the 21st century

4 contrast education as it exists today with your conception of education in the future

5 give evidence of a favorable attitude toward educational change as a concept, and as a goal to strive for, by listing specific changes you would adopt in your own area of responsibility

In a nation that speaks of inalienable rights, the right to learn must be paramount. Yet that right, in its full meaning, has been denied to many in this nation. It has been denied because of color, religion, poverty, infirmity, and residence. And it has been denied because of our often mindless adherence to many unproductive teaching concepts and practices.

The right to learn is the goal we seek for the 21st century. We want for our children a range of learning opportunities as broad as the unknown range of their talents. We want a learning environment that nurtures those talents. We want our children to know themselves and, secure in that knowledge, to open themselves to others. We want them to have freedom, and the order, justice, and peace that the preservation of freedom demands....

What and How to Learn. Schools and teachers have been with us for so long that they have often been equated with education and, worse, with learning. Yet the infant learns to walk and to talk, to trust and to distrust; he learns fear and love and hate—all without benefit of school. By the age of five, the child has sat before a television set for at least the number of hours he will spend in the first three grades of school. Yet we still equate learning with school.

Although we believed, until recently, that school was the most powerful part of the learning environment, we know now that it is not.

But school is still the formal instrument created for the explicit task of educating our young, and in many ways it is the most important educator. Its answers to the questions of what and how to learn have both reflected national strengths and weaknesses and contributed to their formation.

The world has become increasingly complicated by technological advances and challenged by inequities in the human condition, all unfolding against the backdrop of an unknowable future.

As preparation for coping with these uncertainties, much of the subject matter of today's learning is unrealistically narrow and antiseptic. Those who have selected and prescribed it have done so through the biases of their Western culture, looking more to the past than to the future. For example, by denying to the young the richness of African, Asiatic, or Latin American heritages, to say nothing of the exciting variations of our own

The Future of Learning

Into the Twenty-first Century

John I. Goodlad

black and brown and yellow and red cultures, we have too often ignored and implicitly denigrated other cultures at an inestimable cost to all our children.

The full extent of the denial of the right to learn is even greater, however, for we tend to paint only pretty pictures of life, out of deference, supposedly, to the tenderness of children. In so doing, we magnify our hypocrisy for all to see. Even the youngest of our offspring soon become aware that we wage war while talking peace, that children go hungry in the richest land on the face of the earth, that even leaders cheat and lie. They come to understand that what we say and what we do are very different things. They see with the uncluttered vision of children the gap between rhetoric and reality.

What is to be learned is refined by our filtering system until, too often, it has little power to grip the learner and thus defrauds or cheats him. From the truly exciting possibilities of a culture—or conscience—embracing mankind, we slide to the homogenized "adventures" of Dick and Jane and a field trip to the supermarket.

With regard to the "how" of learning, we have only begun to question the outworn notion that certain subjects or concepts are to be learned by all individuals at successive stages of growth at stipulated times in sterile places. Reading is for the first grade, long division for the fourth, and fractions for the fifth and sixth. All of this takes place between the hours of nine and three in a big box divided into cells. Preschool prepares for adjustment to the first box, and six or seven years in that box prepares for adjustment to a next larger box.

In this lockstep, as in so many other ways, we teach that each phase of life is instrumental to the next rather than of ultimate value in itself. We see the man we want the child to become rather than the child seeking to become himself. In the words of Hannah Arendt, "Man sees wood in every tree."

Toward Better Schools.   This is the winter of our educational discontent. Until recently, we believed that we had only to provide some new subject matter here, inject a heavier dose of phonics there, or tighten the discipline a little, to improve both the system and society. Better schools (defined in largely quantitative terms) would mean more jobs, a brisker economy, safer cities, and more aware, dedicated citizens. Or so we thought. Dwindling confidence in these relationships reflects both declining public confidence in the schools and the tenacity with which we cling to the "learning equals school" equation. Painfully, we are coming to realize that grades predict grades, that success in school begets success in more school but is no guarantee of good workers, committed citizens, happy mothers and fathers, or compassionate human beings.

The schools have been poked and probed, judged and weighed—and found wanting. Whereas for many years they fulfilled brilliantly the primary purpose for which they were founded—the creation of one nation out of millions of immigrants—recent decades brought them new kinds of clientele whose needs could not be met with the formulas and procedures that had been used previously.

For a brief span of years, we believed that serious problems existed only in the schools of our great cities. Increasingly we have come to understand that suburban and, to an even greater degree, rural schools do not assure the diet or provide the vitality our children deserve. Even the middle-class school around the corner reveals ragged edges surrounding a soft center. The failures of our schools are apparent in dropout rates, in barely minimal learning on the part of many who do remain in school, and in growing alienation among the young of all colors and classes.

At the root of the problem is an implicit denial of diversity. The schools have become great sorting machines, labeling and certifying those who presumably will be winners and losers as adults. The winners are disproportionately white and affluent. The losers, too often, are poor and brown or black or red.

But many of the winners are losers, too. For they are shaped, directed, and judged according to a narrow conception of what is right and proper. This process begins very early; the environment of expectations, rewards, and punishments is established before mother and child leave the hospital. And in the home, infants are encouraged in their efforts to walk and talk, but their responses to sound, color, and smell are ignored or stifled. This process of channeling energy and talent is refined and perfected in the schools through a network of expectations, rules, grades, required subjects, and rewards for what is wanted and the subtle extinction of the great range of talents and achievements which are not wanted.

Do we paint an unduly dark picture? Perhaps, for sunny islands of contrasting practice are known to all of us. But study and reflection reveal that the contrasting examples are, indeed, islands in an otherwise gray sea. Those few must be tended and nurtured because of both their precious rarity and their potentiality for guiding change.

Massive Task of Change. A massive task of change lies ahead. We cannot take joy from these islands of success while we kill at home and abroad. We cannot point pridefully at those who have "made it" while half of us believe that life has passed us by. We cannot rejoice with our sons and daughters when their brothers and sisters do not graduate with them. We cannot congratulate ourselves on our talents when half of our talents have withered or died.

The inflated rhetoric we have used in describing our accomplishments far exceeds their nature and extent. Among many of our people there is a sense of outrage induced by the discrepancy between what is and what could be. Thankfully, however, not all our energies are used up in anger. We have more than a little hope that a new era can be both described and created. At the core of this hope is a fresh awareness of children: of their intrinsic rather than instrumental value, of their ability to learn, and of the kind of learning they could and should have as we look to the 21st century.

Other generations believed that they had the luxury of preparing their children to live in a society similar to their own. The primary—although seldom attained—aim of education was thus to transmit the existing culture to the young. Ours is the first generation to have achieved the Socratic wisdom of knowing that we do not know the world of the year 2000, in which our children will live. Although it is only 30 years in the future, we cannot truly envisage it and the range of demands it will impose on 21st-century man.

Requirements for the 21st Century. To speak, as we have in the past, of giving our young the "tools" with which to survive, to speak of techniques and "subjects" as the essential components of education, is to speak of trivialities. And, it is to send our children unequipped into the unknowable.

All that we can predict with certainty is that the central issue of the 21st century, as it is of this one, will be the struggle to assert truly human values and to achieve their ascendancy in a mass, technological society. It will be the struggle to place man in a healthy relationship with his natural environment; to place him in command of, rather than subservient to, the wondrous technology he is creating; and to give him the breadth and depth of understanding which can result in the formation of a world culture, embracing and nurturing within its transcending characteristics the diverse cultures of today's world.

We ask first, then, not what kind of education we want to provide but what kind of human being we want to emerge. What would we have 21st-century man be?

We would have him be a man with a strong sense of himself and his own humanness, with awareness of his thoughts and feelings, with the capacity to feel and express love and joy and to recognize tragedy and feel grief. We would have him be a man who, with a strong and realistic sense of his own worth, is able to relate openly with others, to cooperate effectively with them toward common ends, and to view mankind as one while respecting diversity and difference. We would want him to be a being who, even while very young, somehow senses that he has it within himself to become more than he now is, that he has the capacity for lifelong spiritual and intellectual growth. We would want him to cherish that vision of the man he is capable of becoming and to cherish the development of the same potentiality in others.

The education of this kind of human being is necessarily an enabling process rather than an instructional process. It requires opening the whole of the world to the learner and giving him easy access to that world. This implies enormous respect for the child's capacity to learn, and with the granting of respect goes, by implication, the granting of freedom.

Learning in the Year 2000

When we look to education in the century to come, we see learning not as a means to some end but as an end in itself. Education will not be an imitation of life but life examined and enjoyed. A prescribed age for beginning to learn—or for ceasing to learn—will be meaningless. So will age as a criterion for determining what needs to be learned. And so will the standard school day and the standard academic year.

Diffused Learning Environment. Compulsory education—or compulsory attendance, as it might better be called—will be a thing of the past. School as we now know it will have been replaced by a diffused learning environment involving homes, parks, public buildings, museums, business offices, guidance centers. Many such resources that are now unendorsed, unofficial, unrecognized, unstructured, or unsupervised—and unused—will be endorsed and made fully available for learning. There will be successors to our present schools, places designed for people to gather for purposes of learning things together.

The mere availability of a broad range of options will signify what we believe will be an important, and essential, change in our national value system. The word *success* will have been redefined, and a far wider range of choices—of study, of taste, of career, of "life style"—will be legitimized and seen as praiseworthy. Little boys will not be made to feel that they must grow up to be aggressive, or even affluent, men. Little girls will not need to feel that domesticity is the necessary end-all and be-all of existence. A career in science will not have higher status than a career in the creative arts. We will, in short, give substance to our longstanding but never fulfilled commitment to honor and develop the entire range of human talent.

Effects of Technology. Modern technology will help us realize our goals. The profound significance of the computer, when properly used in learning, is that it introduces an entirely new source of energy into the educational process. It is energy which is not affected by the night before, by viruses, or by unmanageable children. Subjects missed this year can be picked up next year. Single subjects can be pursued intensively for periods of time governed only by the whim of the learner. The 50-year-old need not humble himself by going back to school with 12-year-olds to get what he wants. He may go directly to the energy system, which is not aware of age, color, place of birth, or time of day.

It is possible that advanced technology will return the family to the center of the stage as the basic learning unit. Each home could become a school, in effect, via an electronic console connected to a central computer system in a learning hub, a videotape and microfilm library regulated by a computer, and a national educational television network. Whether at home or elsewhere, each student, of whatever age, will have at the touch of a button access to a comprehensive "learning package," including printed lessons, experiments to be performed, recorded information, videotaped lectures, and films.

Role of Schools. The moment so much teaching energy is made available throughout the 24-hour span of the day to all individuals at any place, school need no longer be what we have known it to be. It may then be used for latent and other functions we have not until now fully recognized. It will be the place where human beings come together, not for the formalities of learning subject matter, but for the higher literacy that goes far beyond reading, writing, and arithmetic.

And so the schools of the 21st century, by whatever name they are known, will continue to play a major role in advancing insight and knowledge. But these "school learnings" will center more closely on developing man's ability to know himself and to relate to others. We expect that students will come together to speak and to listen, but in a greater variety of ways than they now do in schools. Heavier stress will be laid on learning different forms of rationality and logic and on ways to deal with crisis and conflict. The individual will be helped to develop a greater consciousness of his thoughts and feelings, so that he may feel and experience life and at the same time stand outside his immediate experience, so to speak. For 21st-century man would be a sentient being with both the freedom that comes from understanding and the accompanying control of impulse. The schools of the 21st century will have as part of their "curriculum" helping the young to understand their own antecedents, as they do today, but in infinitely more direct and vital ways.

Function of Teachers. In such an educational world, everyone will be from time to time both teacher and learner, but there will still be great need for teachers who, for the first time, will be free to engage in truly human tasks. No longer will they need to function as ineffective machines imparting "facts" by rote, since real machines will have taken over that function.

Some will spend many hours preparing a single lesson, to be viewed by thousands or even millions of individuals of every age. Others will evaluate such instructional programs. Some will staff counseling centers. Others will be engaging with groups of all ages in dialog designed to enhance human communication and understanding. The freedom and sense of potency we want for our children will be experienced, at long last, by their teachers. The entire enterprise will be directed toward increasing the freedom and the power of each individual to shape himself, to live at ease in his community, and in doing both to experience self-fulfillment.

We have sketched a kind of learning Utopia. Achieving it will not be easy. In fact, without massive, thoughtful, social reconstruction, we will not get

From Today into Tomorrow: Recommendations

there at all. To stand aside—unconcerned, uncommitted, and unresolved —may very well be to assure no 21st century, least of all our Utopia.

We must actively aim toward a future in which the promise of American public education is truly fulfilled; when quality education, broadly conceived, is accessible to every American of every age and in every walk of life. We believe that the following three recommendations summarize what must be done if we are to move toward our Utopia.

Reordering National Priorities. *We recommend that national priorities be reordered, with spending of money, materials, and energy for war and defense subordinated to wars against racism, poverty, and pollution, and action on behalf of education.*

Department of Education. *We recommend that a Department of Education, with full Cabinet status, be established and backed by a National Institute of Education in addition to the present United States Office of Education.* The Department of Education shall contribute significantly to the reordering of national priorities, establish national educational policies, and promote constructive change in educational practice, all directed toward the full development of individual potential and the welfare of our society.

The immediate charge to this Department is

1. provision of resources for salvaging the growing number of school districts now on the verge of financial collapse
2. comprehensive implementation of what we now know to be quality education
3. increased educational experimentation through a wide variety of educational institutions, with public accountability

We make our recommendations in light of our conviction that school is a concept, not a place, that schooling and education are not synonymous.

Continuing Dialog Culminating in our 200th Birthday. *We recommend that a continuing dialog on our findings and conclusions be commenced now, to be held in towns and cities throughout the land, and culminating in the celebration of our 200th birthday as a nation with learning as the theme.*

Moral and Financial Commitment. The first step toward implementing these three recommendations is moral commitment. Like all moral commitments, it must be backed by resources and action. There is much talk about the need to reorder national priorities. We add our voices to the millions seeking life-giving rather than death-dealing, conservation rather than the wanton pillaging of our resources, and the freeing and nurturing of the human spirit rather than the proliferation and worship of material objects. We sound a special call for full and genuine commitment to the right to learn.

The signal announcing this commitment will be the long-awaited injection of large-scale government funds into learning: for encouraging experimentation in the schools we have, for the creation of schools specifically charged with experimentation, and for transcending the schools by bringing new learnings into them and by taking boys and girls to the whole range of resources outside of them. For a time, at least, we must infuse these funds as though we were at war—because, of course, we are at war: with ignorance, prejudice, injustice, intolerance, and all those forces crippling and restricting young and old alike.

Reform in the Schools. The first phase of reconstruction pertains to the schools we have. Supposedly, the decade of the sixties was one of school reform: in the curriculum, in the organization of school and classroom, and in instruction. But recent studies reveal that the appearance of change far outruns the actuality of change. Put simply, the list of unfinished business is formidable.

In spite of emphasis on the need for identifying goals, few schools have a clear sense of direction. In spite of the obvious futility of "teaching" the world's knowledge, schools still emphasize the learning of facts rather than how to learn. In spite of our golden era of instructional materials and children's literature, the textbook is still the prime medium of instruction. In spite of growing knowledge about individual differences in learning, what children are to learn is still laid out by grades, years, months, and even days. In spite of increased insight into how learning occurs, teaching is still largely telling and questioning. In a diverse, complex society, our schools demonstrate almost monolithic conformity and enormous resistance to change. Close scrutiny reveals a deep-seated inability to come to grips with the problems those in the schools say they have.

The top agenda item, then, in seeking to enhance learning in the seventies is unshackling the schools. The process must begin by decentralizing authority and responsibility for instructional decision making to individual schools. Simply dividing large school districts into smaller districts is not the answer. Schools, like individuals, are different in size, problems, clientele, types of communities served, and the like. They must create programs appropriate to their local circumstances, encouraged and supported in the diversity such a process necessarily entails.

Experimental Schools. Many schools are not ready to take quick advantage of sudden freedoms. Too long fettered by the larger system, their staffs will be timid and uncertain. *We recommend, therefore, that substantial government funds be allocated for the deliberate development of schools, accountable to the public, whose sole reason for being is experimental.* Designed for purposes of providing alternatives, such schools could provide options in the community and thus would attract more supportive parent groups. In time, such schools would provide models for replication in networks of cooperating schools seeking to learn from each other.

Such schools need not arise solely within "the system." We are at a time in history when the need to break out of established patterns is critical. We need alternatives wherever we can find them. Some of the "free" schools springing up around the country offer diversity and should be encouraged to the point where their practices truly reflect their underlying philosophies.

We urge that support be given to schools endeavoring to abolish grade levels, develop new evaluation procedures, use the full range of community resources for learning, automate certain kinds of learning, explore instructional techniques for developing self-awareness and creative thinking, reschedule the school year, and more. Most of all, we urge that substantial financial support be given to schools seeking to redesign the entire learning environment, from the curriculum through the structure of the school to completely new instructional procedures.

Early Childhood Learning. Especially needed are well-developed models of early learning. We know now that the first five years of life largely determine the characteristics of the young adult. And yet we fail these years shamefully through neglect, through narrow, thoughtless shaping, or through erratic shifts from too little concern to too much concern. . . . We believe that it is impossible to provide the kind of learning environment we envisage in the absence of coherent, well-planned, and integrated health services to children from birth on. We believe also that early childhood centers are appropriate places for mothers-to-be to receive prenatal medical care and education and we urge their widespread establishment. There is ample evidence that commercial interests exploit the undiscriminating drive of many Americans to see to it that their children are well prepared for school. There also is abundant evidence that millions of parents fail to provide their children with the guidance, support, and social and intellectual skills they need for productive independence.

Two successive governments have promised and failed to deliver on a vast effort for expansion and improvement in the education of young children. A National Laboratory in Early Childhood Education suffered a crippled birth under one administration and is now starving to death under another. *We need research on the developmental processes of the young: educational programs based on what we now know; thousands of adequately prepared teachers to staff nursery and play schools; and exemplary models of programs stressing cognitive, aesthetic, motor, and affective development.*

Teacher Education. High on our list of "old business" is the overhaul of teacher education from top to bottom. The continuing debate over the value of "methods" courses, whether to have more or fewer of them, and how to regulate teacher education by legislative fiat only reveals the poverty of our approaches to the problem. Shuffling courses about is not the answer. Required are change strategies which take account of the fact that preservice teacher education, in-service teacher education, and the schools themselves are dependent, interrelated, and interacting components of one social system, albeit a malfunctioning one.

It becomes apparent, therefore, that financial resources must be directed toward those strategies that link schools seeking to change with teacher-education institutions seeking to shake out of established patterns. In brief, the teacher for tomorrow's learning must be prepared in school settings endeavoring to create a new kind of tomorrow. Most of today's teachers are prepared for yesterday's schools.

The tasks for the seventies may not have the heady appeal of the slogans for the sixties but they have a meaty substance about them, an "action" appeal for students, teachers, parents, private foundations, and all levels of government. Those who prefer doing to talking should find challenge enough in simultaneously redesigning the schools we have, creating alternative models, and arranging for teachers to find their role in these new settings for learning.

Electronic Education. But we need not wait for the 1980s to get a good start on other components of our visions for the year 2000. In fact, some roots are already taking hold. School, however reformed, is but one of the child's resources for learning. He spends more time and perhaps learns more, for better or for worse, in the electronic embrace of another—television. Television, in turn, is but one of several powerful teachers of electronic genre. The computer has even greater potential because of its ability to coordinate an array of devices: filmed or videotaped cartridges, records, graphic symbols, paper printouts, and responsive surfaces—devices for sight, sound, touch, and even smell.

We must stop talking about the possibilities of electronic educational aids and engage in experimentation on a much broader scale. To date, educational television has teetered on the brink of disaster, its limp fare failing to compete with commercial products, especially advertising. "Sesame Street" demonstrates vigorously that this need not be. It also demonstrates that successful use of television for desirable learning by children requires substantial financial backing for air time, for production, for evaluation, and especially for research into what constitutes appropriate subject matter. Ten years from now, the initial use of this instrument to teach children numbers and the alphabet will appear primitive indeed.

One of the major tasks involved in bringing electronics productively into children's learning involves a kind of research; namely, determining appropriate roles for human and machine teachers. The cant of audiovisual education insists that equipment be only an extension of human teachers. For computers, for example, to be mere extra arms of human teachers is to cripple both. We must recognize the fact that electronic devices constitute a new kind of instructional energy that is indefatigable, relatively immune to changes in the weather, and contemptuous of time of day or day of week. The human teacher, on the other hand, is sharply limited in energy pattern, highly susceptible to chills, immobile in times of flood and snow, and sensitive to time of day. Clearly, the tasks for human and machine teachers should be both different and complementary.

When we come to recognize fully the characteristics and possibilities of electronic energy, most of the "givens" of schooling collapse. Learning need not take place in a box, from nine to three each day, five days a week, 180 days per year. There need not be a school beginning at age five, a graded school, or a "balance" of subjects throughout the day. Nothing need be "missed" because of absence: it can be picked up tomorrow by asking the machine to retrieve whatever is wanted. Something resembling a school—and this something might take many forms—is needed for those important human activities of interaction, exploration, finding one's self through others and others through one's self.

A needed form of experimentation, beginning now and continuing unabated into the 21st century, is that of creating options to schooling and legitimizing them. Soon, it will be common practice to show a variety of cassette tapes through a home television set. CATV promises a new set of options. And just behind both of these developments lies the home computer television terminal plugged into several video outlets, capable of playing its own records and cassettes, and providing printouts of the learning and cultural options currently available in the community. Taking advantage of these alternatives must be accepted and encouraged.

One way for us to begin to grow accustomed to this nonschool freedom is to use much more vigorously the learning resources lying outside of school. Children should be excused from school for blocks of time in order to gain access to a nonschool teacher, to serve as apprentice to an artisan, or to practice a hobby in depth. The biggest block to the kind of learning future we are endeavoring to describe is not its availability. It is our individual difficulty in seeking to shake ourselves loose from the viselike grip of our present stereotyped thinking. Let us begin simply, with the young man who wrote: "All the world is a school, and you don't need permission slips to get out into the halls, and everybody should exchange classrooms, and——Hey! What about the lawns?"

Call to Action. We had better begin now because we will need all of our imagination and our wisdom to cope with some of the critical moral questions soon to be thrust upon us. We now know that drugs are being used deliberately, under medical supervision, to intervene in the learning processes of children. Electronic means are being used to assist in the treatment of childhood disorders. The field of biochemistry is breaking new ground in seeking to understand and improve learning processes. Independent of these activities, drug use ranging from mild exploration to dangerous abuse is now a fact of life. Who is to be judged deviant and needful of chemical or electronic treatment? What restraints are to be placed upon the use of drugs for educational, self-serving, or destructive purposes? And who is to make what decisions for whom?

The question of who is to make what decisions for whom probably is the most pressing educational question both today and tomorrow. It is at the core of current discussions of accountability, voucher systems, and the like, in schooling. It is at the core of any minority-group demand for self-determination and equality. Ultimately, it brings us into the matter of who owns the child and who is to determine his freedom. To come back to where we began, the right to learn means the freedom of each individual to learn what he needs in his own way and at his own rate, in his own place and time.

This interpretation of the right to learn will not be easily understood. Nor are we likely to come easily to full acceptance and support of the flexibility and experimentation required to design the future of learning. We urge our leaders at all levels to work toward public understanding and support. We urge that celebration of this nation's 200th birthday in 1976 be taken as the culmination of a nationwide dialog about and assessment of our entire learning enterprise, a dialog that might well find its initial focus in the discussions and recommendations of the 1970 White House Conference on Children and Youth. Such a theme would herald the placement of human concerns at the top of our national priorities and would focus the eyes of our citizens on this accomplishment. The 20 million people expected to attend the year-long celebration could be given the opportunity to participate in a reasonable facsimile of the learning we have described for tomorrow.

We can think of no more appropriate celebration of the birth of a free nation than a demonstrable commitment to make real the most fundamental freedom: the right to learn.

Author

"A Systematic Approach to Instruction," by Barton R. Herrscher, is a revised version of Chapter 2 of Dr. Herrscher's *Implementing Innovative Instruction*. Dr. Herrscher is the president of Mitchell College, Statesville, North Carolina.

2 Accountability-Based Instruction

One of the major shortcomings of educational accountability is the difficulty of parctical application. Many teachers agree with the concept but have been unable to apply it in the classroom. The systematic approach to individualized instruction outlined in this unit is a practical guide and framework for designing accountability-based instructional practices.

After completing this unit, you should be able to

1   explain or diagram the six components of the instructional system that are described

2   develop a case outlining the advantages of a systematic approach to instruction over the conventional approach to teaching

3   demonstrate a favorable disposition toward the systems approach as a framework, and individualized instruction as a methodology, by suggesting specific applications to your own teaching

A lthough the systems approach to instruction is a comparatively new concept to many educators, it does not represent new thinking. Ralph Tyler conceptualized such an approach to instruction as early as 1935. Shortly thereafter the military demonstrated the feasibility and effectiveness of this approach. Recently, the field of education has seriously considered its implications and applications and has begun to implement systematic approaches.

The systems approach as conceptualized here [1] involves six basic steps: (1) rationale, (2) specific instructional objectives, (3) pre-assessment, (4) learning activities, (5) post-assessment, and (6) revision. These steps can be combined to produce a viable and efficient learning system where success can be demonstrated by measurable learner achievement.

An Instructional System

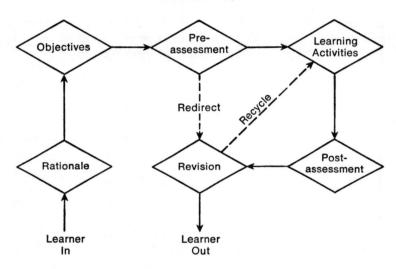

The view of an instructional system shown here is at the operational rather than the theoretical level. In essence, it is a map that charts the

---

A Systematic Approach to Instruction

Barton R. Herrscher

path followed by the learner as he strives for mastery of a course or a unit of instruction. The system is not a teaching methodology, but a rational framework into which any mode of instruction will fit whether it be a lecture, discussion, audio-tutorial material, small group seminar, laboratory work, programmed instruction, or any other approach that incorporates self-paced learning.

Anyone who is concerned with instruction should have an understanding of these steps since they are the key to increased instructional efficiency and to providing sound, organized direction for improvement of instruction. A detailed examination of each part of the system follows.

Rationale

The content of each course should be selected on the basis of its relevance to the needs of the students and its fulfillment of the purposes of the institution. Students should be told *why* it is important that they master the material presented. Without a stated purpose, learning activities become simply hurdles to clear rather than meaningful educational endeavors to experience. By clarifying for the student the reason why it is important for him to cover the material the instructor makes it easier for him to attain the instructional objectives.

Students usually find course work relevant if it relates to their personal interests, applies to job or career objectives, provides background for future study in a subject area, enriches their everyday lives, or develops personal skills in areas recognized as important for social or professional mobility (for example, communications). Relevance is enhanced when material is presented in an exciting, stimulating, challenging manner, with a maximum opportunity for success.

Objectives

Objectives are the basic building blocks of any course. It is through a statement of objectives that the instructor communicates a specific set of expectations to his students, that provide direction and encourage learning.

The objectives for a learning experience are written in terms of student behavior; that is, they state what the student will be able to do *after instruction* that he could not do before. All learning, and thus all instructional objectives, may be classified in three groups: (1) cognitive (intellectual processes), (2) affective (feelings and attitudes), and (3) psychomotor (manual skills).

The specification of instructional objectives gives focus to teaching and direction to the assessment of learning. Objectives also determine the test questions that are used to provide evidence of behavior change (learning), thus verifying the effectiveness of instruction.

Pre-assessment

Pre-assessment of learner capability should come before formal instruction. Pre-assessment, based on instructional objectives for a particular learning sequence, helps to determine whether a student has the prerequisite background and capabilities to profit from the instruction; whether he already possesses the skills, attitudes, or knowledge specified in the objectives; and where he should be placed in the graduated sequence of learning activities if he possesses some but not all of the specified behaviors. A student should be *redirected* when the pre-assessment reveals that he lacks the prerequisites or that he has already mastered the material.

Learning Activities

Learning activities are means to an end rather than ends in themselves. They become the terrain over which a student travels in pursuit of the objectives of the course. Since research indicates that traditional lecture and discussion teaching methods tend to be less effective with nontraditional students, nontraditional approaches should be investigated and a variety of instructional techniques incorporated in the learning activities. Consider, for example, the following list.

environmental
field trips
demonstrations / role playing
laboratory work

verbal
audio recordings
small-group work
lecture discussion
printed materials (textbooks, articles)
programmed instruction
tutoring

pictorial
pictures / slides
motion pictures / TV
maps / charts / diagrams

Regardless of the approach used, however, the following factors should always be given serious consideration.

Explicit Directions. The learner should be given exact details of policies and procedures for the course. He should know what he is expected to do and how he is to proceed at every step of the way.

Learning Units of Appropriate Length. The length of the segments (units) presented in a course depends on the group for whom they are intended. Units designed for college seniors would naturally differ from those intended for sixth graders. On the other hand, the sixth grader who has been working in an area for some time may be able to handle a longer and more complex segment than a mature student who is returning to college after a long absence from educational routines.

Frequent Practice. Practice gives the learner an opportunity to engage in the activity he is to master. The frequency and amount of practice should be consistent with the skills, attitudes, or knowledge called for in the objectives, and in the criterion measures used to assess mastery.

Knowledge of Results. Feedback to the learner regarding his performance is essential. Knowing that he is performing well permits him to move on with confidence; with information readily available on where and why he is incorrect, he can take the necessary steps to improve his performance.

Positive Reinforcement. Positive reinforcement is anything **that** is done or said that can be interpreted as praise to the learner, and that increases the probability that he will act in the same desired way in the future. Knowledge of success is excellent positive reinforcement.

Appropriate Media. Media may include all of the controllable influences that are designed to enhance learning. Broadly defined, media can be persons (e.g., instructors, paraprofessionals, peers), materials (audiotapes, films, charts, books), or activities (reading, laboratory work, projects).

If learning is the goal of education, then the assessment of learning becomes an extremely important process. It is only through such assessment that we are able to determine the success of our teaching endeavors. Robert Mager asks, "If it's worth teaching, isn't it worth knowing if we have succeeded?" [2] We must have measurable evidence of student learning in order to document the fact that learning (which is the overriding purpose of teaching) has occurred.

Post-assessment

In the past few years measurement experts have evolved a variety of approaches to testing practices. These approaches are at considerable variance with the measurement procedures used by educators in the past. It is, therefore, imperative that people involved with the assessment of learning (and this includes most educational personnel) know the implications of these new procedures. [3]

The differences between the norm-referenced approach to evaluation traditionally used in classrooms, and the new criterion-referenced approach are shown in the following chart.

Norm-Referenced Approach	*Criterion-Referenced Approach*
Testing is used to ascertain a student's level of performance in relation to the performance of others.	Testing is used to ascertain a student's performance with respect to an established criterion or performance standard.
The normal curve is a guide in assigning grades—it serves to sort students.	Mastery of objectives is the basis for grading, with instruction adapted to individual learning rates.
Aptitude is viewed as the capacity for learning.	Aptitude is viewed as the time required to master objectives.
Testing is used to assess individual students.	Testing is used to assess teaching.

The theoretical base undergirding this entire instructional system is Bloom's concept that mastery of a subject can be achieved by most students if they are given sufficient time and appropriate instruction. [4] Thus, the normal curve as a guide in assigning grades and the view that aptitude is the capacity for learning are no longer valid. Most students are capable of mastery, and an instructional system should accommodate this concept.

If instruction is adapted to individual learning rates of students, the need for a criterion-referenced approach to evaluation is apparent. If a student performs poorly on a test it simply means he has not yet learned and nonpunitive grading must be adopted. The fact that no learning has occurred means that the instruction for that sequence must be revised, and the student must be *recycled* into the revised system until he demonstrates mastery of the subject matter. The practice of indelibly branding *F* on students who have not learned must end.

Revision

If Carroll's view that aptitude is the amount of time required to attain mastery of a learning task is correct, then mastery is theoretically available to all. [5] This formulation holds the fundamental implications for education. One of these implications is that instructional processes or sequences that fail to instruct must be revised until they become effective teaching tools. Revision of instruction is based on a systematic process of obtaining feedback from the learner. Data regarding error rate and interviews with the learner are two such sources.

Another important element is a systematic attempt to assess student *affect*—the learner's attitude toward the learning activities and toward the subject being studied. What has been achieved if the student, while mastering the objectives of a course, has learned to hate the subject? Attention must be given to student attitudes.

The concept of instructional systems as presented here has focused on an operational rather than a theoretical approach. The six components of this system (rationale, objectives, pre-assessment, learning activities, post-assessment, and revision) form a rational framework that accommodates all modes of instruction. Flexibility is its hallmark. The system, when effectively implemented, increases the efficiency of instruction and produces measurable learner achievement.

Notes

1. This instructional system is a synthesis of ideas from the writings of Ralph Tyler, W. James Popham, Bela Banathy, and Jerrold Kemp.
2. Robert F. Mager, *Developing Attitude Toward Learning* (Belmont, Calif.: Fearon, 1968), p. 9.
3. W. James Popham, *Modern Measurement Methods,* filmstrip–tape program, Instructor's Manual (Los Angeles: VIMCET, 1969), p. 1.
4. Benjamin S. Bloom, "Learning for Mastery." See pp. 94–113 of this book.
5. Ibid.

Authors

"Minicourses—The Style of the Future?" by S. N. Postlethwait and James D. Russell. Both authors are in the Department of Biological Sciences at Purdue University, where Dr. Postlethwait has pioneered the audio-tutorial approach.

"Practical Approaches to Individualizing Instruction," by Philip G. Kapfer. The author is now with the Bureau of Educational Research at the University of Utah.

3 Individualized Instruction

A course composed of a series of individualized modules (minicourses) **Rationale**
frees the instructor from his traditional role of lecturer and provides
time for him to act as a manager, diagnostician, catalyst, tutor, or leader
and to work with students individually. Students, in turn, are freed to pace
and direct their own learning.

After completing this unit, you should be able to **Objectives**

1 contrast conventional courses with minicourses on the basis of the 20
   characteristics of college instruction that are listed here (Postlethwait
   and Russell)

2 state a rationale for utilizing minicourses (self-instructional units, learning packages, etc.) in the design of a college course (Postlethwait and
   Russell)

3 present a model of the systems approach that incorporates various learning alternatives implemented through self-paced, self-directed learning
   packages (Kapfer)

4 formulate a case for teacher involvement in building learning packages,
   and point out pitfalls to be avoided by the builder of such packages
   (Kapfer)

Introduction

A new word is appearing with increased frequency in educational publications and is heard more often when teachers gather to "talk shop." The term is *minicourse*. What does it mean? Where did it come from? How does it differ from a traditional course?

A minicourse is a self-contained instructional package dealing with a single conceptual unit of subject matter. It is an attempt to individualize learning by enabling the student to proceed independently through the material. The multifaceted learning experiences are for the most part presented in a self-instructional format. The student controls the rate and intensity of his study. Since it usually involves materials that are portable, the student can take the minicourse to the library, to a study carrel, or to his home. Minicourses are typically designed for use by one or two students, but they can be used by a larger group. The length of minicourses varies from 15 minutes of student time to several hours. They can be used individually or combined in a variety of different sequences.

Programmed Instruction (1950s)

The development of minicourses dates from the 1950s and the early days of programmed instruction. Most of the early paper-and-pencil programs were designed to teach small units of subject matter—operating a slide rule, playing chess, writing a declarative sentence, using the Pythagorean theorem, etc.

The research of B. F. Skinner at Harvard University and the studies of others in the middle and late 1950s led to the formulation of several teaching principles that became characteristic of programmed instruction—small steps, active student involvement, immediate confirmation or reinforcement, and self-pacing. These principles are used in making minicourses.

Minicourses— The Style of the Future?

A Comparison of Conventional Courses and Minicourses

S. N. Postlethwait and James D. Russell

In 1961, S. N. Postlethwait began using audiotaped presentations to supplement the instruction in his freshman botany course at Purdue University. During the next decade he developed his audio-tutorial approach, which is structured around a self-instructional learning carrel. The system he developed incorporated objectives, a programmed audiotape, printed study guides, visual aids, and real materials. As used in his courses, the system also provides for teaching assistants who can aid students in understanding complex concepts. This audio-tutorial approach has proven to be a very effective and successful learning experience.

The thrust for the 1970s is the design and development of minicourses. Purdue University has received a three-year grant from the National Science Foundation to produce minicourses for its core program in undergraduate biology. Similar modular units are being developed elsewhere under the titles "concept-o-pac," "microcourse," "instruct-o-pac," "uni-pak," and "concept sets."

In considering conventional courses and minicourses, there are a number of characteristics to consider.

Conventional Courses	Minicourses
Learning Experiences	
Conventional courses are usually characterized by lectures, reading the text, group discussions, and sometimes an isolated laboratory experience. The learning experiences are oriented toward teacher performance and group instruction, with emphasis on teaching.	Minicourses provide a combination of learning experiences in an integrated sequence, so that each learning activity can enhance and complement the others. The learning experiences are oriented toward student performance and individual instruction, with the emphasis on learning.
Role of Teacher	
The role of the teacher is one of disseminator of information.	The role of the teacher is one of diagnostician, prescriber, motivator, and resource person.
Objectives	
Objectives are usually *not* stated in specific, behavioral terms. They must be inferred from the content of the subject matter and the tests.	Objectives are stated in terms of student performance and are usually presented to the student before the instruction begins.

Conventional Courses	Minicourses

Selection

Materials (texts, etc.) are selected first, tests are designed to sample this material, but desired behavior with respect to the materials is not always clearly defined in advance.	Objectives are stated first, test items are designed to measure mastery of these objectives, then instructional materials are selected to assist the student in mastering the objectives.

Rate

Students are forced to go through the course "in a lockstep manner" (all going at the *same* rate). They all begin at the same time and are expected to finish simultaneously.	Each student can proceed at his own rate. He is free to skip any portion of the minicourse as long as he can demonstrate mastery of the objectives. He is also free to repeat any portion of the minicourse as often as necessary.

Strategies and Media

Teachers tend to use just one or two strategies such as lecture and written assignments, regardless of the many different types of learning in the course (psychomotor manipulations, cognitive skills, and attitudinal changes). Media are prepared and used on the basis of familiarity (texts, films, 2 x 2 slides, etc.) and are chosen by the teacher on the basis of his feeling comfortable with certain media (usually printed).	Different learning strategies are used for objectives representing different kinds of learning. Several instructional strategies are used to optimize learning on a given topic. Media are selected to complement the type of objective and type of learner, then student-tested. Use of a large variety of media is incorporated into each minicourse.

Individualization

Conventional courses are group-oriented. Students are usually provided with a limited number of instructional resources. Usually the teacher specifies exactly how the student should proceed—read 20 pages of the text, answer 10 questions, etc.	Minicourses are highly individualized. Each student can use any or all of the media and materials available. The selection of the most appropriate approach is often left to the student—listen to a tape, read a text, look at diagrams, view a film, examine real objects, or any combination thereof.

Conventional Courses	Minicourses

Participation

The student's role is usually passive —reading the text or just listening to the teacher. | Minicourses provide for active student participation. The student learns by doing. The student is actively involved in manipulating the instructional materials.

Individual Differences

Individual differences in achievement are expected. If a student wants enrichment materials, he usually must dig them out on his own. Tools and time for individual diagnosis and remedial help are normally lacking or not available. If a student is having difficulty, the teacher must work with him to help him keep up with the class or let him fend for himself. | A minicourse is considered a failure if a significant number of students fail to reach the criterion performance. If a student wants to study a particular topic in greater depth, he can secure supplementary materials and proceed without interrupting the progress of an entire class. Remedial help and extra time are also available to help slow learners reach mastery. If a student is having difficulty mastering a lesson, he can spend the additional time and get individual help from the teacher without delaying the entire class.

Time

Time spent on a topic is usually constant for all learners, resulting in no time variance. Thus achievement scores correlate highly with IQ. | The students spend as much time as necessary to master the topic. Time required for mastery is usually distributed normally and tends to correlate highly with IQ.

Freedom

Traditionally 45–60 minutes are scheduled each day at a fixed time for instruction. Students must attend lectures and laboratories when these are in progress (e.g., 8:00–8:50 on Monday, Wednesday, and Friday). | Instruction can be at the student's convenience and at the time of day when the student learns "best." Minicourses provide greater freedom for students to adjust study time and subject-matter content to individual needs and peculiarities of interest.

Conventional Courses	Minicourses

Reinforcement

In traditional courses students are reinforced or corrected only after major examinations. Many times there is a considerable delay after the exam is taken before it is graded and returned to him.	The small size of the minicourse permits immediate reinforcement and correction.

Testing

Tests usually sample the content that has been covered. The student is often at a loss as to how to prepare (study) for the test. The student sits through the course, then takes an examination to determine his grade. Tests are too often used only to "give grades," instead of for feedback or diagnosis.	Learners are given the objectives and told how attainment of them will be evaluated. Tests are designed to measure mastery of the objectives. The student receives credit when he can demonstrate mastery even if he has *not* gone through the minicourse. Test items (questions) are used for assessing prerequisite skills, for diagnosing difficulties, and for confirming mastery.

Reference

Norm-referenced tests are used where success is dependent upon the performance of others in the class.	Criterion-referenced tests are used where success of the student is independent of the performance of other students who are taking the minicourse.

Mastery

Most learners know at least a little about everything. It is not expected that all students can achieve mastery.	Slow learners master some of the objectives but may not have time to master others in an arbitrary period. Given time, even slow learners are able to master most, if not all, of the objectives.

Conventional Courses	Minicourses

Portability

Course is usually based upon the teacher's lecture and is portable only by moving the teacher to a new location (sometimes accomplished via videotape). The lecture is usually lost forever once the class period ends. If a student misses part of a conventional course, he must talk with the teacher, review a fellow student's notes, or miss the instruction entirely.

Minicourses are portable and easily available at a variety of locations— in the field, at home, in a hospital. They can easily be exchanged and disseminated to other schools. Since the minicourses are in individual packages, make-up lessons and review sessions can be arranged with a minimum of effort. All students are exposed to the same instruction, regardless of the hour of the day or the day of the week.

Revisions

Revisions often reflect preferences of the teacher for topics to be covered. Many times revisions necessitate a complete rewriting of the text or study guide and a major revision of all study material.

Revisions of materials are based on student performance. If students are not mastering the material, it is revised. Subject matter that is constantly changing can be updated with a minimum of cost and effort.

Flexibility

Conventional courses are structured around a semester or year-long study guide or textbook and tend to be inflexible.

Minicourses can be structured into a greater variety of patterns consistent with different approaches or themes.

Course Success

Lacking the features of systematic design and specific objectives, there is no built-in provision for judging success of the course other than the teacher's subjective judgment.

Having a design goal and an evaluation plan, the minicourse developer is able to correct faulty instructional materials and to know when he has succeeded in developing a successful minicourse.

Conventional Courses	Minicourses

Student Failure

Failure is usually not detected until the end of an examination period (six weeks or even a semester). Students often try to build hierarchical skills upon an inadequate foundation. As a result, students may have to repeat an entire semester or course.

Inadequate achievement can be identified at each critical step in the student's progress. Consequently the subject matter is mastered before the student proceeds to subsequent studies. Failure can be pinpointed specifically to both subject matter and instructional material and subsequently remedied in a minimum of time and effort. The student has to repeat just that minicourse that he failed, not an entire course.

Rationale

One of the most important advantages of minicourses is the opportunity to develop, evaluate, and use a variety of instructional strategies to optimize instruction for students on a given topic. The approach can be carefully and deliberately sequenced, tried out with students, and revised until the maximum achievement is demonstrated by the greatest number of students. Careful evaluation makes it possible to measure and predict the effectiveness of each minicourse. Minicourses utilize a wide variety of activities:

1. conducting experiments
2. reading textbooks and articles
3. examining diagrams and photographs
4. viewing films and colored slides
5. handling real objects and models
6. studying demonstration materials
7. listening to audiotapes

All sensory inputs can and should be available to the students in meeting the objectives of the minicourse. Each student can use any or all of the media and materials available. The selection of the most appropriate approach is often left to the student.

Minicourses are highly individualized. Yet they can provide uniform instruction for a large number of students on an individual basis. The approach allows each student to study at a pace and time convenient and effective for him. He can pace his study according to his own ability to assimilate the information and master the objectives. Exposure to difficult subject matter can be repeated as often as necessary. Thus, all students can master the material; the slower ones are not forced to move on prematurely to new material.

In addition to student freedom, minicourses provide flexibility for both the student and the teacher. The small units of subject matter can be arranged or sequenced in a variety of formats. One minicourse might meet part of the requirements for several regular courses. The student might have the option of completing any 10 of a total of 15 or 20 minicourses to meet the requirements of a "total course." The student might also be free to select the order in which he studies some of the minicourses.

Minicourses can provide a maximum of student freedom for independent study. Minicourses also place the responsibility for learning squarely on the shoulders of the student. The emphasis is on student learning rather than on the teacher's teaching. The activities of the student are directed, not the activities of the teacher. A disadvantage of minicourses can be a lack of interest on the part of the students. Since the teacher is not always present and watching over his shoulder, the student may not be motivated—or forced, in some cases—to pursue the learning activity. It is still necessary for the minicourse and the teacher to create an environment in which the learner is inspired to become involved in the process of learning.

One of the characteristics of a minicourse is active student participation. The student learns by doing. Minicourses should provide active involvement, replacing passive reading or just listening to the teacher with handling learning materials, manipulating equipment, and responding frequently to pertinent questions.

Active Student Participation

Since minicourses are in an individual, self-instructional format, make-up lessons and review sessions are accomplished with a minimum of effort. All students can be exposed to the same material, regardless of the hour of the day or the day of the week.

Some critics feel that minicourses are void of human interaction. This criticism is true if the teacher uses minicourses as an excuse to spend class time in the teacher's lounge or in his office. Rather, the teacher should be available to answer students' questions and provide encouragement when needed. Once the minicourses are available, the teacher is freed from the routine and repetitive activities of teaching the same material again and again. He is then available to devote more time to the really important activities of teaching—inspiration, motivation, orientation, and personal contact. The teacher serves as a diagnostician, prescriber, and resource person—providing that information which he can present better than any other source. In minicourses teacher guidance is important since the student has greater responsibility for his own education than he has had in the past. The teacher's role thus becomes more humanistic and less mechanical than before.

Minicourses can be designed to provide student-to-student interaction. It is very difficult, if not impossible, for a student to learn interpersonal skills, such as salesmanship, counseling techniques, teacher competencies, etc., without having an opportunity to practice with another person. For a minicourse on salesmanship, the students might study in pairs, with one as the salesman and the other as the client. Students should also be encouraged to work together on complex learning activities. They can discuss difficult subject-matter areas and quiz each other on the topic. Many students find it helpful to tutor and assist one another in developing mastery of minicourses.

We strongly believe that minicourses *are* the style of the future. They need not be limited to formal education since their "packageable" nature makes them usable in continuing education and correspondence study. With increased leisure time people are forming study clubs—informal groups for pursuing hobbies and interests. Minicourses offer a vehicle for involving all these "students" in active, meaningful learning. With a little ingenuity and creative application, minicourses can provide equal-opportunity education for people in all walks of life. The utilization of minicourses is limited only by the imagination of their users.

Every educator should provide his students with the sound of different drums. Educators are obligated to make schools into places where more than the isolated drums of the adopted textbook and the teacher at the lecture podium are heard. Teachers need to find their creative and exciting new role by stepping away more frequently from these traditional drums in order to develop an integrated, practical human environment for personalized learning. Learners must be given the opportunity to hear different drummers, to find the learning content that is meaningful to them in an atmosphere that promotes learner choices. A climate must be established that protects the student's right to progress at his individually most productive pace, however measured. At the same time he should use and develop his own learning style, however "far out" by conventional standards. If individualized learning is to occur, the learner must be cognizant of the en-route and terminal behaviors expected of him. Likewise, he must be apprised, if not convinced, of the reasonableness of what he is to do.

Nontextbook media should not be "tacked on" at the end of a textbook chapter or hidden away in the teacher's guide to be used on a group basis rather than individually. Instead, nontextbook media should be organized and provided as *honest* alternatives to the textbook. The teacher and the textbook are only two of many diverse book, nonbook, and human learning resources. However important the teacher and convenient the textbook, other resources should be *equally available* to the learner. Unless they are equally available, they are not honest alternatives. A systems package is needed.

The focus of this article is on a practical curricular approach for organizing all types of learning resources so that they are available for use by individual students and by small learning teams. In other words, the goal is to examine,

---

Practical Approaches
to Individualizing Instruction

Philip G. Kapfer

If a man does not keep pace with his companions,
Perhaps it is because he hears a different drummer.
Let him step to the music which he hears,
However measured or far away.

Henry David Thoreau

at an operational rather than theoretical level, a "systems approach" to media utilization.

Descriptions of at least two different types of curricular systems packages have appeared recently in professional literature. Both of these types of packages [1, 2] reflect the systems approach to education.

A simple systems diagram, which illustrates a possible learning package sequence frequently employed, is given here. This diagram was developed for the purpose of acquainting parents, students, and teachers with some of the available learning alternatives offered through the systems approach.

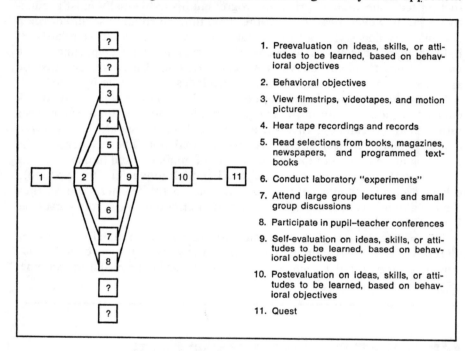

1. Preevaluation on ideas, skills, or attitudes to be learned, based on behavioral objectives

2. Behavioral objectives

3. View filmstrips, videotapes, and motion pictures

4. Hear tape recordings and records

5. Read selections from books, magazines, newspapers, and programmed textbooks

6. Conduct laboratory "experiments"

7. Attend large group lectures and small group discussions

8. Participate in pupil–teacher conferences

9. Self-evaluation on ideas, skills, or attitudes to be learned, based on behavioral objectives

10. Postevaluation on ideas, skills, or attitudes to be learned, based on behavioral objectives

11. Quest

When the student, with the assistance of a teacher, selects a particular systems package in his personalized sequential learning program, he takes a pretest based on the behavioral objectives in that package. If the pretest results indicate that the ideas, skills, or attitudes included in the package have not already been achieved by the student, he selects from suggested alternative subject matter, media, and methodology in order to fit his own unique learning style. The behavioral objectives guide him in his learning; when he feels that he has achieved one behavioral objective, he proceeds to the next one and again selects from suggested alternatives in subject matter, media, and methods.

When the student feels that he has achieved all of the behavioral objectives in the package, he takes a self-test. If the self-test results indicate that he is ready for teacher evaluation, the student can request the post-test for the package. Upon successful completion of the post-test, the student may proceed to his next systems package or he may participate in quest activities. If the student elects to engage in quest, he defines a problem for in-depth or in-breadth study, conducts his research, and thereby achieves some level of resolution of the problem.

During the entire learning sequence the teacher provides as many opportunities as possible for student–teacher and student–student interaction during conferences and seminars. Small learning teams, made up of from two to six students, are formed whenever feasible. The teacher monitors each student's progress, diagnoses learning problems, prescribes possible alternative learning media and methods from suggestions listed in the package, and evaluates progress in achieving stated behavioral objectives.

For years teachers have developed instructional units and lesson plans. By rewriting such lesson plans for student rather than teacher use, combining several such lessons into a systems package, and adding pre- and self-evaluation to the usual postevaluation that occurs, curricular materials for self-paced learning can be developed. Several such systems packages then could comprise a typical unit of instruction, with the units based on required state or school district courses of study. A sample lesson format that has proved useful for writing systems packages [in various subject areas] is given here.

Lesson Topic: _____

  I. Component Idea, Skill, or Attitude: _____

    _____

 II. Behavioral Objective: _____

    _____

III. Instructions: _____

    _____

IV. Learning Activities: _____

    _____

    A. Media: _____

    _____

    B. Methodology: _____

    _____

 V. Self-Evaluation _____

    _____

Slight modification of this format makes possible various approaches to learning along a continuum from presentation to discovery, and along a second continuum from teacher direction to self-direction. For example, if Part I is completely omitted from the student's package and if Part II is written as an en-route behavioral objective rather than as a terminal objective, a discovery approach (with regard to content or process) instead of a presentation approach can be used. Further, if the student possesses the necessary research skills, Part IV can be left blank so that he must search for his own learning resources, thus extending his self-direction in learning.

It should be noted that teacher involvement in *building* systems packages is usually necessary before teachers can make effective, practical classroom use of such materials prepared by others. The management concepts seem to grow with the systems-package concepts. For this reason most teachers who have never prepared self-paced instructional materials, when provided with such materials, tend not to use them at all or else to use them for group-paced instruction. By contrast, teachers who have prepared their own systems packages very quickly succeed in breaking out of the group-paced instruction pattern.

The most serious barrier to successful teacher-development of packages is the beginner's tendency to "write the textbook." Instead of simply identifying media already available commercially and providing citations for such media for easy use by students, much textual material also is written and included. In the first place, this tendency to "write the textbook" offers little advantage over the format currently used in textbooks. Second, the likelihood of equal availability of all media is lost. Third, textbook authors are provided assistance from a publisher's highly trained editorial staff; teachers are not. And fourth, teachers very quickly and understandably run out of time and patience when unrealistic time demands are placed on them and when they are asked to accomplish tasks for which they are not prepared by experience or training.

On the other hand, teacher-prepared material can be most valuable and, at times, absolutely necessary. A brief monograph, a videotape, a filmstrip, 35-mm slides, an 8-mm film, a programmed booklet, or an audiotape are only a few examples of possible teacher-prepared media. Such media should be cataloged and housed in the library or resource center so that equal availability of all media becomes a reality.

Systems packages are designed to help individual students achieve in individually ideal ways. Whether one refers to this as individualized instruction, continuous progress, or as self-paced learning, the intent is clear: given systems packages, students will be able to achieve measurable performances under given conditions, at or above specified minimum levels, and at *rates*, in *styles*, and in *sequences* unique to each student.

The individuality of learning rates and learning styles has been mentioned repeatedly in the literature on self-pacing. A topic that is treated less frequently, however, is individualization of the sequence of learning. What *is* the best sequence of acquired behaviors in learning to read, in learning to multiply, in studying chemistry, in learning about the social studies? Variations among programmers and textbook authors attest to the fact that many different teaching sequences are available. In fact, much learning is not sequential. However, group-paced instruction necessitates a single sequence that every student in the group must follow.

The concept of educational systems for individualizing instruction is being developed at many locations throughout the country. As a result, formats may differ. However, an important outcome, due to common purpose, is that the various systems have more curricular similarities than differences.

The systems approach in curriculum development is based on two preliminary and related steps—establishment that a need exists for changing human behavior, and identification and description of the required new behavior. In view of the importance of behavioral objectives to the systems approach, the practice of including behavioral objectives in the student portion of the learning package is essential. Thus, the format used in some other types of systems packages in which behavioral objectives are omitted from student materials is open to serious question.

Ideally, a systems package should provide for at least three diversifications. In the lesson format, only two of these diversifications are evident; namely, media and methodology. Diversified subject matter includes such alternatives as varying levels of difficulty, varying degrees of depth and breadth, conflicting points of view, and approaches that appeal to a wide range of interests. These three diversifications provide the student with the desired different drummers to which he can listen and respond.

Notes

1. Ray L. Talbert, "A Learning Activity Package—What Is It?" *Educational Screen and Audiovisual Guide* 47 (January 1968): 20–21; *see also* Jan McNeil and James E. Smith, "The Multi's at Nova," *Educational Screen and Audiovisual Guide* 47 (January 1968): 16–19, 43.
2. Philip G. Kapfer, "An Instructional Management Strategy for Individualized Learning," *Phi Delta Kappan* 49 (January 1968): 260–263; *see also* Philip G. Kapfer and Gardner Swenson, "Individualizing Instruction for Self-Paced Learning: A Commitment by the /I/D/E/A Materials Dissemination Center," *Clearing House* 42 (March 1968).

Authors

"Ten Untenable Assumptions of College Instruction," by Robert Glaser. Dr. Glaser, Professor of Psychology and Education and Director of Learning Research and Development at the University of Pittsburgh, has long been a leading figure in individualized instruction.

"Alternatives to the Invalid Assumptions of Current Educational Practice," by Barton R. Herrscher. As president of Mitchell College, Dr. Herrscher has put some of these alternatives into practice.

4 Changing Approaches to Teaching

P ost-secondary teaching tends to suffer from two basic weaknesses: **Rationale**
(1) it is usually based on invalid assumptions, and (2) it usually results
in "schooling" (a system of certification and classification) rather than in
"genuine education" (learning that is self-directed and continuous). An
understanding of these weaknesses is the first step to improvement.

After completing this unit, you should be able to **Objectives**

1 list the untenable assumptions of college teaching, and propose changes
   in practices to overcome these assumptions (Glaser)

2 discuss the reasons why college instructors continue to base their teaching on invalid assumptions even though most of them know better
   (Glaser, Herrscher)

3 challenge the three common invalid assumptions that are used to guide
   classroom practice, by suggesting alternatives to each (Herrscher)

My intention in preparing these comments was to examine what present knowledge of the learning process has to suggest for the conduct of instruction in a university classroom. In the course of doing this, I examined the characteristics and the conditions under which I conduct my own college classes, which I believe are no better and no worse than a good many of the classes of my colleagues. What stood out in my analysis were the assumptions underlying present general teaching practices—assumptions that, by and large, do not represent things we believe or things that we preach. Ten of these assumptions of college teaching seem particularly prevalent.

First, I should present a very general statement of what I consider to be four basic elements of the instructional process: (1) definition of course objectives and goals of instruction—the knowledge and skills we want our students to attain; (2) the student's entering behavior—the repertoire of talents and competencies with which the student begins a course of learning; (3) instructional procedures—how we teach and guide the student toward specified educational objectives; and (4) assessment of student performance—examination to determine how well the student has attained certain knowledge and skills in the subject matter.

The development of a course of instruction is initiated with the first component, that is, with some specification of the goals of instruction. These goals constitute the objectives to be accomplished and the purpose for which the course is designed. The main input, so to speak, into the course is the entering behavior of the student. This consists of the student's existing level of achievement, his aptitudes, and his background, from which instruction must begin. The next phase includes the actual instructional procedures and learning experiences employed to modify student behavior. The final phase is some sort of quality control, that is, assessment of the extent to which the end-of-course behavior achieved by the student approximates the performance required by the specified course objectives. This picture of the gross elements of the instructional process appears to limit my scope

---

Ten Untenable Assumptions of College Instruction

Robert Glaser

and it may be (although I am not quite sure this is so) that I am talking about knowledge and disciplines that have been called "consensual." In consensual disciplines, there is a reasonable amount of agreement on basic methods and findings and little disagreement on the competence of scholars in the fields. Typically, these are mathematics, the sciences, engineering, and the like. In contrast, my remarks may be less relevant to "dissensual" knowledge, where teachings are generally open to debate and individual interpretation.

With the foregoing in mind, the assumptions I would like to present are the following. I submit that, in the usual conduct of our college classes, we act as if these things were true: **Ten Major Myths**

1. That the specific knowledge acquired by the student is related to the long-range educational goals that exist in the mind of the instructor.
2. That the aptitudes, achievements, and backgrounds of the students in a classroom are approximately equal.
3. That aptitude is more important than previous achievement for the attainment of knowledge.
4. That all people learn in the same way and take approximately the same amount of time to learn the same thing.
5. That listening to lectures and reading books are powerful means for changing student behavior.
6. That students retain knowledge without requiring much review and relearning.
7. That course grades tell what a student knows and can do.
8. That a college professor is, by virtue of the title, a good professor of knowledge.
9. That teaching is an art that requires no tools and no underlying technology.
10. That the structure imposed upon knowledge by a discipline is the best structure for transmitting that knowledge to students.

Let me now briefly discuss each of these assumptions.

The knowledge with which the student leaves the classroom is related to the educational goals envisioned by the instructor. This assumption states that we know the long-range educational goals that we wish our students to attain in the future and that the behavior with which they leave the course actually contributes to their attainment of these goals. The fact of the matter is that the long-term relationship between the kind of thing the student is taught and the way he is eventually required to behave in our society or in his job is not very clear. It is useful to distinguish between the long-term goals of education and the terminal behavior that the student should display at the end of a specific instructional situation. It is this **Relation of Knowledge to Goals** immediate terminal behavior of the student that is the tangible aspect upon which a teacher can operate and that is the only tangible evidence to indicate that he is performing an adequate teaching job. In the absence of knowledge about the behavior necessary for students to be able to abstract, generalize, and be creative and inventive with their knowledge over the long term, we can only *assume* certain relationships between the specific behaviors we produce and our expressed long-term educational goals.

All Animals Are Equal?

Aptitudes, achievements, and backgrounds of the students in a classroom are roughly equal. Because, in our lectures and seminars, all students are taught by the same means for the same period of time, this assumption must be made. The only leeway provided is that some students need more outside study time than others. This is a primary belief that underlies the general uniformity of college instruction, and nothing could be less true. Individuals differ from one another in ways that influence how they learn from a uniformly presented lesson. One way in which they might differ is in the extent to which they have already learned some of the things we wish to teach them. A second point of difference might be the extent to which the individual has acquired the necessary knowledge that is prerequisite to learning what is taught in the lesson. A third difference refers to the extent to which the student has previously learned not only the solutions to specific problems, but the generalized responses necessary for solving a class of problems or for applying a general concept. A fourth difference may involve motivation and learning style. If individuals differ in all these aspects, then this second assumption of equality of background is untenable and a standard sequence of instruction, even after students have been selected for college, seems too rigid and constricting.

Aptitude and Achievement

Aptitude is more important than previous achievement for the attainment of knowledge. By and large, the primary information used in selecting students for college is the high-school grade average that indicates a rough measure of attainment and tests of verbal and arithmetic aptitude. Much less detailed assessment is made of a prospective student's competence in the subject matter prerequisites before he takes a required freshman course. It would seem that a student earns the right to take these courses by virtue of having mastered the prior knowledge and skills that are required. If this is so, then what is required is detailed diagnostic assessment of the student's strengths and shortcomings regarding the subject matter so that he can be asked to master the entering behavior required for a course. In all fairness, however, it is true that universities are increasingly concerned with differential placement on the basis of achievement tests, but I submit that this needs to be done with more precision.

The Sacredness of Time

All men learn in the same way and roughly take the same amount of time to learn the same thing. Because colleges provide the same facilities for each student—lectures, books, and laboratories—and allow about the same amount of time for each student for all methods of instruction, we must assume this. Otherwise, we would provide a great variety of learning conditions and let the student choose the one from which he could profit most and take the amount of time he needs to master a subject. It is interesting to consider some of the things that would happen if time for learning and individual modes of instruction were allowed to vary. We might find, for example, that, as the time allowed for learning increased, the lower-aptitude students would have more and more chance to catch up with the higher-aptitude students, and the correlation between aptitude and attainment in college would decrease. If the time allowed for learning were decreased, then lower-aptitude students would have less and less chance to catch up, and as the time allowed for mastery became less, the correlation between aptitude and attainment would increase. Furthermore, as the adequacy of instruction for each student changed, the relationship between achievement and student differences would be affected. As instructional presentation approached optimal adequacy for each student, individual differences would have less relation to established levels of achievement because many students would reach these base levels of competence. If instruction were less than optimal, individual differences would be brought into play to cope with the instructional situation and hence would have much more influence upon achievement.

Listening to lectures and reading books are powerful means for modifying student behavior. Little needs to be said about this assumption other than the fact that lectures and reading from books are extremely useful for certain purposes. They are not, however, as useful for everything as the very extensive use of the lecture method and the reading assignment procedure would seem to imply. A corollary assumption here is that in our technological society, books are good means for storing and communicating information. As far as storing information is concerned, libraries of the future will be much different places from what they are today and will actually become places for information retrieval and self-instruction. As far as communicating information is concerned, present notions of instructional technology are modifying the ways in which "textbooks" are constructed.

The Lecture and the Textbook

Humans retain knowledge without requiring much review and relearning. By mentioning this assumption, I mean to point to the fact that the educational progression from grade school through graduate school makes little provision for the built-in review and relearning of knowledge that is used at a particular time or will be used later in life. The general effectiveness with which students are taught at the present time can undoubtedly be improved to facilitate retention of knowledge. However, we have very little basic data at the present time on just how well we are doing in this respect. Studies are required to determine—for specific kinds of knowledge, for

We Do Forget

specific kinds of curricula, and for individuals with particular life patterns—how much and what kind of basic knowledge is retained as a result of instruction. In other words, how much and what kind of practice and review results in a certain degree of retention or facility to relearn? The conditions of effective practice need to be tried and their effects identified so that they can be used with surer knowledge of their results.

Grades and Performance

The grades that a student receives in a course tell how much he knows and what he can do. When a grade is based upon a measure of achievement such as a final examination, the scores obtained from this test provide primarily two kinds of information. The first is the degree to which the student has attained the instructional objectives of a course—for example, whether he can satisfactorily prepare an experimental report or solve certain kinds of mathematical problems. The second is the relative ordering of individuals with respect to their test performance, for example, whether student A can solve more problems than student B. The principal difference between these two kinds of information lies in the standard used as a reference. What can be called criterion-referenced measures depend upon an established standard of subject matter competence, while what can be termed norm-referenced measures depend upon a standard relative to the performance of other students. The standard against which a student's performance is compared in order to obtain the first kind of information is increasing subject-matter competence along a continuum of achievement. The specific knowledge and skills that define each level of achievement are identified in terms of the criterion behavior that a student must be capable of performing before he achieves a particular level of knowledge. A student's score on such a criterion-referenced measure provides explicit information as to what he can or cannot do. Information is provided as to the degree of competence attained by a student, independent of reference to the performance of others. We are thus informed that the student can perform certain algebraic operations and not *just* that he is average or above average in algebra.

On the other hand, achievement measures convey the second type of information about the capability of one student compared with the capability of other students. It is possible to provide this type of information (i.e., a student's relative standing) without making reference to performance criteria. Educational achievement examinations, for example, are administered for the purpose of ordering students in a class or school, and a particular student's achievement is evaluated in terms of a comparison between his performance and the performance of other members of the reference group. Such norm-referenced measures need provide little or no information about the degree of proficiency exhibited by the tested behaviors in terms of what the individual can do. They indicate that one student is more or less proficient than another but may not tell how proficient either of them is with respect to the subject-matter knowledge involved. In large part, achievement measures currently employed in education, and especially course grades, are solely norm-referenced, and it is difficult to ascertain the levels of performance that describe at least the basic end-of-course competence that a student is expected to attain or that he should have in order to go on to the next course.

Professors As Artists

A college professor is, by virtue of his title, a good professor of knowledge. A corollary to this is that all college professors teach effectively by lecturing. None of us really believes these assumptions, but we act as if we do. Knowledge of the learning process recommends a more responsive environment for education. Learning occurs most effectively when the learner interacts with his instructional environment; he works with it, manipulates it, changes it, and is changed in turn by the consequences of his actions.

The ninth assumption, that *teaching is an art that requires no tools and no technology*, is attested to by the fact that, for many subjects in college, professors are required to teach with their bare hands. By this I mean that it is usually easier to get funds for research equipment and office supplies than it is to get money for things to teach with so that lectures and seminars can be made more effective. I refer to the use of the developments of modern technology, such as automated demonstration apparatus, films, slides, televised demonstrations we buy or devise ourselves, computer terminals and self-instructional kits, and other materials with which the students can work. However, the application of technological advances to instruction is in the wind, although it is highly probable that these advances will reach the grade schools and high schools before they penetrate into the more conservative educational climate of university teaching. Furthermore, it seems that the increasing knowledge of the learning process will contribute to the development of improved pedagogical practices. As such improvements come into being, the potential of the professor as a teacher can be enhanced with the aid of tools and techniques for teaching, just as the physician and engineer have tools for aspects of their trades.

Structure for Learning

The way in which a discipline structures its knowledge provides the best structure for transmitting it to students. It seems to me that when we teach, we organize our courses in a way that satisfies the epistemological purposes of the body of knowledge involved. Sometimes this organization is theoretical and logical, and sometimes it is chronological or fortuitous. The requirements of the subject matter have dictated this organization, and requirements for transmitting this subject matter to the student have entered little into consideration. A problem arises when one starts to build an integrated learning sequence and has to analyze the body of knowledge to be covered. A first step is the analysis of knowledge into units that can provide building blocks by which the learner goes through an instructional sequence. It would seem best if the organization of instruction were a joint function of *both* the structure of the subject matter and the characteristics of the instructional sequence that best facilitate retention, concept manipulation, generalizability of knowledge, and so forth. The distinction I wish to make here is between what can be called the logical and epistemological arrangement of a subject matter on the one hand, and the "learning structure" on the other. The learning structure may dictate the kind of sequence and order of both the subject matter and student experiences that have been discovered to produce certain kinds of student behavior. A task for psychological research is to identify appropriate learning structures that can be incorporated into the epistemological structure of the knowledge in order to produce a more ideal learning process. Such a joint analysis might well result in a revision of the organization and presentation of subject matter.

A Commitment to Individuality

In conclusion, two things should be said. First, underlying this discussion is a commitment to the individuality of humans and to the development of educational environments that are adaptable to individual differences. Men are not equal in that they learn in different ways. They require, however, equal opportunity to achieve their ends in ways that are most effective for them. Because the relatively rigid structure of the usual college classroom does not permit this, it must be revised. The second point is that the tone of these remarks may provoke criticism that I am preoccupied solely by one aspect of learning—that aspect concerned with discipline, content, analysis, and precision—and that I ignore what has been called "left-handed" thought—intuition, injury, playfulness, and learning from trial and error. Obviously, in this concern for learning and the improvement of teaching, we must examine both against the broad question of what constitutes the best environment for an individual's maximum understanding of a subject.

E ducation has, for too long, pointed with pride to those who have "made it" while disregarding the many who have "fallen by the wayside." Although we have chosen not to notice the general ineffectiveness of education, the overall failure is glaringly "apparent in dropout rates, in barely minimal learning on the part of many who do remain in school and in growing alienation among the young of all colors and classes."[1]

It has been our practice to equate learning with school. Close scrutiny reveals, however, that no such equation exists in the real world of education. Much of what takes place in school results in little, if any, learning for some students. And a great deal of learning for all students takes place outside of school. The right to learn *in school* is an extremely important issue today and appears likely to become even more important in the future.

In a nation that speaks of inalienable rights, the right to learn must be paramount. Yet that right, in its full meaning, has been denied to many in this nation. It has been denied because of color, religion, poverty, infirmity, and residence. And it has been denied because of our often mindless adherence to many unproductive teaching concepts and practices.[2]

Thanks to massive government action in recent years, many of the barriers to learning, cited above, no longer exist. Civil-rights legislation has eradicated discrimination on the basis of race and religion. The Basic Opportunity Grants, the College Work Study Program, and National Defense Student Loans have removed poverty from the list of barriers to higher education. With the advent of state systems of community colleges, place of abode in many states is now seldom a handicap.

The one barrier that has remained and has been seemingly immune to reform is "our mindless adherence to unproductive teaching concepts and practices." The end result has been that "The schools have become great sorting machines, labeling and certifying those who presumably will be winners and losers as adults. The winners are disproportionately white and

Alternatives to the Invalid Assumptions of Current Educational Practice

Barton R. Herrscher

affluent; the losers, too often, poor and brown or black or red. But many of the winners are losers, too." [3]

The accountability movement in education is a recognition of the need for more productive teaching. In its stress on demonstrated student accomplishment, accountability has as its primary objective an increase in the number of "winners." Under this concept, the teacher shares responsibility with students for learning and as such assumes at least partial responsibility for the "losers." Educators who see in accountability a challenge rather than a threat tend to be those who have accepted (*a*) Benjamin Bloom's concept that most students can learn a subject to a high level of mastery if they are given enough time and the right kind of instruction, [4] (*b*) the concept that individual students can best profit from individualized instruction, and (*c*) the idea that even the best instruction allows room for improvement.

An analysis of the assumptions underlying traditional instruction reveals a set of beliefs in conflict with the three concepts just delineated. They have, in effect, tended to protect unproductive teaching and justify the high rates of student dropout and failure. The following are three assumptions that we know to be invalid, yet we have allowed them to guide classroom practice:

1. Mastery of a subject is possible only for a minority of the students in a class.
2. There is one standard classroom format best for all students—25 students grouped by age, seated in rows in a classroom, with one teacher who does most of the talking.
3. The current "instructional system," consisting of little other than directed learning activities and periodic testing, is best simply because it is almost universally practiced.

A brief refutation of each invalid assumption, along with the alternative educational concepts that should guide classroom practice, make up the balance of this paper. The hope is that these ideas will serve as harbingers of change.

Students Can Learn

Support for the "some can't learn" theory has come from aptitude tests.

The use of aptitude tests for predictive purposes and the high correlations between such tests and achievement criteria have led many of us to the view that high levels of achievement are possible only for the most able students. From this, it is an easy step to some notion of a causal connection between aptitude and achievement. The simplest notion of causality is that the students with high levels of aptitude can learn the complex ideas of the subject while the students with low levels of aptitude can learn only the simplest ideas of the subject.[5]

A strong contrasting case has been built by John Carroll and Benjamin Bloom. They view aptitude as "the amount of time required by the learner to attain mastery of a learning task."[6] This assumption, which should guide classroom practice, sees mastery learning as theoretically available to the great majority of students, if these students are granted sufficient time and are provided instruction appropriate to their individual learning styles. Simply stated, students *can* learn. [7]

Individualized Instruction

There is an inverse relationship between grade level and the appropriateness of lockstep group instruction. As student aptitudes and backgrounds become more diverse with the passage of time and advancement in school, individualized instruction becomes more necessary.

To expect 25 college students enrolled in freshman English to persevere equally, to profit equally from group instruction (probably a lecture/discussion approach, with emphasis on the lecture) and to master the course content by the end of the term, is to expect what never will be. "Whatever the amount of time allowed by the school and the curriculum for particular subjects or learning tasks, it is likely to be too much for some students and not enough for other students."[8]

The simple recognition of individual differences in students tends to invalidate the "group instruction" assumption of traditional education. A more appropriate approach is to provide individualized instruction based on the assumption that students are different with regards to every learning variable that can be isolated. As educators, our basic task is one of causing students to learn by determining how individual differences in students can be related to the teaching and learning process.

A Systematic Approach

Every instructor has a "system" that guides his teaching. Most have adopted a two-component system consisting of (1) learning activities and (2) testing. The student engages in learning activities (listening to lectures, reading the textbook, engaging in laboratory work, etc.), after which he is tested. Then, more learning activities and a test over the new content, and so on until the end of the term. Students are then assigned grades in some relative fashion based on test-score averaging and other criteria. The distribution of achievement (grades) usually approximates a normal curve. The cost of this tried-and-true system has been a disproportionate number of "losers" in the form of failures and dropouts.

A more effective instructional system is the six-component one [9] here outlined. Each learning unit of a course is organized as follows:

Rationale. The student is first exposed to the reason that the material has been included in the learning unit. The goals of the unit are thus justified and defended by the instructor, resulting in greater student motivation to learn.

Objectives. The student is next given the specific objectives of the learning unit. These are stated behaviorally, with precise performance indicators, and describe what the student should be able to do after instruction.

Pre-assessment. The student is pretested to determine whether he (*a*) already has achieved mastery of the objectives or (*b*) needs remedial work before being able to profit from the particular unit of instruction. The student is redirected to more appropriate material in either case. Usually, however, the pretest results simply call for him to move directly to the learning activities of the unit.

Learning Activities. The student next engages in a variety of learning activities designed to help him acquire the skills, knowledge, or attitudes specified in the objectives. The different learning styles of the students should be taken into consideration here.

Post-assessment. The student demonstrates mastery (or nonmastery) of the objectives on the post-test. Mastery permits the student to move on to the next unit of instruction. Nonmastery requires a recycling of the student back to the learning activities until such time as he demonstrates mastery. Then, and only then, does he move on to the next unit.

Revision Based on Student Feedback. The student, before going on to the next unit of instruction, provides important data (via his responses in an interview or on a brief questionnaire) used by the instructor to evaluate and revise the unit.

Where this six-component instructional system is being employed [10] the result has been a significant increase in student achievement and thus in the number of "winners." The assumption that the traditional two-component instructional system is best has been proved invalid. Adoption of a true systematic approach to instruction incorporating a rationale, specific objectives, pre- and post-assessment, validated learning activities, and feedback, along with redirection and recycling of students as needed, can be a potent force for instructional improvement.

Conclusion

The recognition of the invalid assumptions of instruction and the acceptance of valid assumptions to replace them is the first step toward improving instruction. With this accomplished, an educational revolution can become a reality. John Gardner sums it up perfectly:

I am entirely certain that, twenty years from now, we will look back at education as it is practiced in most schools and wonder that we could have tolerated anything so primitive. The pieces of the educational revolution are lying around unassembled. [11]

Notes

1. John I. Goodlad, "The Future of Learning: Into the Twenty-first Century." See pp. 2–13 of this book.
2. Ibid.
3. Ibid.
4. Benjamin S. Bloom, "Learning for Mastery." See pp. 94–113 of this book.
5. Ibid.

6. Ibid.
7. For a comprehensive treatment of this concept, cf. John E. Roueche, and John C. Pitman, *A Modest Proposal: Students Can Learn* (San Francisco: Jossey-Bass, 1972).
8. See note 4 above.
9. Barton R. Herrscher, *Implementing Individualized Instruction* (Houston: ArChem, 1971), p. 4.
10. The system is being employed by many college instructors throughout Puerto Rico and the United States. Two colleges in North Carolina are committed to the use of this system on an institution-wide basis: Mitchell College and Kittrell College.
11. John Gardner (former Secretary of Health, Education, and Welfare), from a speech delivered at the U.S. Department of Agriculture Graduate School, Washington, D.C., 8 September 1967.

Authors

"Defining Instructional Objectives," by Arthur M. Cohen, who is Associate Professor in the Graduate School of Education, University of California, Los Angeles. Dr. Cohen, the author of *Objectives for College Instruction,* is Director of the ERIC Clearinghouse for Junior Colleges.

"The Meaning of a College Education," by Paul L. Dressel, who is Assistant Provost and Director of Institutional Research at Michigan State University.

5 Specifying the Purposes of Education

G oals and objectives indicate what is to happen to the student as a result of his educational experience. Goals are usually general, objectives specific. Both should be stated operationally. Goals outline the overall skills, attitudes, or knowledge to be gained by the student; objectives specify actions or products of student actions. One of the most important ways an instructor can effect learning is by specifying instructional objectives and communicating them to students.

After completing this unit, you should be able to

1 discuss the background of the process of defining instructional outcomes (Cohen)

2 enumerate the advantages of precisely stated instructional objectives (Cohen)

3 differentiate between broad institutional goals, long-range objectives, and specific instructional objectives (Cohen, Dressel)

4 develop a statement of institutional goals representing a set of competencies to be attained by students, competencies applicable to both a liberal education and an occupational education (Dressel)

Direction is the hallmark of every instructional system. Whether the reason for the existence of a particular educational structure is to induct youngsters into the mysteries of a tribal culture, to train them to exercise technical skills in a world of specialized work, or to prepare them to apply complex cognitive processes to an infinite variety of tasks, goals may be found as guiding principles of the establishment. There must be purpose or there can be no organized process of education, and the underlying purpose of all education, formal or informal, is to bring about change in students. [1]

Within the open-door college, many forces effect such change. Counseling services help the student select from the many opportunities and paths available to him in the college and in the world outside. Student activities, planned and unplanned, temper him as he attempts to organize his life, his thoughts, and his beliefs. The whole campus community has an effect in ways which are still largely unknown. [2]

But it is for others, laboring elsewhere, to discuss the ways the many facets of college affect each student.... [By] learning about various educational approaches applicable to college curriculum and instruction... we will know something of the theories from which instructional systems are drawn, be aware of beginning attempts to apply systems approaches to education, and learn of results and future directions in colleges in which these deliberate attempts to effect educational innovation have been made.

My own effort is to outline the core of a process whereby courses and instruction within those courses may be arranged so that all is geared to institutional purpose. The process is one of defining instructional objectives in terms of observable change in the students. [3] Outcomes thus specified may serve as bases for the design of any educational system, innovative or conventional, automated or ordinary, as broad as the college's whole effort or as limited as a single instructional session. The construction and use of complete sets of objectives so defined can bring all curriculum and instruction sharply into focus, for the entire endeavor may then continually be weighed against institutional purpose—against what is actually happening to the students.

Defining Instructional Objectives

Arthur M. Cohen

The process of which I speak has not enjoyed a long history. One might consider that a need for defining instructional outcomes in terms of observable student change came into American education less than a century ago, at a time when providing a setting for the student dilettante ceased to represent the major purpose of colleges. As universities accepted a charge to train members of the professional community—architects, lawyers, teachers —programs of demonstrable relevance to students' future activities had to be built. [4] The democratic ideal of a form of higher education for all gave impetus to the process; as the doors swung open, it became increasingly necessary to define particular directions each of the newly developing college programs would take.

One might also find a reason for specified instructional objectives in the scientism characteristic of the 20th century. No more willing to accept on faith the phenomena of developmental processes in the human organism, we now try to understand and to predict patterns of learning. This is obviously impossible unless we first consider what is supposed to be learned.

Currently, some form of the art of specifying objectives is practiced in industrial and armed-services training schools and by writers of programmed texts. In each of these cases, it is impossible to design deliberate programs without considering the outcomes of the instruction. The equipment repairman must be able to make the machine operate after his training, the gunner must hit the target a specified number of times, [5] and the student who works through the program must answer the criterion questions correctly or the program has failed. [6] In all cases, the outcomes are specified before the instructional sequences are established. [7]

In the preceding paragraphs, I have used several terms—purpose, goal, aim, objective—without clear referents. I would like to single out two of these terms and give them particular definitions. Let us say first that the term *goal* here indicates generally what is to become of the students. It indicates the broad range of their abilities. Typical goals, for example, could be: (1) students will be able to communicate effectively; (2) students will understand scientific methodology; (3) students will learn to think critically; (4) students will appreciate American democratic processes; and so on, always considering that, in this case, educational goals indicate actions to be taken, skills to be learned, abilities to be gained, attitudes to be held or modified by the students as a result of having attended the institution.

The second term to be defined is *objective*. An objective as used here is a specific, observable student action or product of student action. To satisfy our definition, it must, first, specify something the student is to do; second, state the circumstances under which he will do it; and, third, note the degree of accuracy with which he will perform the action. [8]

Notice that both *goals* and *objectives* indicate something that is to happen to the student; in the one case, implied attitudes or abilities to be gained; in the other, specific actions or definite products of student actions. Under no circumstance will we consider a goal or an objective to be something provided by the college or the instructors. To say, in this context, that a college goal is "to provide opportunity for students to fulfill themselves" or that an objective is "to offer courses that meet university requirements" is inappropriate. Those and similar terms come under the heading of institutional purpose and should not be confused with goals and objectives.

How can goals and objectives be established within the open-door college? It is not difficult, once one accepts the premise that the basic reason for any education is to allow—or, if you will, cause—people to change. All instruction is designed to lead students to perform tasks they could not perform previously, to have them think different thoughts, dream different dreams. If it does not do that, or purport to do it, then it is not instruction but something else—call it "total experience without definable meaning" or "inward evolution" or by some term that identifies it as being process and product, means and end combined. Identify it, label it, and then ask honestly, "Is the providing of a setting for this indefinable something the *sole* purpose of the junior college?" If so (and I am not going to discuss here the full implications of a positive answer to that question), then any attempt to specify outcomes is meaningless—the process is its own product. If not, then some attempt to specify objectives must be made. Defining outcomes involves separating ends from means so that each may be considered for its own value.

I have gone to great lengths to define the terms *goals* and *objectives* because they must be recognized and dealt with apart from processes. They should not be confused with means and methods or with generalized and nebulous aims.

College Goals

Junior college goals are drawn from sources both extra- and intrainstitutional. [9] Whether programs are labeled liberal or general education, vocational preparation or community service, goals are influenced by board policies, social pressures, types of students, administrative orientation, and a host of other factors. Whatever the source of the goals, however, objectives may be derived from them. Rather than dwell on sources of goals, I would explain how objectives may be generated from goals that stem from any source. For this purpose, I have selected a common goal as an example and will show how it may be broken into separate objectives.

"The student will be able to communicate effectively in writing." That goal, or one similar, stems from a commitment to general education and is broad enough to be found in most college statements of direction. [10] But objectives must be built, for several instutional needs are not served by the goal statement alone. Attempts, for example, to evaluate the college's success in effecting the designated ability in its students could not be undertaken on the basis of the goal as stated. Construction of curriculum might take any direction, for interpretations of effective communication vary widely. And instructional procedures could not be established with any assurance of direct relevance. The specification of objectives is prerequisite to all those undertakings.

An objective, you recall, must meet three criteria—it must specify a student action or product of such action, it must state the conditions under which the performance will occur, and it must establish a minimum performance criterion, a standard. There are many forms of writing that could be interpreted as "effective communication." For instance, if the student produces a coherent composition, he is giving evidence of his ability to communicate effectively in writing. To meet the first criterion for the objective, then, we need to specify the type and approximate length of the composition and certain other pertinent facts. For example:

> The student will write a descriptive essay of 500–1000 words on a topic to be assigned.

That is the task performance by means of which the student shows he can communicate. Several other student actions may be derived from the same goal; for example:

> The student will write a 300–500 word set of specifications for construction of a model airplane.

> The student will write a 75–125 word description of one of 20 plants that may be found on the campus.

In each of these examples the action to be taken by the student is specified. In each case he is giving evidence that he can communicate effectively in writing, and in each case the nature of the communication is specified in advance.

The second criterion is a statement of the conditions and circumstances of the action. Do we want the student to gain ability to write his paper in class in a specified period of time? Do we want him limited to the use of certain reference materials? Conditions may be stated thus:

> Essay will be written in two hours under examination conditions; dictionary may be used.

> Description will be written as an overnight assignment.

> Student will be allowed three days and all library resources to write the paper.

> Essay will be written in 50 minutes with no aids and no rewrites permitted.

We have established the circumstances under which the action will take place.

Having set the task and the conditions, only the standard remains to be specified. We may want to allow a few errors:

> No gross grammatical errors (fragments, run-ons); not more than two errors in spelling and three in punctuation.

We may want the student to communicate effectively regardless of his grammar:

> Description will enable the instructor to identify each of the plants from a set of 20 pictures.

We may require that the essay be mechanically near-perfect:

> No gross grammatical errors (fragments, run-ons); no errors in spelling or in punctuation.

Setting the criterion depends on many factors—importance of the task, previous abilities of the students, time available for instruction, and so on. The point is, some minimum standard must be included in each objective. Put all together, here is an objective as it might be stated in practice:

> In a two-hour examination, the student will write a 500–1000 word descriptive essay on a topic to be assigned. No gross grammatical errors and a maximum of two errors in spelling and three in punctuation will be allowed. Dictionary may be used.

Note that there remains little ambiguity as to the nature of the task by means of which the student demonstrates his ability to communicate. Here are others:

> Given three days and the resources of the library, the student will write a 300–500 word set of specifications for construction of a model airplane. Specifications will be such that any woodworking student would be able to build and fly the plane.

> Given 20 pictures of plants, the student will write a 75–125 word description of one of them so that the instructor can identify the plant. Paper may include no gross grammatical or spelling errors. Dictionary will be allowed. Time: 30 minutes.

Note that in all these tasks terminal to a particular instructional sequence, the student is acting under a definite set of conditions when he demonstrates his ability to communicate. We are not speculating on whether or how well he can do it. His abilities to organize his thoughts, to handle language, to use rules of grammar, to spell, and so forth, are demonstrated in the task he has performed.

Interim Objectives

After the terminal task has been specified, interim objectives must be built. What are the several abilities prerequisite to the student's writing a composition? One can think of dozens, and each of them needs to be defined as a separate task. A set of interim tasks or objectives may be plotted so that the student is led to the desired end ability. As in the case of terminal objectives, each must meet three criteria—a task indicative of a gained ability must be specified, conditions under which the performance will occur must be noted, and a minimum achievement standard must be set.

Here are a few examples of objectives designed to demonstrate abilities prerequisite to the task of writing an essay:

1. The goal is that the student recognize appropriate titles:

   Given a 500-word descriptive essay and eight titles, two of which may be considered appropriate to the essay, the student will select one of the two titles. Time allowed, eight minutes. No reference works are permitted.

2. The student must recognize the flow of ideas:

   Given six paragraphs, the student will order them in sequence appropriate to form a coherent composition. Time allowed, ten minutes. No reference works permitted.

3. Does the student understand paragraph structure?

   Given a paragraph and six possible topic sentences, the student will select the sentence that best applies. Five minutes, no reference works.

   Given six sentences, the student will, within seven minutes, order them in sequence to form a paragraph. No reference works permitted.

There are, of course, many more, but a critical point in curriculum construction is that each of the prerequisite abilities be itself stated as a specific objective. Only in that manner can checks be applied to the system at every point and the entire sequence of relevant experiences be efficiently directed and appropriately evaluated.

Long-Range Objectives

A criticism sometimes applied to the process of specifying instructional objectives is that performances which may be tested in the classroom are too limited—that the truly important outcomes of instruction are exhibited in student behaviors beyond college walls. Defining long-range effect may, even so, be undertaken in terms of specific objectives. Tapping the student's mind directly to determine whether he has gained certain abilities is impossible—instead, we arrange for him to perform certain tasks that we agree are indicative of his holding those abilities. A similar process applies to the attitudes that affect his out-of-class actions. *If* we accept the premise that the open-door college is charged with affecting attitudes, and once we agree on the nature of those attitudes—two rather significant assumptions—it but remains for us to arrange the curriculum accordingly and to determine from the student's actions whether and how his feelings have been affected.

A long-range goal found in some college catalogs is: "The student will exercise the privileges and responsibilities of democratic citizenship."[11] Again, it is not my purpose to argue for or against the statement as a definition of purpose, but it seems sufficiently broad to be generally acceptable. What remains is to translate the stated goal into operational terms—into one or more specific objectives.

Many behaviors may be indicative of students' exercising the responsibilities of citizenship. Voting is one. Consider this specific objective:

> The student, if eligible, will voluntarily register to vote within the six months following the course.

We have an action suggesting an attitude, the circumstances (voluntarily, within six months), and a criterion (either he registers or he doesn't). A specific objective has been derived from a general goal.

Here is another behavior that might stem from a similar attitude toward democratic processes:

> Prior to the next general election, the student will voluntarily campaign for a candidate by working in his office or distributing handbills for a period of not less than 40 hours.

The student is acting in a particular manner, the conditions (voluntarily) are indicated, and a criterion (for not less than 40 hours) is suggested. There is little ambiguity about whether or not the student has gained the desired attitude; he is indicating by his actions that he has.

The issue of acquired tastes also arises in discussions of curricular organization. We may want our students to gain appreciation for forms of art other than those commonly presented in the popular media. Consider these objectives:

> Within the next year, the student will voluntarily attend three legitimate stage productions.
>
> The student will voluntarily purchase two books of contemporary poetry within the six months following the course.

The behaviors, the conditions, and the criteria are all specified.

These and similar objectives may be built for particular courses, or they may be part of a departmental charge. In all cases, however, the first consideration is to determine what observable student actions we will accept as indicative of certain attitudes. We may then set out to plan interim objectives designed to lead the student in the desired direction. It may not always be expedient to collect data on the achievement of out-of-class objectives. Nevertheless, they should be deliberately constructed, for they serve as excellent guiding principles for curriculum development.

Considerations

There are many variables to consider in defining objectives. Here are a few:

1. What is the relative importance of one objective to another, to the total of all college objectives?
2. How pertinent is the objective to the community from which the college draws its support?
3. What are the base abilities of the entering student population?

4. What percent of the students enrolled in a particular program will reach certain objectives?
5. How relevant is the objective to the student this year? five years from now?

These and other factors must be assessed time and again as objectives are constructed and revised. Defining objectives for the two-year college is not a one-time task. It must be done continually at regular intervals, and it should be undertaken by everyone who has concern for the curriculum and for instructional processes. Consider the advantages:

1. A continuing dialog on institutional goals and purposes will ensue—a dialog based on actual outcomes.
2. Gaps and overlaps in the curriculum may be identified and reduced. Is the college committing too much to certain goals, not enough to others?
3. Organizational patterns and physical-plant arrangements may be planned in terms of what is really happening to the students. Resources may be appropriately directed.
4. Methods and media may be selected and used according to their demonstrated value. A whole basis for experimentation can be established.
5. The giving of grades may be made relevant to actual, defined accomplishments. Marks will take on particular meanings.
6. Student self-study may be economically and appropriately directed.

Determining complete sets of specific objectives and communicating them to students may be the single most significant thing an instructor can do to effect learning. [12]

The process is not without its pitfalls. For one thing, ambiguous goals and aims have great defensive value. It is impossible for a critic to snipe at a college program with any great degree of accuracy if he does not know what the program is designed to accomplish. If we say the students will learn to communicate effectively, to think critically, and to appreciate democracy, and stop short of translating those goals into specific objectives, who can say that the students do not so communicate, think, and appreciate? The accusation that they have not reached those fortunate cognitive and affective states of mind is easily rebutted if for no other reason than that the charge must be based on terms and data capable of widely varying interpretation.

A corollary to be considered here is that once outcomes are specified, the college must stand ready to defend each of them. There is a public relations plus in nebulous concepts. Anyone who challenges the college's statement that it intends to lead its students to "exercise the privileges and responsibilities of democratic citizenship" is attacking Flag Day and the Fourth of July. But translate that exercise into particular habits of voting, campaigning, and becoming involved in public issues, and someone in the community will not approve. Once communicated, specific objectives will be questioned, and the more successful the institution is in bringing its students to the ability to perform the designated tasks, the more intense the questioning will become. Paradoxically, ambiguity, inefficiency, and instructional procedures of unknown effect are, in this case, institutional strengths.

There are matters of internal import also. Once objectives are spelled out in specific, measurable terms, instructional methods will become considerably more efficient. Having gone through the deliberate process of constructing the objectives, instructors will become intensely aware of what they are trying to do and seek more appropriate ways of doing it. They may wish to prepare replicable media, so that when they find effective means of meeting their objectives they can use the materials again. Staff requests for mechanical equipment will be weighed on the basis of demonstrable value. One or more measurement specialists will have to be assigned to help the faculty gather evidence of student achievement. The work of the college research director will gain new dimensions, for it will then involve much more than his computing grade-point averages to the second decimal place. These matters represent adjustments that can and should be made within the framework of existing educational structures as junior colleges proceed to define outcomes.

I have listed some of the considerations that arise once objectives are defined, because the system is so very different from that in most of our educational institutions. Specifying objectives means separating process from product in the classroom. It means examining student change rather than teacher performance. It means sharpening our views of students—looking past their implied abilities to their specific actions, beyond their unknown attitudes to their observed behaviors.

Conclusion

The process of defining objectives is neither a fad nor a mere transient approach. It is a deliberate attempt to focus instructors' and administrators' attention on their actual intent—and for timely reasons. Formerly, when instruction was all lecture–textbook, learn or don't, it was so ill-defined that it was immune to assessment. Learning took place in or out of class —few knew or particularly cared. It was easy to hide behind the "normal ability curve" and to say "We put it before them. Sorry if they were unmotivated to learn."

But changes have occurred. Our institutions are filled with all types of students, and it *is* possible to teach them, for we know much more about human learning than we did a generation ago. It is feasible, for example, to arrange instructional sequences so that a measurable change comes about; to alter instructional forms in accordance with the nature of the tasks the student will be asked to perform; to design and to effect change. [13] As materials of a programmed instructional nature become better developed and more widely used, the process of influencing outcomes will become quite familiar in all colleges. [14] And as computer-assisted instruction becomes a reality, the ultimate in directing learning will be achieved. [15]

Will junior college educators lead in the process of demonstrably effective education? Defining instructional objectives is only the first step, already overdue. Will instructors specify the goals of their own instruction? They must work through the process in their own courses—build the objectives, specify the outcomes, collect the evidence—or be guilty of abandoning to others the responsibility they implicitly accepted when they entered the profession.

What is offered here is a set of tools for use by people concerned with what happens in education. It is not necessary for one to accept an instructional system based exclusively on defined goals; the indefinable, the unmeasurable will be with us, I expect, for generations. But as beginning points for assessing impact of the curriculum, as minimum levels to which we can commit our resources, specific instructional objectives must be considered by everyone in the two-year college.

Notes

1. Jack R. Frymier, *The Nature of Educational Method* (Columbus, Ohio: Charles E. Merrill, 1965), p. 7.
2. Philip E. Jacob, *Changing Values in College* (New York: Harper, 1957), p. 111.
3. The process was pioneered by Ralph Tyler and his associates at the University of Chicago during the 1930s.
4. Frederick Rudolph, *The American College and University* (New York: Vintage Books, 1962), p. 241.
5. Robert G. Smith, *The Development of Training Objectives* (Washington, D.C.: George Washington University, Human Resources Research Office, 1961).
6. C. A. Thomas, *Programmed Learning in Perspective* (Chicago: Educational Methods, 1961), p. 37.
7. Benjamin S. Bloom, ed., *Taxonomy of Educational Objectives* (New York: David McKay, 1956), p. 26.
8. Robert F. Mager, *Preparing Instructional Objectives* (Belmont, Calif.: Fearon, 1962).
9. Clyde E. Blocker et al., *The Two-Year College: A Social Synthesis* (Englewood Cliffs, N. J.: Prentice-Hall, 1965), p. 205.
10. B. Lamar Johnson, *General Education in Action* (Washington, D.C.: American Council on Education, 1952), p. 140.
11. *Catalog and Announcement of Courses* (Palm Desert, Calif.: College of the Desert, 1963), p. 4.
12. Paul Douglas, *Teaching for Self-Education As a Life Goal* (New York: Harper, 1960), p. 29.
13. Robert M. Gagné, "The Analysis of Instructional Objectives for the Design of Instruction," in *Teaching Machines and Programed Learning*, edited by R. Glaser (Washington, D.C.: National Education Association, 1965).
14. B. F. Skinner, "Teaching Machines," *Scientific American* (November 1961).
15. John Coulson, "Automation, Electronic Computers, and Education," *Phi Delta Kappan* 47 (March 1966): 310–311.

Each year I preside over a graduate seminar examining problems of instruction and curriculum in American higher education. For some years it had been my custom to initiate the discussion with the question "What does a student get out of college?" It caused consternation among some students, but it led to a stimulating discussion of various results of a college education. And then one year there appeared a brash and obviously bored young doctoral candidate whose quick and cynical response brought greater consternation to me than to his fellow students. To my question "What does a student get out of college?" he responded tersely, "Himself." Inclined, as are many professors, to reject the unanticipated response as both inappropriate and incorrect, I barely restrained a cutting response. And then, in a flash, I realized that the answer was exactly right. Ultimately all students who enter college do get out of it—by death, by dropout, or by baccalaureate degree. My cynical friend had stated the truth. Every student who enters college does sometime, somehow, get out of it.

Having arrived at this conclusion, I complimented my perspicacious friend (note how I have promoted him) and admitted that I had not posed the question I intended. And so I tried again: "How would you determine whether an individual had received a baccalaureate degree?" With a smirk, my intelligent, incisive, but slightly irksome friend responded, "By examining a certified copy of his college transcript." Again, in my desire to get to the anticipated discussion I was tempted to suggest we dispense with the humor and get down to business. But then, as I silently and quickly reviewed my own practice in determining whether an individual had received a degree, I had to admit to myself, to my irksome friend, and to the group that once again the answer was precisely right.

The Meaning
of a College Education

A Set of Competencies
and a Degree of Attainment in Each

Paul L. Dressel

Somewhat chastened, I now attempted to phrase a question that could not thus easily be answered: "If I tell you that an individual has a baccalaureate degree from a college in the United States, what else do you know about that individual?" I glanced confidently toward my discerning friend, who responded quickly and tersely, "The individual has attended some college." My friend was precisely right once again. Despite all of the discussion of credit by examinations, I know of no institution in these United States that will grant a baccalaureate degree to a student until that student has spent some period of time—usually a minimum of one academic year—on its campus. If one knows that a person has a baccalaureate degree from an American college or university, he knows that that person has been to college somewhere for some period of time. And so, once again I complimented my ready and realistic respondent, but now pointed out that my question had asked, "What else do you know?" Accepting the answer as correct, the question still remained as to whether there might be other facts that would be definitely known about that baccalaureate recipient. So I then raised the question: "What would one surely know about the college experiences of anyone with a baccalaureate degree?" Answers included paying fees and listening to lectures, but some argued that athletes paid no fees and individuals might sleep through lectures, and here my original respondent somewhat belligerently reasserted that the only certainty was that the degree recipient had attended college.

On this dismal note our first session ended. After two hours we had concluded (1) that the only thing a student certainly gets out of college is himself; (2) that one can be sure that a person has a baccalaureate degree only by examining a certified transcript; and (3) that possession of a baccalaureate degree indicates that a person has spent some limited time on a college or university campus.

What Are the Standards?

Other than credits, grade-point requirement, and a few specific course requirements, most institutions of higher education have no standards of award for a diploma. There is no basis for awarding a baccalaureate degree except that a student serve time and meet the specific requirements. In at least one state, university students, mental institution patients, and prisoners in the state penitentiary are referred to in statements of budget and financial procedure as inmates. Obviously, this is not a reasonable grouping, for it is much easier for the student to get out without showing any improvement. Our whimsical, somewhat cynical, but essentially correct conclusions suggest that the extensive statements of objectives in college catalogs have had, as John W. Gardner once observed, as little impact on the achievements of most colleges and universities as the chaplain's prayers have on the conduct of business in the United States Senate.

Yet the purpose of educational objectives is to give direction to an educational program, to provide guidance in the development of that program, and to indicate the anticipated results in behavioral terms detailed enough to determine whether students have attained the objectives in sufficient degree. Objectives do not do this, because they are too esoteric and too inexplicit, hence unattainable. In all such statements, to satisfy the young faculty members, each of whom is convinced that the knowledge developed in his own discipline is the most important thing for a student to acquire, knowledge plays a big role. The student personnel staff, distraught by student demands for freedom, is concerned with citizenship and personal responsibility. Older faculty members and deans, no longer competent in their disciplines and no longer sure that these are the most significant things in life, are sure that critical thinking, attitudes, and values should be given a major place in statements of objectives. Humanists in literature and the arts still insist on the inclusion of such terms as appreciation and creativity, perhaps hoping thereby that their own self-acknowledged creativity will be more widely appreciated. No one really knows what a university president hopes for his undergraduates, other than that they leave his office and return to their classes, but private liberal arts college presidents continue to insist that, for the sake of their boards and benefactors, statements of objectives include religious commitment. Thus one finds such anomalies as an institution extending, on one page of its catalog, a hearty invitation to Jewish and Catholic students and on another page indicating that one of the desired outcomes is a commitment to Protestant Christianity.

Asking more than the college can possibly provide and being so unspecific that no evaluation is possible, it is not surprising that objectives have become exercises in pompous verbosity. Humanists may defend such excesses by asserting, with credit to Browning, that "a man's reach should exceed his grasp." But the engineer or the scientist to whom *Browning* means a type of machine gun may well wonder whether a man who goes around reaching but never grasping might be only an unsuccessful beggar.

It is time that institutions of higher education justify the confidence and generous support given them by defining some minimal set of competencies and a degree of attainment in each in order to give meaning to a college education. If an individual has a baccalaureate degree, he should be aware of some competencies he possesses, and he should be aware that these competencies are of significance in many different fields of activity. In stating such competencies, we should avoid becoming involved in the vocational–liberal education debate. Surely when vocational education is so specific in its attention to the development of skills that the individual's vision is seriously limited and his possibility of flexible adaptation to changing technology negated, it is bad education; it is not even college education. A liberal education that is irrelevant to the current scene and to the individual's future career has never been and is not now acceptable in our society. There are abilities, skills, and insights that are valuable in most occupations and also essential in the personal development of an individual and in his effective performance as a citizen. If we can attain such a statement of competencies and provide experiences by which each student attains these competencies, the individual will not only have attained a liberal education but be able to earn a living.

Up to this point I have been destructively critical, and the obligation now rests with me to contribute some positive alternative by offering such a statement of competencies. I shall suggest six—six being the smallest perfect number.

What of the Competencies?

1. *The student should know how to acquire knowledge and how to use it.* Acquiring knowledge includes utilization and evaluation of source material; analysis and interpretation of data; experimentation; firsthand observations; interviews and discussion. Using knowledge includes evaluation of accuracy and relevance of evidence; solution of problems; explanation of events; analysis of possible courses of action; prediction. The competency is to be interpreted as applicable to problems arising in any aspect of living: vocational, social, or personal. The acceptance of such a competency as an outcome of an undergraduate program has immediate implications with regard to the relevance of the learning experiences provided. In the broad interpretation given, formal course work, particularly of the lecture–recitation type, has limited value. Students can learn how to acquire knowledge and use it through community-service experiences and through working with other students in the study, analysis, and solution of problems originating on the campus or in society at large. Independent study is a highly relevant concept and becomes, within the framework of this competency, a major final required experience by which the student demonstrates that he has developed the initiative and the ability to acquire knowledge and to use it with minimal direction and supervision by a professor.

2. *The student should have a high level of mastery of the skills of communication.* The phrase *high level* may be a stumbling block, for colleges have always accepted this competency as a desired outcome, but they have not defined or demanded actual accomplishment. I suggest that high-level mastery should include such more specific competencies as perceptivity and sensitivity in recognizing attitudes; accuracy in the use of technical vocabulary; facility with grammar; adaptability to audiences; flexibility in style. The skills of communication, of course, include reading—with facility and appropriate critical reactions—both popular and scholarly materials; listening in formal and informal situations; speaking to large assemblies and small groups; writing formal research papers and critical essays; participating in discussion and dialog. This competency is applicable to communication in every aspect of living. The range of relevant learning experiences is, therefore, almost limitless: analysis and evaluation of newspapers, magazines, and scholarly research papers, interviewing, group discussions, preparation of technical reports, critical analyses or statements of personal points of view. Certainly one of the most potent experiences

in communication for students is in teaching other students, for one's mastery and his ability to communicate are simultaneously challenged. The active involvement of students in educating others also motivates students to become involved in their own education. Only as an individual is capable of communication is it possible for us to really assess the extent to which he has mastered other significant competencies.

3. *A student should be aware of his own values and value commitments; and he should be aware that other individuals and cultures hold contrasting values that must be understood and to some extent accepted for satisfactory interactions.* Every individual has some set of values, even though he may curry favor and avoid difficulty by accepting or appearing to accept the values of those with whom he is in contact at the moment. However, values may go unrecognized because they are implicit in unexamined behavior or are habitual because of precept and prescription. The statement of this competency is based on the assumption that values are in large part culturally determined, that there are no absolutes, and that meaningful interaction among individuals and cultural groups requires understanding and acceptance rather than mere tolerance. The statement also assumes that colleges and universities must be dominated by a spirit of continuing and critical inquiry, a value commitment that underlies all six competencies, and acceptance of which is a prerequisite for continuance and development in college.

Values refer to the bases, considerations, or points of view, conscious or unconscious, that are involved in or appear to underlie a person's choices and actions. A person's value commitments may interact or clash so that behavior is, at best, an ambiguous guide to value. A truthful husband may still tell a lie when his wife requests a comment on her new dress. Our inferences of others' values are bounded by our own. Recognizing this, we should be hesitant about rejecting the values of other individuals and cultures as untenable or wrong simply because they differ from our own.

The competency is applicable to all behavior engaged in by the student, but individuals should not become so self-conscious and introspective about their reactions and thoughts that they are incapacitated for action. Rather, they should recognize and weigh the effects of those environmental constraints and sanctions that often determine views, attitudes, or behavior without awareness of the values thereby supported. Social mores and personal habits are efficient and often effective in permitting time for more significant thought and pursuit of deeper meaning, yet the life that is unexamined in its details may become unexaminable in any fuller or more complete sense. Acceptance of value differences also involves the valuing of the worth and dignity of the individual, and hence of individual originality and creativity which, along with critical inquiry, are basic value commitments of higher education.

The limitless range of application of this competency means that any experience, in or out of class, on or off campus, can have relevance. Some will be more effective than others, however, because they confront the individual with a situation in which the values revealed force a confrontation with them. For some individuals, differences in speech, food, dress, aesthetic standards, use of leisure time, politics, or religion will serve as the initial stimulation. For others, some probing into the rationale of their own views and those of other students and professors may be required. In order to sense fully the meaning of value differences, an individual may require a "culture shock," such as is attainable only by living in a community of radically different pattern and customs. Although courses and other structured experiences can contribute to value consciousness and awareness of motivations, community service, team learning experiences, and study abroad are likely to have even more effect.

If students are to develop concern, awareness, and competency in recognition and analysis of value differences and their implications in decisions, colleges must clarify their own values and, by consistency in relating decisions to them, demonstrate the meaning of this competency. Many decisions in our colleges are not actually made; they result only from the gradual accretion of specific actions from day to day and the ultimate verbalization of the consequences. Even in major decisions, expediency, opportunism, and competition often play a determining role. Many institutions currently are yielding reluctantly to student demands for greater freedom only because the pressures make it expedient to do so. Institutions acquire new programs and new buildings simply because the money is made available, although the operating costs rise and the programs may dilute or negate the central concerns of the institution. A liberal arts college president recently told me that, against his better judgment, his college will add graduate programs in order to maintain equality with another college in the same community which has announced that intent. Students are disillusioned with higher education, at least in part, because the values we preach are too often denied by our practice.

4. *The student should be able to cooperate and to collaborate with others in studying, analyzing, and formulating solutions to problems and taking action on them*. The difficulty of stating educational outcomes and agreeing on them is demonstrated by two reactions to this competency. One professor argued loudly and at length that learning is essentially an individual enterprise and that the idea of cooperation or collaboration was inappropriate to higher education. Another rejected the use of the word *collaborate* on the grounds that it had communistic overtones. One is tempted to conclude that the great difficulty in planning undergraduate education is that too many of the professors themselves lack the competencies that should result from undergraduate education.

This competency, cooperation and collaboration, is closely related to the first competency. which places emphasis on the individual and expresses the concern that he be able to acquire and utilize knowledge and relate it to problems. It does not debar the individual from seeking the assistance of others or collaborating with others, but it demands that he have this competency in his own right. Competency 4, on the other hand, is explicitly concerned that the student be able and willing to cooperate and collaborate with others because our democratic society and its associated technology place increasing emphasis on the ability of individuals to relate themselves to others effectively and to find thereby self-realization and self-expression rather than self-obliteration.

Again, this is a far-reaching competency. It involves effective communication, and it depends upon valuing each individual and capitalizing on the individuality and creativity of each. This competency uses several words that would require some careful definition and elaboration. *Cooperate* implies joint action, concurrence, agreement, personal contribution, and possibly compromise. *Collaborate* means working together, acting jointly, agreeing upon a division of labor—a procedure for combining individual efforts into a single product. Collaboration is, therefore, a more active interaction with others than cooperation, which can be largely passive.

The range of application of this competency is again extensive, including vocational, social, and personal activities. Problems may arise in preparation for courses, in the laboratory, in the determination of college policies, in residence halls, in the interaction of the college and the community, or in society at large. If one accepts this competency as important, then team or group projects and reports in courses and in independent study projects, committee assignments in colleges or residence halls, community-service projects, seminars, and surveys become some of the more obvious relevant learning experiences.

5. *The student should have awareness, concern, and a sense of responsibility regarding contemporary events, issues, and problems.* Acceptance of this competency rejects the "ivory tower" conception of a college for a more dynamic conception, which regards the college experience not only as a preparation for life but as a period of carefully planned and directed internship for reflections upon, and interactions with, society. Certain terms command our attention. *Awareness* denotes no more than knowledge that events are occurring or have occurred, that certain issues or problems exist. *Concern* involves conscious direction of attention to these events and some degree of regard, solicitude, or anxiety about the consequences. *Sense of responsibility* indicates acceptance of some personal obligation to assess the implications of events and to contribute to the resolution of issues or solution of problems. Issues are frequently timeless and can be studied in the classics of ancient Greece, but the student will not live in ancient

Greece and, unless these issues are related to events around him, his education will not—in a term frequently used by restless students—be relevant. The range of application of this competency is limitless, but each student must practice and attain the competency within some limits. While awareness, concern, and sense of responsibility include problems of all types, no individual can be expected to be equally aware of and concerned with all. His range of concern, however, is some indication of the extent to which he perceives his education as relevant to his total role as a person. Awareness, concern, and responsibility are not readily inculcated by learning experiences specifically developed and directed to those ends. Rather, they result from a projection of a program or a college image that attracts students concerned more with problems than with mastery of a discipline, and from a faculty that demonstrates, in and out of class, alertness to and concern with events outside academe. The competency implies that education is useful only as it is relevant to and contributes to the improvement of the life of an individual and of society. The competency is developed through experiences, decisions, and actions that are consciously related to ultimate results and to the values they appear to support. An educational program that fosters this competency must provide for each individual a balance between disciplines and individual concerns; between ideas and theories and problems, or the issues they serve to illuminate or explain; between the isolated item of data, the discrete fact, and the essential but elusive interrelationship of all knowledge in the life of the individual. Any learning experience can provide opportunity for development of this competency provided it is a continuing and conscious concern of the faculty who, by their insistence, make it also a continuing and conscious concern of the students.

6. *The student should see his total college experience as coherent, cumulative, and unified by the development of the broad competencies already indicated and by the accompanying realization that these competencies are relevant to his further development as an individual and fulfillment of his obligations as a responsible citizen in a democratic society.* Thus the student sees his college experience as cohesive, interrelated, connected, additive, and unified by his concern and the faculty's concern that he develop these competencies. His college education becomes meaningful to him because he has some ends in view. He can see his day-to-day experiences in relation to these ends, and he can, with assistance, appraise his own progress toward them. There is no longer a dichotomy between means and ends. The competencies to be acquired determine the experiences to be provided, and the experiences are obvious exercises in the competencies.

In a college in which such competencies are emphasized, the student will have gotten something out of college besides himself. The faculty can assert confidently that the individual who acquires a baccalaureate degree has done something more than serve time and acquire credits. Education in such a college will have some tangible meaning, expressed in the competencies that its graduates exhibit.

What of the Faculty?

In presenting this conception of a college education, I may be charged by some with having reached farther than I can grasp and by others with having reached farther than most faculties can or want to grasp. Certainly faculty commitment is a necessity. Currently faculties not only reach for but tenaciously grasp at specialization, departmentalization, course proliferation, decreased teaching loads and increased salaries, pretentious and petty scholarship, and an increasing share of governance. There is abroad these days a point of view, openly and succinctly expressed by one professor who, in rejecting an appeal for a renovation of undergraduate education, asserted that the college or university exists for the sake of the professor and not the student. He further asserted that only this emphasis could insure a strong faculty and that the undergraduate was thereby benefited. This statement was a forthright profession, but I believe that faculties should profess a renewed commitment to a meaningful undergraduate education and demonstrate this by providing a coherent, cumulative, unified undergraduate educational experience. Then and only then can meaning be restored to a college education and to the baccalaureate degree that signifies its completion.

Authors

"Are Children Born Unequal?" by William H. Boyer and Paul Walsh. Both are Professors at the College of Education at the University of Hawaii.

"The Teacher As Pygmalion: Comments on the Psychology of Expectation," by Peter Gumpert and Carol Milligan. (This is a condensation of the original article.) Peter Gumpert is Assistant Professor in Social Psychology at Teachers College, Columbia University, New York. Carol Milligan is teaching in the Department of Psychology of Providence College in Providence, Rhode Island.

6 Student Learning: An Emerging View

H istorically poor teaching has been protected by the assumption that students fail because they lack ability. This assumption is no longer valid. Students can achieve a high level of mastery, and there are means for promoting mastery learning. Not all of the means are "instructional." Some are psychological. One of these is teacher expectation for student achievement. This unit looks at the psychology of expectation against a backdrop of human equality—equality of intellectual potential. The concepts developed here and in the unit following form a foundation on which a new educational structure will inevitably rest.

Rationale

After completing this unit, you should be able to

Objectives

1 discuss the historically accepted concept of the natural inequality of man and its application to education (Boyer and Walsh)

2 enumerate the four types of evidence typically offered to prove that people are innately different in their capacity to learn, and build a case refuting such evidence (Boyer and Walsh)

3 select, after considering three "ability models," the one to which you personally subscribe, and state the rationale for your selection (Boyer and Walsh)

4 formulate a case in support or rejection of the statement "Poor teaching is protected in the American educational system through the assumption that the student doesn't have the ability" (Boyer and Walsh)

5 discuss the educational implications of Rosenthal and Jacobson's study regarding the effects of teacher expectation on student attainment (Gumpert and Milligan)

6 formulate a case for or against the concept that teacher expectation leading to selectivity of attention, perception, response, interpersonal warmth, and encouragement, might actually result in superior student learning and performance (Gumpert and Milligan)

7 use the "teacher expectation" concept to evaluate old classroom practices such as tracking, homogeneous grouping, class size, group instruction, and stress on learning speed, as an index of student intelligence (Gumpert and Milligan)

8 discuss the effects of "reward success" and "punish failure" on the learning environment (Gumpert and Milligan)

In societies where power and privilege are not equally distributed, it has always been consoling to those with favored positions to assume that nature has caused the disparity. When man himself creates unequal opportunity, he can be obliged or even forced to change his social system. But if nature creates inequality, man need only bow to supreme forces beyond his control, and the less fortunate must resign themselves to their inevitable disadvantage.

The metaphysics of natural inequality has served aristocracies well. The Greeks had wealth and leisure as a result of the labor of slaves. Plato expressed the wisdom of the established order with the claim that nature produces a hierarchy of superiority in which philosophers, such as himself, emerge at the top. Aristotle's belief that all men possess a rational faculty had more heretical potential, but it was not difficult to believe that some men are more rational than others.

In later periods, nations that possessed economic superiority explained their advantages on the basis of innate superiority. Sir Francis Galton was convinced that the English were superior and that the propertied classes were even more superior than the general population. They were the repository of what was the most biologically precious in mankind.

The democracies of the new world shattered many elements of the old order, and brought a new, radical, equalitarian outlook. In principle, if not always in practice, man became equal before the law, and the idea of "the worth of the individual" established a principle of moral equality. Yet legal and moral equalitarianism did not necessarily mean that men were intellectually equal. So the assumption upon which American schools and the American marketplace developed was that democracy should mean *equal opportunity for competition among people who are genetically unequal*. This creed has satisfied the requirements of modern wisdom even for the more

---

Are Children Born Unequal?

William H. Boyer and Paul Walsh

liberal founding fathers such as Thomas Jefferson, and it equally fit into the social Darwinism of an emerging industrial society.

In contemporary American education many of these assumptions remain. People are usually assumed to be not only different in appearance but also innately unequal in intellectual capacity and therefore unequal in capacity to learn. The contemporary creed urges that schools do all they can to develop *individual* capacities, but it is usually assumed that such capacities vary among individuals. Ability grouping is standard practice and begins in the earliest grades. Intelligence tests and the burgeoning armory of psychometric techniques increasingly facilitate ability tracking, and therefore the potentially prosperous American can usually be identified at an early age. If it is true that people have inherently unequal capacities to learn, the American educational system is built on theoretical bedrock, and it helps construct a social order based on natural superiority. But if people actually have inherently equal capacities, the system is grounded in quicksand and reinforces a system of arbitrary privilege.

Four types of evidence are typically offered to prove that people are innately different in their capacity to learn. The first is self-evidential, the second is observational, the third is logical–theoretical, and the fourth is statistical.

The self-evidential position is based on high levels of certainty, which include a strong belief in the obviousness of a conclusion. Many people are very certain that there is an innate difference between people in intellectual capacity. However, such tenacity of feeling is not itself a sufficient basis for evidence, for it offers no method of verification. The mere certainty of a point of view regarding the nature of intelligence must be discounted as an adequate basis for verification.

The observation of individual differences in learning capacity cannot be dismissed as a basis for evidence; useful information for hypotheses requiring further verification can be obtained in this way. For instance, parents may notice different rates of learning among their children. People from different social classes learn and perform at different levels. The city child may learn particular skills more rapidly than the rural child. Observations require some care if they are to produce reliable evidence, but it is possible to observe carefully, and such observation can be verified by other careful observers.

But if people learn particular tasks at different rates, does it follow that people must therefore be *innately* different in their learning capacity? It does *not* necessarily follow. Increasingly, as we know more about the role of environment, we see that there are not only differences between cultures but also differences within cultures. Even within families, no child has the same environment as the others. Being born first, for instance, makes that child different; he is always the oldest sibling. A whole host of variables operates so that the environment as perceived by an individual child has elements of uniqueness (and similarity) with that of other children raised in proximity.

Observational evidence can be a useful part of the process of understanding when it raises questions that can be subjected to more conclusive evidence, but it is often used as a way of selectively verifying preconceived notions endemic in the culture. Western culture is strongly rooted in the belief in a natural intellectual hierarchy. Few observers have been taught to make observations based on assumptions of natural intellectual equality. Observational evidence must be carefully questioned, for it is often based on a metaphysic of differential capacity, which encourages selective perception and *a priori* categories of explanation. Yet these preconceptions are rarely admitted as an interpretive bias of the observer.

Data-Based Theories

Theories based on carefully obtained data provide a more adequate basis for reaching a defensible position on the nature-nurture controversy than either of the previous procedures. A general theory in the field of genetics of psychology that fits available information would be a relevant instrument for making a deduction about the nature of intelligence. If a logical deduction could be made from a more general theory about heredity and environment to the more specific question of innate intellectual capacity, the conclusion would be as strong as the theory. Such deduction is a commonly used procedure.

Both genetic and psychological theories have often been used to support the belief in inherited intelligence. Genetic connections between physical characteristics such as eye color, hair color, and bodily stature are now clearly established. Certain disease propensity has a genetic basis, yet the best established research is now between single genes and specific physical traits. It is commonplace to assume that if a hereditary basis for differential physical traits has been established, there is a similar connection between genes and intelligence. The conclusion, however, does *not* necessarily follow. Intelligence, defined as the capacity to profit by experience or as the ability to solve problems, is not a function of a single gene. Whatever the particular polygenetic basis for learning, it does not follow that intellectual capacity is variable because physical traits are variable. Current genetic theory does not provide an adequate basis for deducing a theory of abilities.

Similarly, the Darwinian theory of natural selection is often used to ascribe superiority to those in the upper strata of a hierarchical society. Yet a system of individual economic competition for survival is actually a very recent phenomenon in human history, characteristic of only a few societies, primarily in the 18th, 19th, and early 20th centuries. It is very probably irrelevant to genetic natural selection because of its recent origin. American immigration came largely from the lower classes, a fact that could condemn America to national inferiority if the Darwinian theory were used. In the long span of human history, most societies have relied mainly on cooperative systems or autocratic systems for their survival, and individual competition is an atypical example drawn largely from the unique conditions of Western, particularly American experience.

Psychological theories that emphasize individual difference have often assumed that the descriptive differences in physical characteristics, personality, and demonstrated ability are all due largely to heredity. Psychology has had strong historical roots in physiology, but as social psychologists and students of culture have provided new understanding of the role of experience, hereditarian explanation has shifted toward environmentalism. Even the chemical and anatomical characteristics of the brain are now known to be modifiable by experience. . . .

Anthropologists, with their awareness of the effects of culture, are the least likely to place credence in the genetic hypothesis. Claude Levi-Strauss, a social anthropologist, claims that all men have equal intellectual potentiality and have been equal for about a million years. Whether or not this is true, it is clear that the best-supported general genetic or psychological theory does not validate the conclusion that individual intellectual capacity is innately unequal.

Statistical studies under controlled conditions, on the other hand, can provide some of the most reliable information. For instance, when animals are genetically the same, there is the possibility of inferring genetic characteristics through experimental studies. Identical twins develop from the separation of a single egg and have identical genetic inheritance. If human twins could be raised under controlled experimental conditions, much could be learned about the respective role of heredity and environment. Many studies have been made of twins, but none under sufficiently controlled experimental conditions. The results, therefore, permit only speculative conclusions. Most twins are so similar that unless they are separated they are likely to be treated alike. When they are separated, in most cases one twin is moved to a family of the same social class as the other twin. And people of similar appearance tend to be treated similarly—a large, handsome child is not usually treated the same as a short, unattractive child. The resultant similarity of IQ scores of separate twins has not been surprising.

Studies of Twins

Even if particular identical twins were to show marked differences in ability when they live in substantially different environments, as they occasionally do, the evidence does not prove the *environmentalist* thesis unless a significantly large number of random cases is compared with a similarly random selection of nonidentical twins. In a small sample, difference could be due to the experience deprivation of one twin. It is possible to stultify any type of development, and so the variation between identical twins, identified in some studies up to 40 points, by no means disproves the hereditarian position. Consequently, current studies do not provide conclusive statistical evidence to support either position over the other.

The second most common statistical evidence used to show the hereditary basis of intelligence is the constancy of IQ scores at different age periods.

Usually, IQ scores do not change appreciably, but occasionally the changes are dramatic. It is now understood that a standard IQ test is culturally loaded toward middle-class values, and so the general constancy of most IQ scores can be explained as the expected result of limited mobility between social class and the resultant constancy of subcultural experiences. So even the statistical "evidence," so often used to support a belief in innate intelligence, is really not conclusive.

Studies of innate intelligence, then, have not produced conclusive evidence to justify the claim for an innate difference in individual intellectual capacity. Equally, there has not been conclusive evidence that the innate potential between people is equal. The research is heavily marked by the self-serving beliefs of the researchers. Psychologists have usually created "intelligence" tests that reflect their own values, predetermining that their own scores will be high. When they have discovered they are high, they have often proclaimed such tests to be indicators of innate superiority.

Many studies are built on simple-minded assumptions about the nature of environment. Physiological environment is related to the subject. A researcher who says that two children live in the "same" environment is quite wrong, for the environment that each child perceives may be quite different from that perceived by the researcher.

Assumptions about Environment

Also, it is often assumed that environment is only postnatal, but evidence is now available on the role of prenatal environment, both psychologically and nutritionally. Malnutrition of a pregnant mother can, and often does, have permanent debilitating psychological and physiological effects on her child. Certain diseases contracted by the mother (measles, for example) and certain drugs (thalidomide, for instance) can produce destructive "environmental" effects that limit intellectual capacities. Clearly, people do demonstrate varying capacities to learn, but they have had varying prenatal and postnatal opportunities. If they are female, they are generally treated differently than if they are male. Negroes are treated differently from whites—one social class is treated differently from another. The *kind* of employment people engage in has a profound effect on what they become. They probably become different through different treatment and different experience, yet our institutions, reflecting our culture, usually operate on the assumption that such differences in ability are innate.

Ability Models

There are at least three ability models that can be supported by current evidence. Each is based on different assumptions about human nature and therefore provides a basis for different social philosophies and different conceptions of government and education.

The first model assumes a great variety of innate ability and a high level of intellectual demand on the average person. In this model, there are hereditary geniuses and idiots, while most people have an intellectual capacity about equal to the demands of their society.

The second model assumes that the innate ability potential of everyone (who has not been injured pre- or postnatally) is equal and far exceeds the normal demand level. (The actual opportunities a person has may produce differential *performance* similar to the first model.)

The third model assumes the possibility of some variation, but since all of the ability potential is well beyond the normal demand level, the variation makes virtually no operational difference.

In an economic or educational system, the first model would justify the usual culling, sorting, and excluding through screening devices to create a "natural" hierarchy of ability. It would also justify the common belief in "equal opportunity for competition between unequals," where sorting is achieved through competition.

Applying Ability Models

Both the second and third models would justify maximum social effort to develop the abilities of all people, and the failure to achieve high levels of ability in all people would constitute social failure rather than individual failure. American society, with its considerable disparity of wealth and power, is largely a success based on the inequality assumed in the first of the three models. It is largely a failure based on the equality assumed in the second and third models.

Schools make little effort to develop the kind of equal ability assumed in models two and three. IQ tests are widely used to identify presumed differences in innate ability so that culling and grouping can make the management of the school easier and more efficient. The disastrous effects of the schools on lower-class children are now finally becoming known. The "compensatory" concept has gained some headway, but most educators are so overloaded with work and so traditional in outlook that the schools have become partners with the economic system in reinforcing a system of privilege that usually panders to the children of those in power and finds metaphysical excuses to make only minor gestures toward the less fortunate. The "special programs for the gifted" would be more accurately labeled "special programs for the privileged," for the gifted are primarily the children from socioeconomic classes that provide the most opportunities. The less fortunate (usually lower-class children) are ordinarily neglected or convinced that they are innately inferior. Once they become convinced, the prophecy is soon realized.

Part of the problem is the way *intelligence* is defined. It can be defined in many different ways, each leading to a somewhat different educational direction. We can view intelligence as environmental adaptation, as ability to solve problems, as ability to use logical convergent thinking. Or our definition can emphasize divergent thinking and the creation of ideas and problems. When *intelligence* is defined as abstract verbal–conceptual ability drawing on the modal experiences of middle-class environment, as it is in most IQ tests, a selection has been made that excludes many other plausible and often more useful definitions.

Persistence of the Elitist Tradition

The capacity to become intelligent does, of course, have a genetic basis. A cat is not capable of becoming a psychologist. But this does not mean that demonstrated differences in intelligence among psychologists are innate. What is particularly important is whether intelligence is defined primarily as the input or the output. The input is not subject to control, but the output depends on experience; so it is intelligence as output that should be the central concern of the educator.

Until the particular beliefs—which are endemic in many cultures, including American culture—are seen to be part of the heritage of an ancient, anachronistic, elitist tradition, there is little likelihood that the official liberal and equalitarian goals of many modern nations will be realized, even though the wealth of modern technology gives every promise that they are capable of being achieved. Government, industry, education, and virtually all other institutions are now part of the problem, hobbled by a metaphysics of innate inequality. Elitist assumptions about the meaning of ability permeate all fields of education. When teachers of music, mathematics, art, or physical education find that a student doesn't demonstrate the requisite ability, they often reject him (low grades can be a form of rejection). Then counselors shuttle the student to courses where he shows "ability." All this assumes that the school should not develop abilities, but only grant them the opportunity to be expressed. The Rousseauian belief in the preexisting self is widespread.

The environmental hypothesis may be wrong, but if it is, it should be shown to be wrong only after a society has done everything possible to develop the abilities of people. We should begin with prenatal care and should eliminate the experience of economic deprivation, ghetto living, and elitist schools and businesses. *Lacking definitive scientific evidence about human potentialities, social policy should be based on moral considerations*. We should base our policy on the most generous and promising assumptions about human nature rather than the most niggardly and pessimistic. Men will do their best only when they assume that they are capable. Liberal assumptions and conservative assumptions about human nature create their own self-fulfilling prophecies. We now create millions of people who think of themselves as failures—as social rejects. Their sense of frustration and despair is a travesty on the potentialities of an affluent nation.

Poor teaching is protected in the American educational system through the assumption that the child doesn't have ability. An American environmentalist commitment (toward liberal rather than totalitarian goals) would aim at *creating* ability, at *increasing* intelligence, at *developing* interests. The meaning of *education* would need to be broader than merely institutional schooling. It should also include community responsibility, especially for business and the mass media, which must supplement the work of the school if Americans are to receive more equal educational opportunity. This requires more social planning and more public responsibility than Americans have previously been willing to undertake.

Most American institutions, including the schools, still base their policy largely on the old conservative ideology. This outlook resists change and condemns many to inferiority. Ideological rigidity is not exclusive to the United States; in fact, many other nations are even more rigid. Yet the expanding wealth produced by modern technology is beginning to encourage the have-nots within the United States and throughout the world to demand their share by force and violence if necessary. Violence is likely to be an increasingly common road to social change unless a new public morality based on new assumptions about human potentiality is translated into both foreign and domestic policy. It is not merely racism that bogs down American progress, but also the more pervasive belief in intellectual inequality. The failure to develop the abilities of people was useful to the early American aristocracy and to the power elite of an industrial-scarcity economy. But modern economies of abundance flourish through the maximum development of the abilities of people. There is potentially plenty for all. More widespread development of the capabilities of people would not only add greatly to the wealth of nations, but also permit people to participate in a social and cultural renaissance.

Aside from the compelling moral obligation to create equal opportunities within nations and even between nations, the excluded millions in the world are starting to force the changes that should have occurred long ago. Some of them don't believe they are inferior, and they are understandably impatient about changing the old processes of exclusion. All institutions, including the schools, will either need to reexamine their self-consoling elitist beliefs and create real and equal opportunity, or else risk violence and revolution as the dominant instruments of social change.

n *Pygmalion in the Classroom*[1], Robert Rosenthal and Lenore Jacobson present an experimental investigation of an interesting and provocative question: Do teachers' expectations of how well or badly their students will perform actually influence the intellectual development of the students? The background of the study is introduced by a reminder that prophecies are sometimes instrumental in bringing about their own fulfillment. This reminder is followed by a discussion of evidence for the operation of self-fulfilling prophecies drawn from medical, psychiatric, and behavioral science research. The evidence as compiled by Rosenthal and Jacobson is impressive: it is clear that what one person expects of another often has subtle, yet powerful, effects on the other. Since the teacher often "knows" (expects) which of her pupils will be brighter than the others, e.g., that white middle-class children will do better than the lower-class or Negro children, the critical question arises: can her expectation, *by itself,* bring about its own fulfillment?

To test the hypothesis that teacher expectations do, in fact, have such an effect, the investigators administered a group test of intelligence to several classes of children who were to enter grades one through six in "Oak School." The children's teachers were told that the test had been developed to predict forthcoming "spurts" in intellectual growth. At the beginning of the fall term each teacher was given the names of several children in her classroom who could be expected to make unusual strides in intellectual development during the coming year. The specially designated children were actually no different from their contemporaries, having been selected randomly from the population of pupils at the school. The intelligence test was readministered to the children after a semester, after a year, and again after two years.

The Teacher As Pygmalion
Comments on the Psychology of Expectation

Peter Gumpert and Carol Milligan

The major finding of the study was that the undesignated children, the control group, gained an average of more than eight IQ points after a year, while the special children, the experimental group, gained an average of more than 12. Statistical tests suggested that this difference was one that could not reasonably be ascribed to chance variation alone. Rosenthal and Jacobson concluded that their major hypothesis was confirmed.

They also report a great deal of additional data on the more specific effects of the expectations they induced among the teachers of Oak School. **Effects of Expectations** Some of these ancillary results are intriguing, particularly some of the observations concerned with teachers' perceptions of their students during the first year of the experiment. However, looking carefully at all the results reported by Rosenthal and Jacobson—how the strength of teacher expectation varied with the sex of the students, their group status (minority or otherwise), their ability track, and so on—is a complex and confusing business. It is fairly easy to interpret each result taken alone, but the reader who attempts to make his interpretations consistent with one another will be in for a good deal of difficulty. The situation becomes even more confusing when we add to the Oak School results those obtained in the three similar studies in other schools reported by Rosenthal and Jacobson (pp. 96, 138, 145). Here we find apparent reversals of some of the effects that are given much emphasis in the Oak School study. One of these, to which Rosenthal and Jacobson pay special attention, is the result that after one year, Oak School girls in the experimental group showed greater gains on the reasoning subtest of the IQ test than did boys. The reverse was the case on the verbal subtest, where the boys showed evidence of greater improvement than girls. Since initially boys had shown slightly higher verbal scores and girls had shown slightly higher reasoning scores, Rosenthal and Jacobson interpret their results as indicating that each group tends to benefit most from favorable teacher expectations in those areas in which it is somewhat advantaged at the outset. However, in a previous experiment, while the initial scores for the sexes show the same pattern, the pattern of gains is reversed.

Rosenthal and Jacobson respond to this by postulating that their explanation for the Oak School result is not applicable to the earlier experiment, presumably because the schools in that study drew their pupils from a "substantial middle-class community," while Oak School's pupils came from a lower-class community. They do not explain how the socioeconomic class difference could account for the discrepancy in results between the two studies. The authors do not abandon their faith in the relationship between sex and subtest in either of the two studies, even though the results are by most people's standards mutually contradictory. They see the discrepancy in results as another demonstration of the "probable complexity of the operation of teacher-expectancy effects" (p. 162).

This points to what we consider to be a major flaw of the book. The authors somehow give the impression that the "expectancy effect" is a mysterious and profoundly complex entity, defying attempts by behavioral science to account for it. From such a viewpoint, it is not surprising that the importance of statistical significance is overemphasized by these investigators and the importance of replicability underemphasized. We would have preferred their showing less tolerance for ambiguity and logical contradiction while pressing harder to find some consistent principles to explain their data.

Data Reanalyzed

Some of the confusion disappears if one takes another approach to Rosenthal and Jacobson's statistical analysis. In the Oak School experiment each child in each of 18 classrooms was used either as an "experimental" or a "control" subject in the study. Clearly, this was the easiest and most natural way for the researchers to obtain a reasonably large sample of children. But children affect one another, and many things teachers and children do can affect classroom atmosphere; so there is reason to suspect that each child's test gains cannot be seen as an independent observation for statistical purposes. If the assumption of independence were, in fact, not tenable, we could conclude that they overestimated the degree of statistical stability of much of their data. Accordingly, we reanalyzed some of their major results using the analysis of variance to discover whether a child's performance gain could be partially accounted for by the particular classroom he happened to be in, independent of his grade level or whether he was in the experimental or the control group. As we suspected, the effect of classroom membership is very stable in the analyses we did, which means that strictly speaking, the proper "unit of analysis" for the study is the classroom average rather than the individual child (see the footnotes on pp. 95, 96, 118, 119, 145, and 146). Looking at the data this way, many of the results that were statistically significant, using the analysis of variance as Rosenthal and Jacobson used it, do not reach significance when the more usual and, in fact, more proper test is applied.

On the other hand, even if we confine Rosenthal and Jacobson to these more conservative statistical techniques, we find that the most important results of their study remain statistically stable. Further, these results are reasonably easy to interpret consistently. First, it remains clear that a semester after the teachers had been given information about the "spurters" in their classrooms, the children designated as spurters showed somewhat greater improvement on the intelligence test than did the control children. This overall effect of teachers' expectancies became much greater at the end of one year but a good deal less marked (and no longer statistically stable) at the end of two years. By and large, these effects were more pronounced in the first and second grades than they were in the later grades. Second, the experimental children tended to show greater gains in reading grades on their report cards and were judged by their teacher to be, on the average, more intellectually curious than the control children. Finally, the average degree of improvement shown by the experimental children in a classroom was strongly associated with the average degree of improvement shown by the control children in the same classroom: if the experimental children did especially well, so did the control children. So it would seem that the general classroom "atmosphere" generated by all concerned has something to do with what happens. The second and third set of results are of particular interest because they provide us with clues as to how some of the classroom expectancy effects observed in the Oak School study might have taken place, a consideration to which we shall return.

Let us note what we consider to be some of the book's other weaknesses. First, Rosenthal and Jacobson speak repeatedly of "IQ gains," thus implying that changes occurred in children's intellectual "capacity" or intellective functioning as this is usually understood by the layman. Such a claim would, of course, be unjustified. A discussion of the nature of intelligence and theories about its measurement is not possible within the scope of this paper. Suffice it to say that a change in IQ score can be interpreted simply as a change in performance on a test for which age-norms exist. Since rather little normative information is available (especially on younger children) for the intelligence test used in their research, the IQ gains reported by Rosenthal and Jacobson must be interpreted with particular caution.

Second, there is implicit confusion throughout the book about the difference between the "strength" of a variable and the level of statistical significance associated with its effects. Though the two things often go together, it is important to note that a statistical significance level is an index of the probable stability of a result, and not of its magnitude. A very weak effect that is extremely stable will be detected at a high level of statistical significance even though it may not be very meaningful in practical terms. If, for example, we were to weigh a large number of automobiles on a very sensitive scale, add a thimbleful of gasoline to the gas tanks of most of them, and weigh them again, the changes in their weight would turn out to be highly significant statistically, though the thimblefuls of gasoline would still have contributed little, relatively speaking, to the total weight of the automobiles. In assessing the importance of a variable, then, one must take into account not only the stability and the apparent magnitude of its effects, but also the significance of a result of that magnitude in the total context of the research.

These points aside, *Pygmalion in the Classroom* is an important and thought-provoking book. Anyone concerned with the problems and practices of education should certainly take the trouble to read it. The study provides a perfectly satisfactory demonstration that the teacher-expectation effects hypothesized do indeed take place. Though the Oak School experiment is not as sophisticated as it might be, it was done in a "natural" setting (which, incidentally, usually makes it difficult to do elegant research) rather than under the more artificial circumstances of the laboratory. The fact that the effect can be demonstrated in the actual classroom under very ordinary conditions is convincing. That the effect appears to be quite strong and stable in spite of the subtlety and simplicity of the experimental induction is especially dramatic. The results of the experiment fairly demand that much serious attention, thought, and research be devoted to the effect on children of the beliefs and attitudes held about them by school administrators, supervisors, and teachers. It also points up the crucial importance of conducting research on just *how* people's expectations of children become realities. It is possible that we will learn to change teachers' behavior toward children before we learn how to change their attitudes toward them, and thus their expectations of them. It is on this last general consideration—how the expectation of the teacher might have led to modifications of her pupils' performance and classroom behavior—that Rosenthal and Jacobson are weakest in their analysis. Though they do speculate about some aspects of the problem, the heart of the matter remains untouched. In short, they have shown us that teachers' expectations of their students' performances have definite consequences for these (subsequent) performances. But they have not shown us how this process works.

In the remainder of our article, we propose to do some more or less systematic speculating about how the Oak School teachers may have fulfilled the researchers' prophecies. We shall begin by arguing that expectation leads to selectivity of attention, perception, and response, and end by discussing just how increases in interpersonal "warmth" and encouragement might actually lead to superior learning and performance.

Some Psychological Effects of Expectation

The study of the influence of expectation upon thinking and behavior has been of interest to psychologists for many years in a variety of contexts. There are literally hundreds of studies that are relevant to the notion that a person's attitude, set, or expectation will affect his perceptions and responses. One tentative conclusion that can be drawn from these studies—of particular interest in thinking about expectancy in the classroom—is this: a person is more likely to perceive a barely perceptible stimulus if he expects it than if he does not. For example, if an experimental subject is given a list from which words are to be presented tachistoscopically, the recognition threshold for words on the list (i.e., the words he is expecting) will be lower than for those not on the list [2]. A related study is reported by Bruner and Minturn [3]. When shown an ambiguous stimulus that resembled both a letter and a number, for example *B* and *13*, subjects who were told to expect letters saw *B* and those who were told to expect numbers reported seeing *13*. Neither of these results is surprising, possibly because they both confirm what we often observe in our everyday activities—that we are likely to see what we expect to see, and that we tend to interpret ambiguous events in such a way as to confirm our own predictions. Similarly, if a teacher expects to see something, she is likely to find evidence of its occurrence sooner or later.

Further, that a person's expectations exert a powerful influence on the behavior of the people with whom he interacts is a well-documented phenomenon. (A review of literature on this point is contained in Rosenthal. [4]) In the laboratory, for example, if a group of experimenters is told to expect that their subjects will most likely perform well on a particular task, and another group is told to expect their subjects to perform poorly, the subjects in the former group will tend to have significantly higher scores than those in the latter. Expectation effects have even been demonstrated when the experimental subjects were animals (Rosenthal [5]; also reported in *Pygmalion in the Classroom*). Strupp and Luborsky [6] make the point that a therapist's expectations about the prognosis of treatment may have much to do with its actual outcome. The teacher, similarly, may have a personal stake in seeing what she expects to see in the classroom.

It appears that a person who is in a position to exercise over another the subtle interpersonal influence we have been talking about may do so without being aware either of the content of the message he transmits or the ways he transmits it. The recipient of influence may be equally unaware that any transaction other than the obvious overt one is taking place; he may well do what is expected of him without even realizing that a demand on him is being made. It also appears likely that some people are more effective "covert persuaders" than others. Such things as the physical appearance, confidence, warmth, friendliness, amount of experience or competence, interest, and status of the persuader seem to affect the extent to which expectancies are influential [7]. Some of these personal characteristics are also related to a person's effectiveness as an overt persuader. So it seems plausible that some teachers may be better covert persuaders in the classroom than others. It is also possible that the teacher who is warm, friendly, and sure of herself is a better covert persuader than her less friendly and less competent colleagues, and that the highly skilled and successful teacher is also good at helping make her prophecies come true.

Subtlety of Interpersonal Influences

The manner in which one person influences another is not determined entirely in advance by previously existing attitudes and beliefs. Expectation may change, vary, increase, or decrease, depending on the nature of an ongoing social interaction and the reciprocal influence that two people have upon one another. In the classroom, for example, it is likely that a teacher's behavior toward a particular child will not depend consistently on previously existing beliefs about what he can or will do, but may be modified by what occurs between them.

In order to imagine how such variables might affect an interaction, let us construct an oversimplified situation. Imagine that one of Rosenthal and Jacobson's teachers is told that Johnny Second-Grader, an unremarkable-appearing boy, is about to experience a period of intellectual blossoming. Given a situation in which the teacher is trying to communicate a difficult bit of information to Johnny, she is now more likely to expect an indication of comprehension than if she had been told nothing about potential academic progress. (In fact, she might not otherwise have attempted the communication in the first place.) A minor change in Johnny's behavior at this point, say a nod or smile, may be interpreted as a glimmer of understanding so that, encouraged, the teacher intensifies her efforts to reach him. Consequent subtle changes in the teacher's behavior and attitude, such as alterations in body posture, tone of voice, perceived interest, facial expression, or verbal praise, may similarly interest and encourage Johnny, leading to his increased motivation and attention, and finally to the reward of mastering something new—as well as the fulfillment of his teacher's expectation. The point is that psychological expectation may have a catalytic effect, evoking interactions and leading to events that depend upon much more than the effects of expectation alone, but which might not . . . have occurred without the belief that such events were possible.

We have discussed something about the effects that a person's expectations may have on his own behavior and thinking and on the behavior and thinking of others. It seems very clear also that the nature of the social structure itself often has similar effects. One of the findings of a study of the British school system reported by Hilde Himmelweit and Judy Wright [8] involved a comparison of two schools with different policies regarding assignment to tracks (or streams, as they are referred to in England). In one school, assignment to a stream was based on ability. In the other, assignment was based on criteria other than intellectual ability. Yet the effect of stream placement on further academic advancement and final performance was identical for the two schools. Thus, the effect of streaming seemed to be a more powerful determinant of performance than were the attributes that led to the pupils' initial placement in streams; streaming turns out to be a potent "leveler" in Britain. This result can be interpreted as indicating that the meaning for an individual of being allocated to a particular stream, and the influence exerted by the experience of stream membership, can be major determinants of his progress. The expectation for a person's behavior that is implicit by virtue of his place in the social structure may exert a powerful influence over what he does, in that he will not only respond to the expectation but may also help to create an environment within which it will be fulfilled.

Let us be very clear. As common and powerful as these so-called "expectation" effects seem to be, virtually nothing is known about how they are communicated. We know that the classroom teacher expects Johnny to be a "spurter" this year, and we know that she therefore probably wants him to improve. We can guess that she does something which communicates itself to Johnny, and it seems clear that Johnny responds to whatever it is she does. But we don't know what she does, or exactly what Johnny picks up. Furthermore, how does Johnny's "receiving the message," whatever it might be, actually lead to his improvement? These questions are just beginning to come under the scrutiny of research psychologists. . . .

Summary

Let us return now to the classroom and to the teacher who expects to see startling improvement in the performance of a particular pupil. As we have argued above, if she expects a pupil to begin to improve, she may be avidly watching for signs of improvement while ignoring the pupil's usual inadequacies or failures. If she should see something that indicates improvement, she might be especially quick to reward it by her special attention and by her excitement at seeing her expectations begin to be fulfilled. This in turn might give the child new interest in this kind of performance, and might spur him on to new attempts to fulfill an expectation that he might now begin to perceive. Since the teacher is no longer paying as much attention to the child's failures, the child may now feel new room to grow, and indeed might grow with his burgeoning confidence about new learning and new power over his environment. As the child's performance improves, his teacher's standards for his performance may become higher; thus, what Rosenthal and Jacobson term the "benign circle" might develop. And here is an added dividend: a teacher who spends relatively more time rewarding success in the classroom, and therefore relatively less time punishing failure, may be improving the learning environment not only for the few children of whom she expects new things, but for all the children in the room—as is suggested by the results in Rosenthal and Jacobson described above.

Our discussion in this section has been very speculative; certainly, many links are missing in the chain that connects what the teacher expects the student to be able to do and what the student becomes able to do. And surely, there is not just one thing happening in the entire process, but many things. The phenomenon of subtle interpersonal influence guiding progress in the classroom is as complex as it is fascinating. Our plea is merely that these matters, adumbrated by *Pygmalion in the Classroom,* are researchable now, at our present level of research sophistication, and are especially deserving of a major laboratory and field research effort at this time.

Notes

1. Robert Rosenthal and Lenore Jacobson, *Pygmalion in the Classroom: Teacher Expectation and Pupil's Intellectual Ability* (New York: Holt, Rinehart and Winston, 1968).
2. U. Neisser, "On Experimental Distinction Between Perceptual Process and Verbal Response," *Journal of Experimental Psychology* 47 (1954): 399–402.
3. Jerome S. Bruner and A. L. Minturn, "Perceptual Identification and Perceptual Organization," *Journal of Genetic Psychology* 53 (1955): 21–28.
4. Robert Rosenthal, *Experimenter Effects in Behavioral Research* (New York: Appleton-Century-Crofts, 1966).
5. Ibid.
6. Hana H. Strupp and L. Luborsky, eds., *Research in Psychotherapy* (Washington, D.C.: American Psychological Association, 1962).
7. See note 4.
8. Hilde Himmelweit and Judy Wright, "The School System, Social Class and Attainment after School," paper presented at the Annual Conference of the British Psychological Society, 1967.

Author

"Learning for Mastery," by Benjamin S. Bloom, Professor of Education at the University of Chicago. The wheels Dr. Bloom set in motion in 1956 with *Taxonomy of Educational Objectives* are still turning.

7 Learning for Mastery

Bloom's paper "Learning for Mastery" is one of the most important educational treatises of recent years. It deserves close scrutiny by everyone who is concerned with education. The paper has great potential for influencing views and practices in the design of instruction. The model clearly demonstrates that the majority of students can be expected to achieve mastery of a subject up to a high level.

After completing this unit, you should be able to

1 discuss the implications of teacher expectations regarding student achievement; that is, that the students in a class represent a normal distribution

2 identify the theoretical concepts that underlie Bloom's instructional model

3 design an instructional system that accommodates the five major variables of learning

4 outline the affective consequences of mastery learning and formulate a case supporting the view that learning mastery must be both a subjective recognition by the student of his competence and a public recognition by school and society

5 display a positive attitude toward the following tenets by proposing at least two specific changes in the area of your educational responsibility:

   a. most students can learn to a high level of mastery

   b. the use of the "normal curve" must be reevaluated, particularly in regard to its inappropriate use in grading individual students

Each teacher begins a new term (or course) with the expectation that about a third of his students will adequately learn what he has to teach. He expects about a third of his students to fail or to just "get by." Finally, he expects another third to learn a good deal of what he has to teach, but not enough to be regarded as "good students." This set of expectations, supported by school policies and practices in grading, becomes transmitted to the students through the grading procedures and through the methods and materials of instruction. The system creates a self-fulfilling prophecy such that the final sorting of students through the grading process becomes approximately equivalent to the original expectations.

This set of expectations, which fixes the academic goals of teachers and students, is the most wasteful and destructive aspect of the present educational system. It reduces the aspirations of both teachers and students; it reduces motivation for learning in students; and it systematically destroys the ego and self-concept of a sizable group of students who are legally required to attend school for 10 to 12 years under conditions that are frustrating and humiliating year after year. The cost of this system in reducing opportunities for further learning and in alienating youth from both school and society is so great that no society can tolerate it for long.

Most students (perhaps over 90 percent) can master what we have to teach them, and it is the task of instruction to find the means that will enable our students to master the subject under consideration. Our basic task is to determine what we mean by mastery of the subject and to search for the methods and materials that will enable the largest proportion of our students to attain such mastery.

In this paper we will consider one approach to learning for mastery and the underlying theoretical concepts, research findings, and techniques required. Basically, the problem of developing a strategy for mastery learning is one of determining how individual differences in learners can be related to the learning and teaching process.

Background

Some societies can utilize only a small number of highly educated persons in the economy and can provide the economic support for only a small proportion of the students to complete secondary or higher education. Under such conditions much of the effort of the schools and the external examining system is to find ways of rejecting the majority of students at various points in the educational system and to discover the talented few

Learning for Mastery

Benjamin S. Bloom

who are to be given advanced educational opportunities. Such societies invest a great deal more in the prediction and selection of talent than in the development of such talent.

The complexities of the skills required by the work force in the United States and in other highly developed nations means that we can no longer operate on the assumption that completion of secondary and advanced education is for the few. The increasing evidence [1,2] that investment in the education of humans pays off at a greater rate than does capital investment, suggests that we cannot return to an economy of scarcity of educational opportunity.

Whatever might have been the case previously, highly developed nations must seek to find ways to increase the proportion of the age group that can successfully complete both secondary and higher education. The problem is no longer one of finding the few who can succeed. The basic problem is to determine how the largest proportion of the age group can learn effectively those skills and subject matter regarded as essential for their own development in a complex society.

However, given another set of philosophic and psychological presuppositions, we may express our concern for the intellectual and personality consequences of lack of clear success in the learning tasks of the school. Increasingly, learning throughout life (continuing learning) will be necessary for the largest proportion of the work force. If school learning is regarded as frustrating and even impossible by a sizable proportion of students, then little can be done at later levels to kindle a genuine interest in further learning. School learning must be successful and rewarding as one basis for insuring that learning can continue throughout one's life as needed.

Even more important in modern society is the malaise about values. As the secular society becomes more and more central, the values remaining for the individual have to do with hedonism, interpersonal relations, self-development, and ideas. If the schools frustrate the students in the latter two areas, only the first two are available to the individual. Whatever the case may be for each of these values, the schools must strive to assure all students of successful learning experiences in the realm of ideas and self-development.

There is little question that the schools now do provide successful learning experiences for some students—perhaps as high as one third of the students. If the schools are to provide successful and satisfying learning experiences for at least 90 percent of the students, major changes must take place in the attitudes of students, teachers, and administrators; changes must also take place in teaching strategies and in the role of evaluation.

The Normal Curve

We have for so long used the normal curve in grading students that we have come to believe in it. Our achievement measures are designed to detect differences among our learners, even if the differences are trivial in terms of the subject matter. We then distribute our grades in a normal fashion.

In any group of students we expect to have some small percent receive A grades. We are surprised when the percentage differs greatly from about 10 percent. We are also prepared to fail an equal proportion of students. Quite frequently this failure is determined by the rank order of the students in the group rather than by their failure to grasp the essential ideas of the course. Thus, we have become accustomed to classify students into about five categories of level of performance and to assign grades in some relative fashion. It matters not that the failures of one year performed at about the same level as the C students of another year. Nor does it matter that the A students of one school do about as well as the F students of another school.

Having become "conditioned" to the normal distribution, we set grade policies in these terms and are horrified when some teacher attempts to recommend a very different distribution of grades. Administrators are constantly on the alert to control teachers who are "too easy" or "too hard" in their grading. A teacher whose grade distribution is normal will avoid difficulties with administrators. But even more important, we find ways of convincing students that they can only do C work or D work by our grading system and even by our system of quiz and progress testing. Finally, we proceed in our teaching as though only the minority of our students should be able to learn what we have to teach.

There is nothing sacred about the normal curve. It is the distribution most appropriate to chance and random activity. Education is a purposeful activity and we seek to have the students learn what we have to teach. If we are effective in our instruction, the distribution of achievement should be very different from the normal curve. In fact, we may even insist that our educational efforts have been *unsuccessful* to the extent to which our distribution of achievement approximates the normal distribution.

"Individual differences" in learners is a fact that can be demonstrated in many ways. That our students vary in many ways can never be forgotten. That these variations must be reflected in learning standards and achievement criteria is more a reflection of our policies and practices than of the necessities of the case. Our basic task in education is to find strategies that will take individual differences into consideration but will do so in such a way as to promote the fullest development of the individual.

The Variables for Mastery Learning Strategies

A learning strategy for mastery may be derived from the work of Carroll [3], supported by the ideas of Morrison [4], Bruner [5], Skinner [6], Suppes [7], Goodlad and Anderson [8], and Glaser [9]. In presenting these ideas, we will refer to some of the research findings that bear on them. However, our main concern here is with the major variables in a model of school learning and the ways in which these variables may be utilized in a strategy for mastery learning.

Put in its most brief form, the model proposed by Carroll [10] makes it clear that if the students are normally distributed with respect to *aptitude* for some subject (mathematics, science, literature, history, etc.) and all the students are provided with exactly the *same instruction* (same in terms of amount of instruction, quality of instruction, and time available for learning), the end result will be a normal distribution on an appropriate measure of achievement. Furthermore, the relationship between aptitude and achievement will be relatively high (correlations of +.70 or higher are to be expected if the aptitude and achievement measures are valid and reliable). Conversely, if the students are normally distributed with respect to aptitude, but the kind and quality of instruction and the amount of time available for learning are made appropriate to the characteristics and needs of *each* student, the majority of students may be expected to achieve mastery of the subject. And the relationship between aptitude and achievement should approach zero. It is this basic set of ideas we wish to develop here.

1. Aptitude for Particular Kinds of Learning. We have come to recognize that individuals do differ in their aptitudes for particular kinds of learning and over the years we have developed a large number of aptitude tests to measure these differences. In study after study we have found that aptitude tests are relatively good predictors of achievement criteria (achievement tests or teacher judgments). Thus, a good set of mathematics aptitude tests given at the beginning of the year will correlate as high as +.70 with the mathematics achievement tests at the end of the course....

The use of aptitude tests for predictive purposes and the high correlations between such tests and achievement criteria have led many of us to the view that high levels of achievement are possible only for the most able students. From this, it is an easy step to some notion of a causal connection between aptitude and achievement. The simplest notion of causality is that the students with high levels of aptitude can learn the complex ideas of the subject and the students with low levels of aptitude can learn only the simplest ideas of the subject.

Quite in contrast to this is Carroll's [11] view that *aptitude is the amount of time required by the learner to attain mastery of a learning task*. Implicit in this formulation is the assumption that, given enough time, all students can conceivably attain mastery of a learning task. If Carroll is right, then learning mastery is theoretically available to all, if we can find the means for helping each student. It is this writer's belief that this formulation of Carroll's has the most fundamental implications for education.

One type of support for this view is to be found in the grade norms for many standardized achievement tests. These norms demonstrate that selected criterion scores achieved by the top students at one grade level are achieved by the majority of students at a later grade level. Further support is available in studies where students can learn at their own rate. These studies show that although most students eventually reach mastery on each learning task, some students achieve mastery much sooner than do other students [12,13].

Can all students learn a subject equally well? That is, can all students master a learning task at a high level of complexity? As we study aptitude distributions in relation to student performance, we have become convinced that there are differences between the extreme students and the remainder of the population. At the top of the aptitude distribution (1 percent to 5 percent) there are likely to be some students who have a special talent for the subject. Such students are able to learn and to use the subject with greater fluency than other students. The student with special aptitudes for music or foreign languages can learn these subjects in ways not available to most other students. Whether this is a matter of native endowment or the effect of previous training is not clear, although this must vary from subject to subject. It is likely that some individuals are born with sensory organs better attuned to sounds (music, language, etc.) than are others and that these constitutional characteristics give them special advantages in learning such subjects over others. For other subjects, special training, particular interests, etc., may develop these high-level aptitudes.

At the other extreme of the aptitude distribution, we believe there are individuals with special disabilities for particular learning. The tone-deaf individual will have great difficulty in learning music; the color-blind individual will have special problems in learning art; the individual who thinks in concrete forms will have special problems in learning highly abstract conceptual systems such as philosophy. Again, we believe these may constitute less than 5 percent of the distribution, but this will vary with the subject and the aptitudes.

In between are approximately 90 percent of the individuals where we believe (as does Carroll) that aptitudes are predictive of rate of learning rather than the level (or complexity) of learning that is possible. Thus, we are expressing the view that, given sufficient time (and appropriate types of help), 95 percent of students (the top 5 percent + the next 90 percent) can learn a subject up to a high level of mastery. We are convinced that the grade of A as an index of mastery of a subject can, under appropriate conditions, be achieved by up to 95 percent of the students in a class.

It is assumed that it will take some students more effort, time, and help to achieve this level than it will other students. For some students the effort and help required may make it prohibitive. Thus, to learn high-school algebra to a point of mastery may require several years for some students but only a fraction of a year for other students. Whether mastery learning is worth this great effort for the students who may take several years is highly questionable. One basic problem for a mastery-learning strategy is to find ways of reducing the amount of time required for the slower students to a point where it is no longer a prohibitively long and difficult task for these less able students.

We do not believe that aptitude for particular learning tasks is completely stable. There is evidence [14,15] that the aptitude for particular learning tasks may be modified by appropriate environmental conditions or learning experiences in the school and the home. The major task of educational programs concerned with learning to learn and general education should be to produce positive changes in the students' basic aptitudes. It is likely that these aptitudes can be most markedly affected during the early years in the home and during the elementary years of school. Undoubtedly, however, some changes can take place at later points in the individual's career.

Even if marked changes are not made in the individual's aptitudes, it is highly probable that more effective learning conditions can reduce the amount of time required to learn a subject to mastery for all students and especially for the students with lower aptitudes. It is this problem that must be directly attacked by strategies for mastery learning.

2. Quality of Instruction. Our schools have usually proceeded on the assumption that there is a standard classroom situation for all students. Typically, this has been expressed in the teacher–student ratio of 1 to 30, with group instruction as the central means of teaching. There is the expectation that each teacher will teach the subject in much the same way as other teachers. This standardization is further emphasized by textbook adoption, which specifies the instructional material to be provided each class. Closely related to this is the extensive research over the past 50 years that seeks to find the one instructional method, material, or curriculum program that is best for all students.

Thus, over the years, we have fallen into the "educational trap" of specifying quality of instruction in terms of good and poor teachers, teaching, instructional materials, curriculum—all in terms of group results. We persist in asking such questions as: What is the best teacher for the group? What is the best method of instruction for the group? What is the best instructional material for the group?

One may start with the very different assumption that individual students may need very different types and qualities of instruction to achieve mastery. That is, the same content and objectives of instruction may be learned by different students as the result of very different types of instruction. Carroll [16] defines the *quality of instruction in terms of the degree to which the presentation, explanation, and ordering of elements of the task to be learned approach the optimum for a given learner.*

Much research is needed to determine how individual differences in learners can be related to variations in the quality of instruction. There is evidence that some students can learn quite well through independent learning efforts, while others need highly structured teaching–learning situations [17]. It seems reasonable to expect that some students will need more concrete illustrations and explanations than will others; some students may need more examples to get an idea than do others; some students may need more approval and reinforcement than others; and some may even need to have several repetitions of the explanation, while others may be able to get it the first time.

We believe that if every student had a very good tutor, most of them would be able to learn a particular subject to a high degree. A good tutor attempts to find the qualities of instruction (and motivation) best suited to a given learner. And there is some evidence [18] that middle-class parents do attempt to tutor their children when they believe that the quality of instruction in school does not enable their children to learn a particular subject. In an unpublished study, the writer found that one-third of the students in an algebra course in a middle-class school were receiving as much tutorial instruction in the home in algebra as they were receiving group instruction in the school. These students received relatively high grades for the algebra course. For these students, the relationship between their mathematics aptitude scores (at the beginning of the year) and their achievement in algebra at the end of the year was almost zero. In contrast, for the students who received no additional instruction other than the regular classroom instruction, the relationship between their mathematics aptitude scores and their algebra achievement scores was very high (+.90). While this type of research needs to be replicated, it is evident in this small study that the home tutoring help was providing the quality of instruction needed by these students to learn the algebra—that is, the instruction was adapted to the needs of the individual learners.

The main point to be stressed is that the quality of instruction is to be considered in terms of its effects on individual learners rather than on random groups of learners. Hopefully, the research of the future may lead to the definition of the qualities and kinds of instruction needed by various *types* of learners. Such research may suggest more effective group instruction since it is unlikely that the schools will be able to provide instruction for each learner separately.

3. Ability to Understand Instruction. In most courses at the high school and college level there is a single teacher and a single set of instructional materials. If the student has facility in understanding the teacher's communications about the learning and the instructional material (usually a textbook), he has little difficulty in learning the subject. If he has difficulty in understanding the teacher's instruction and/or the instructional material, he is likely to have great difficulty in learning the subject. *The ability to understand instruction may be defined as the ability of the learner to understand the nature of the task he is to learn and the procedures he is to follow in the learning of the task.*

Here is a point at which the student's abilities interact with the instructional materials and the instructor's abilities in teaching. For the student in our highly verbal schools it is likely that this ability to understand instruction is primarily determined by verbal ability and reading comprehension. These two measures of language ability are significantly related to achievement in the majority of subjects and they are highly related (+.50 to +.60) to grade-point averages at the high school or college level. What this suggests is that verbal ability (independent of specific aptitudes for each subject) determines some general ability to learn from teachers and instructional materials.

While it is possible to alter an individual's verbal ability by appropriate training, there are limits to the amount of change that can be produced. Most change in verbal ability can be produced at the preschool and elementary school levels with less and less change being likely as the student gets older [19]. Vocabulary and reading ability, however, may be improved to some extent at all age levels, even though there is a diminishing utility of this approach with increasing age. Improvements in verbal abilities should result in improvements in the individual's ability to understand instruction.

The greatest immediate payoff in dealing with the ability to understand instruction is likely to come from modifications in instruction in order to meet the needs of individual students. There is no doubt that some teachers do attempt to modify their instruction to fit a given group of students. Many teachers center their instruction at the middle group of their students, others at the top or bottom group—these are, however, reflections of the teacher's habits and attitudes. They are, by no means, determinants of what it is *possible* for a teacher to do. Given help and various types of aids, individual teachers can find ways of modifying their instruction to fit the differing needs of their students.

Group Study. Group-study procedures should be available to students as they need it. In our own experience we have found that small groups of students (two or three students), meeting regularly to go over points of difficulty in the learning process, were most effective, especially when the students could cooperate and help each other without any danger of giving each other special advantages in a competitive situation. Where learning can be turned into a cooperative process with everyone likely to gain from the process, small-group learning procedures can be very effective. Much depends on the composition of the group and the opportunities it gives each person to expose his difficulties and have them corrected without demeaning one person and elevating another. In the group process, the more able students have opportunities to strengthen their own learning in the process of helping another person grasp the idea through alternative ways of explaining and using the idea.

Tutorial Help. One-to-one relationship between teacher and learner represents the most costly type of help and should be used only where alternative procedures are not effective. However, this type of help should be available to students as they need it, especially where individuals have particular difficulties that can't be corrected in other ways. The tutor, ideally, should be someone other than the teacher, since he should bring a fresh way of viewing the idea or the process. The tutor must be skillful in detecting the points of difficulty in the student's learning and should help him in such a way as to free the student from continued dependence on him.

Another approach to variations in the students' ability to understand instruction is to vary the instructional material.

Textbooks. Textbooks may vary in the clarity with which they explain a particular idea or process. The fact that one textbook has been adopted by the school or by the teacher does not necessarily mean that other textbooks cannot be used at particular points in the instruction when they would be helpful to a student who can't grasp the idea from the adopted textbook. The task here is to be able to determine where the individual student has difficulty in understanding the instructions and then provide alternative textbook explanations if they are more effective at that point.

Workbooks and Programmed Instruction Units. These may be especially helpful for some students who cannot grasp the ideas or procedures in the textbook form. Some students need the drill and the specific tasks that workbooks can provide. Other students need the small steps and frequent reinforcement that programmed units can provide. Such materials may be used in the initial instruction or as students encounter specific difficulties in learning a particular unit or section of the course.

Audiovisual Methods and Academic Games. Some students may learn a particular idea best through concrete illustrations and vivid and clear explanations. It is likely that film strips and short motion pictures, which can be used by individual students as needed, may be very effective. Other students may need concrete material such as laboratory experiences, simple demonstrations, blocks and other relevant apparatus in order to comprehend an idea or task. Academic games, puzzles, and other interesting but not threatening devices may be useful. Here again, the point is that some ways of communicating and comprehending an idea, problem, or task may be especially effective for some students, although others may not use or need such materials and methods. We need not place the highest priority for all on abstract and verbal ways of instruction.

With regard to instructional materials, the suggestion is not that particular materials be used by particular students throughout the course. It is that each type of material may serve as a means of helping individual students at selected points in the learning process—and that a particular student may use whatever variety of materials are found to be useful as he encounters difficulties in the learning.

Throughout the use of alternative methods of instruction and instructional material, the essential point to be borne in mind is that these are attempts to improve the *quality of instruction* in relation to the ability of each student to *understand the instruction*. As feedback methods inform the teachers of particular errors and difficulties the majority of students are having, it is to be expected that the regular group instruction could be modified so as to correct these difficulties. As particular students are helped individually, the goal should be not only to help the student over particular learning difficulties but also to enable him to become more independent in his learning and to help him identify the alternative ways by which he can comprehend new ideas. But, most important, the presence of a great variety of instructional materials and procedures should help both teachers and students to overcome feelings of defeatism and passivity about learning. If the student can't learn in one way, he should be reassured that alternatives are available to him. The teacher should come to recognize that it is the learning which is important and that instructional alternatives exist to enable all (or almost all) of the students to learn the subject to a high level.

4. *Perseverance*. Carroll defines *perseverance* as *the time the learner is willing to spend in learning*. If a student needs to spend a certain amount of time to master a particular task, and he spends less than this amount in active learning, he is not likely to learn the task to the level of mastery. Carroll attempts to differentiate between the amount of time the student spends on learning and the amount of time the student is actively engaged in learning.

Perseverance does appear to be related to attitudes toward and interest in learning. In the International Study of Educational Achievement [20], the relationship between the number of hours of homework per week reported by the student (a crude index of perseverance) and the number of years of further education desired by the student is +.25.

We do believe that students vary in the amount of perseverance they bring to a specific learning task. However, students appear to approach different learning tasks with different amounts of perseverance. The student who gives up quickly in his efforts to learn an academic subject may persevere an unusually long time in learning how to repair an automobile or in learning to play a musical instrument. It would appear to us that as a student finds the effort rewarding, he is likely to spend more time on a particular learning task. If, on the other hand, the student is frustrated in his learning, he must (in self-defense) reduce the amount of time he devotes to learning. While the frustration level of students may vary, we believe that all students must sooner or later give up a task if it is too painful for them.

While efforts may be made to increase the amount of perseverance in students, it is likely that manipulation of the instruction and learning materials may be more effective in helping students master a given learning task, in spite of their present level of perseverance. Frequency of reward and evidence of success in learning can increase the student's perseverance in a learning situation. As students attain mastery of a given task, they are likely to increase their perseverance for a related learning task.

In our own research we are finding that the demands for perseverance may be sharply reduced if students are provided with instructional resources most appropriate for them. Frequent feedback accompanied by specific help in instruction and material as needed can reduce the time (and perseverance) required. Improvement in the quality of instruction (or explanations and illustrations) may reduce the perseverance needed for a given learning task.

There seems to be little reason to make learning so difficult that only a small proportion of the students can persevere to mastery. Endurance and unusual perseverance may be appropriate for long-distance running—they are not great virtues in their own right. The emphasis should be on learning, not on vague ideas of discipline and endurance.

5. *Time Allowed for Learning.* Throughout the world, schools are organized to give group instruction with definite periods of time allocated for particular learning tasks. A course in history at the secondary level may be planned for an academic year of instruction, another course may be planned for a semester, while the amount of instructional time allocated for a subject like arithmetic at the fifth-grade level may be fixed. Whatever the amount of time allowed by the school and the curriculum for particular subjects or learning tasks, it is likely to be too much for some students and not enough for other students.

For Carroll, the time spent on learning is the key to mastery. His basic assumption is that aptitude determines the rate of learning and that most, if not all, students can achieve mastery if they devote the amount of time needed to the learning. This implies that the student must not only devote the amount of time he needs to the learning task but also that he be *allowed* enough time for the learning to take place.

There seems to be little doubt that students with high levels of aptitude are likely to be more efficient in their learning and to require less time for learning than students with lower levels of aptitude. Whether most students can be helped to become highly efficient learners in general is a problem for future research.

The amount of time students need for a particular kind of learning has not been studied directly. One indication of the time needed comes from studies of the amount of time students spend on homework. In our review of the amount of time spent by 13-year-old students on mathematics homework in the International Study of Educational Achievement [21], we find that if we omit the extreme 5 percent of the subjects, the ratio is roughly 6 to 1. That is, some students spend six times as much time on mathematics homework as do others. Other studies of use of time suggest that this is roughly the order of magnitude to be expected.

If instruction and student use of time become more effective, we believe that most students will need less time to learn the subject to mastery and that the ratio of time required for the slower and the faster learners may be reduced from about 6 to 1 to perhaps 3 to 1.

In general, we find a zero or a slightly negative relationship between final grades and amount of time spent on homework. In the International Study [22], the average correlation for 12 countries at the 13-year-old level is approximately $-.05$ between achievement-test scores in mathematics and number of hours per week of homework in mathematics as reported by students. Thus, the amount of time spent on homework does not seem to be a very good predictor of achievement in the subject.

We are convinced that it is not the sheer amount of time spent in learning (either in school or out of school) that accounts for the level of learning. We believe that each student should be allowed the time he needs to learn a subject. And the time he needs to learn the subject is likely to be affected by the student's aptitudes, his verbal ability, the quality of instruction he receives in class, and the quality of the help he receives outside of class. The task of a strategy for mastery learning is to find ways of altering the time individual students need for learning as well as to find ways of providing whatever time is needed by each student. Thus, a strategy for mastery learning must find some way of solving the instructional problems as well as the school organizational (including time) problems.

There are many alternative strategies for mastery learning. Each strategy must find some way of dealing with individual differences in learners through some means of relating the instruction to the needs and characteristics of the learners. We believe that each strategy must include some way of dealing with the five variables discussed in the foregoing.

One Strategy for Mastery Learning

Were it not so costly in human resources, we believe that the provision of a good tutor for each student might be one ideal strategy. In any case, the tutor–student relationship is a useful model to consider when one attempts to work out the details of a less costly strategy. Also, the tutor strategy is not as farfetched as it may seem at first glance. In the preschool period most of the child's instruction is tutorial—usually provided by the mother. In many middle-class homes the parents continue to provide tutorial help as needed by the child during much of his school career.

Other strategies include permitting students to go at their own pace, guiding students with respect to courses they should or should not take, and providing different tracks or streams for different groups of learners. The nongraded school [23] is one attempt to provide an organizational structure that permits and encourages mastery learning.

A group of us at the University of Chicago has been doing research on the variables discussed in the previous pages. In addition, some of us have been attempting to develop a strategy of teaching and learning that will bring all (or almost all) students to a level of mastery in the learning of any subject. Our approach has been to supplement regular group instruction by using diagnostic procedures and alternative instructional methods and materials in such a way as to bring a large proportion of the students to a predetermined standard of achievement. In this approach, we have tried to bring most of the students to mastery levels of achievement within the regular term, semester, or period of calendar time in which the course is usually taught. Undoubtedly, some students will spend more time than others in learning the subject, but if the majority of students reach mastery levels at the end of the time allocated for the subject, mastery will have affective as well as cognitive consequences.

We have had some successes and some dismal failures with this approach. We have been trying to learn from both the successes and the failures. In the near future we hope to have some of these ideas applied to a large number of classrooms in selected school systems. Initially, we have chosen to work with subjects that have few prerequisites (algebra, science, etc.) because we believe it is easier to secure mastery learning in a given time period in such courses. In contrast are subjects that are late in a long sequence of learning (sixth-grade reading, eighth-grade arithmetic, advanced mathematics, etc.). For such subjects, it is unlikely that mastery learning can be attained within a term for a group of students who have had a long history of cumulative learning difficulties in the specific subject field.

In working on this strategy, we have attempted to spell out some of the *preconditions* necessary, develop the *operating procedures* required, and evaluate some of the *outcomes* of the strategy.

Preconditions. If we are able to develop mastery learning in students, we must be able to recognize when students have achieved it. We must be able to define what we mean by mastery, and we must be able to collect the necessary evidence to establish whether a student has achieved it.

Specifying Objectives

The specification of the objectives and content of instruction is one necessary precondition for informing both teachers and students about the expectations. The translation of the specifications into evaluation procedures helps to define further what it is that the student should be able to do when he has completed the course. The evaluation procedures used to appraise the outcomes of instruction (summative evaluation) help the teacher and student know when the instruction has been effective.

Implicit in this way of defining the outcomes and preparing evaluation instruments is a distinction between the teaching–learning process and the evaluation process. At some point in time, the results of teaching and learning can be reflected in the evaluation of the students. But, these are *separate* processes. That is, teaching and learning are intended to prepare the student in an area of learning, while evaluation (summative) is intended to appraise the extent to which the student has developed in the desired ways. Both the teacher and the learner must have some understanding of what the achievement criteria are, and both must be able to secure evidence of progress toward these criteria.

If the achievement criteria are primarily competitive—that is, the student is to be judged in terms of his relative position in the group—then the student is likely to seek evidence on his standing in the group as he progresses through the learning tasks. We recognize that competition may be a spur to those students who view others in competitive terms, but we believe that much of learning and development may be destroyed by primary emphasis on competition.

Much more preferable in terms of intrinsic motivation for learning is the setting of standards of mastery and excellence apart from interstudent competition, followed by appropriate efforts to bring as many students up to this standard as possible. This suggests some notion of absolute standards and the use of grades or marks that will reflect these standards. Thus, it is conceivable that all students may achieve mastery and the grade of A. It is also possible in a particular year in a specific course for few or none of the students to attain mastery or a grade of A.

While we would recommend the use of absolute standards carefully worked out for a subject, we recognize the difficulty of arriving at such standards. In some of our own work, we have made use of standards derived from previous experience with students in a particular course. In one course, students in 1966 were informed that the grades for 1966 would be based on *standards* arrived at in 1965. The grades of A, B, C, D, and F would be based on an examination parallel to that used in 1965 and the grades would be set at the same performance levels as those used in 1965. The students were informed that the proportion of students receiving each grade was to be determined by their performance levels rather than by their rank order in the group. Thus, the students were not competing with each other for grades; they were to be judged on the basis of levels of mastery used in 1965.

We do not believe this is the only way of arriving at achievement standards, but the point is that students must feel they are being judged in terms of level of performance rather than a normal curve or some other arbitrary and relative set of standards. We are not recommending national achievement standards. What is being recommended are realistic performance standards developed for each school or group, followed by instructional procedures that will enable the majority of students to attain these standards.

One result of this way of setting achievement standards was to enable the students to work with each other and to help each other without being concerned about giving special advantages (or disadvantages) to other students. Cooperation in learning rather than competition was a clear result from this method of setting achievement criteria.

In the work we have done, we attempted to have the teacher teach the course in much the same way as previously. That is, the particular materials and methods of instruction in the current year should be about the same as in previous years. Also, the time schedule during the course was about the same. The operating procedures discussed in the next section *supplemented* the regular instruction of the teacher. We have proceeded in this way because we believe a useful strategy for mastery learning should be widely applicable. If extensive training of teachers is necessary for a particular strategy, it is less likely that it will receive widespread use.

Operating Procedures. The operating procedures we have used are intended to provide detailed feedback to teachers and students and to provide specific supplementary instructional resources as needed. These procedures are devised to insure mastery of each learning unit in such a way as to reduce the time required while directly affecting both quality of instruction and the ability of the student to understand the instruction.

Formulative Evaluation. One useful operating procedure is to break a course or subject into smaller units of learning. Such a learning unit may correspond to a chapter in a textbook, a well-defined content portion of a course, or a particular time unit of the course. We have tended to think of units as involving a week or two of learning activity.

Using some of the ideas of Gagné [24] and Bloom [25], we have attempted to analyze each unit into a number of elements ranging from specific terms or facts, more complex and abstract ideas such as concepts and principles, and relatively complex processes such as application of principles and analysis of complex theoretical statements. We believe, as does Gagné [26] that these elements form a hierarchy of learning tasks.

We have then attempted to construct brief diagnostic–progress tests that can be used to determine whether or not the student has mastered the unit and what, if anything, the student must still do to master it. We have borrowed the term *Formative Evaluation* from Scriven [27] to refer to these diagnostic–progress tests.

Frequent formative evaluation tests pace the learning of students and help motivate them to put forth the necessary effort at the appropriate time. The appropriate use of these tests helps to insure that each set of learning tasks is thoroughly mastered before subsequent learning tasks are started.

Each formative test is administered after the completion of the appropriate learning unit. While the frequency of these progress tests may vary throughout the course, it is likely that some portions of the course—especially the early sections of the course—may need more frequent formative tests than later portions. Where some of the learning units are basic and prerequisite for other units of the course, the tests should be frequent enough to insure thorough mastery of such learning material.

For students who have thoroughly mastered the unit, the formative tests should reinforce the learning and assure the student that his present mode of learning and approach to study is adequate. Since he will have a number of such tests, the student who consistently demonstrates mastery should be able to reduce his anxiety about his course achievement.

For students who lack mastery of a particular unit, the formative tests should reveal the particular points of difficulty—the specific questions they answer incorrectly and the particular ideas, skills, and processes they still need to work on. It is most helpful when the diagnosis shows the elements in a learning hierarchy that the student still needs to learn. We have found that students respond best to the diagnostic results when they are referred to particular instructional materials or processes intended to help them correct their difficulties. The *diagnosis* should be accompanied by a very specific *prescription* if the students are to do anything about it.

Problems of Grading

Although we have limited evidence on this point, we believe that the formative tests should not be assigned grades or quality points. We have marked the tests to show *mastery* and *nonmastery*. The nonmastery is accompanied by detailed diagnosis and prescription of what is yet to be done before mastery is complete. We believe that the use of grades on repeated progress tests prepares students for the acceptance of less than mastery. To be graded C repeatedly prepares the student to accept a C as his "fate" for the particular course, especially when the grades on progress tests are averaged in as part of the final grade. Under such conditions, there must come a point when it is impossible to do better than a particular grade in the course—and there is little value in striving to improve. Formative evaluation tests should be regarded as part of the learning process and should in no way be confused with the judgment of the capabilities of the student or used as a part of the grading process.

These formative tests may also provide feedback for the teacher since they can be used to identify particular points in the instruction that are in need of modification. The formative evaluation tests also can serve as a means of quality control in future cycles of the course. The performance of the students on each test may be compared with the norms for previous years to insure that students are doing as well or better. Such comparisons can also be used to insure that changes in instruction or materials are not producing more error and difficulty than was true in a previous cycle of the course.

Alternative Learning Resources. It is one thing to diagnose the specific learning difficulties the student has and to suggest the specific steps he should take to overcome these difficulties. It is quite another thing to get him to do anything about it. By itself, the frequent use of progress tests can improve the achievement of students to a small degree. If, in addition, the student can be motivated to expend further effort on correcting his errors on the progress tests, the gains in achievement can be very great.

We have found that students do attempt to work on their difficulties when they are given specific suggestions (usually on the formative evaluation results) as to what they need to do.

The best procedure we have found thus far is to have small groups of students (two or three) meet regularly for as much as an hour per week to review the results of their formative evaluation tests and to help each other overcome the difficulties identified on these tests.

We have offered tutorial help as students desired it, but so far students at higher education levels do not seek this type of help frequently.

Other types of learning resources we have prescribed for students include: (*a*) reread particular pages of the original instructional materials; (*b*) read or study specific pages in alternative textbooks or other instructional materials; (*c*) use specific pages of workbooks or programmed texts; and (*d*) use selected audiovisual materials.

We suspect that no specific learning material or process is indispensable. The presence of a great variety of instructional materials and procedures, and specific suggestions as to which ones the student might use, help the student recognize that if he cannot learn in one way, alternatives are available to him. Perhaps further research will reveal the best match between individuals and alternative learning resources. At present, we do not have firm evidence on the relations between student characteristics and instructional materials and procedures.

Outcomes.   What are the results of a strategy for mastery learning? So far we have limited evidence. The results to date, however, are very encouraging. We are in the process of securing more evidence on a variety of situations at the elementary, secondary, and higher education levels.

Cognitive Outcomes of a Mastery Strategy.   In our work to date we have found some evidence of the effectiveness of a strategy for mastery learning. Our best results have been found in a course on test theory where we have been able to use parallel achievement tests for the course in 1965, 1966, and 1967. In 1965, before the strategy was used, approximately 20 percent of the students received the grade of A on the final examination. In 1966, after the strategy was employed, 80 percent of the students reached this level of mastery on the parallel examination and were given the grade of A. The difference in the mean performance of the two groups represents about two standard deviations on the 1965 achievement test and is highly significant.

In 1967, using the same formative evaluation tests as used in 1966, it was possible to compare the 1966 and the 1967 results after each unit of learning. Thus, the formative evaluation tests became quality-control measures. Where there were significant negative differences between the results on a particular test from 1966 to 1967, the instructor reviewed the specific learning difficulties and attempted to explain the ideas in a different way. The final results on the 1967 summative evaluation instrument, which was parallel to the final achievement tests in 1965 and 1966, were that 90 percent of the students achieved mastery and were given grades of A.

Similar studies are under way at different levels of education. We expect to have many failures and a few successes. But the point to be made is not that a single strategy of mastery learning can be used mechanically to achieve a particular set of results. Rather, the problem is one of determining what procedures will prove effective in helping particular students learn the subject under consideration. It is hoped that each time a strategy is used, it will be studied to find where it is succeeding and where it is not. For which students is it effective and for which students is it not effective? Hopefully, the results in a particular year can take advantage of the experience accumulated over the previous years.

Affective Consequences of Mastery. We have, for the past century, conceived of mastery of a subject as being possible for only a minority of students. With this assumption we have adjusted our grading system so as to certify that only a small percent of students (no matter how carefully selected) are awarded a grade of A. If a group of students learns a subject in a superior way (as contrasted with a previous group of students), we still persist in awarding the A (or mastery) to only the top 10 or 15 percent of the students. We grudgingly recognize that the majority of students have "gotten by" by awarding them grades of D or C. Mastery and recognition of mastery under the present relative grading system is unattainable for the majority of students—but this is the result of the way in which we have "rigged" the educational system.

Mastery must be both a subjective recognition by the student of his competence and a public recognition by the school or society. The public recognition must be in the form of appropriate certification by the teacher or by the school. No matter how much the student has learned, if public recognition is denied him, he must come to believe that he is inadequate, not the system of grading or instruction. Subjectively, the student must gain feelings of control over ideas and skills. He must come to recognize that he "knows" and can do what the subject requires.

If the system of formative evaluation (diagnostic–progress tests) and the summative evaluation (achievement examinations) informs the student of his mastery of the subject, he will come to believe in his own mastery and competence. He may be informed by the grading system as well as by the discovery that he can adequately cope with the variety of tasks and problems in the evaluation instruments.

When the student has mastered a subject and when he receives both objective and subjective evidence of the mastery, there are profound changes in his view of himself and of the outer world.

Perhaps the clearest evidence of affective change is the interest the student develops for the subject he has mastered. He begins to "like" the subject and to desire more of it. To do well in a subject opens up further avenues for exploration of the subject. Conversely, to do poorly in a subject closes an area for further study. The student desires some control over his environment, and mastery of a subject gives him some feeling of control over a part of his environment. Interest in a subject is both a cause of mastery of the subject as well as a result of mastery. Motivation for further learning is one of the more important consequences of mastery.

At a deeper level is the student's self-concept. Each person searches for positive recognition of his worth and he comes to view himself as adequate in areas where he receives assurance of his competence or success. For a student to view himself in a positive way, he must be given many opportunities to be rewarded. Mastery and its public recognition provide the necessary reassurance and reinforcement to help the student view himself as adequate. It is the opinion of this writer that one of the more positive aids to mental health is frequent and objective indications of self-development. Mastery learning can be one of the more powerful sources of mental health. We are convinced that many of the neurotic symptoms displayed by high school and college students are exacerbated by painful and frustrating experiences in school learning. If 90 percent of the students are given positive indications of adequacy in learning, one might expect such students to need less and less in the way of emotional therapy and psychological help. Contrariwise, frequent indications of failure and learning inadequacy must be accompanied by increased self-doubt on the part of the student and the search for reassurance and adequacy outside the school.

Finally, modern society requires continual learning throughout life. If the schools do not promote adequate learning and reassurance of progress, the student must come to reject learning—both in the school and later life. Mastery learning can give zest to school learning and can develop a lifelong interest in learning. It is this continual learning that should be the major goal of the educational system.

Notes

1. Theodore W. Schultz, *The Economic Value of Education* (New York: Columbia University Press, 1963).
2. M. J. Bowman, "The New Economics of Education," *International Journal of Educational Sciences* 1 (1966): 29–46.
3. John Carroll, "A Model of School Learning," *Teachers College Record* 64 (1963): 723–733.
4. Henry C. Morrison, *The Practice of Teaching in the Secondary School* (Chicago: University of Chicago Press, 1926).
5. Jerome S. Bruner, *Toward a Theory of Instruction* (Cambridge, Mass.: Harvard University Press, 1966).
6. B. F. Skinner, "The Science of Learning and the Art of Teaching," *Harvard Educational Review* 24 (1954): 86–97.
7. Patrick Suppes, "The Uses of Computers in Education," *Scientific American* (September 1966): 206–221.
8. John I. Goodlad and R. H. Anderson, *The Nongraded Elementary School* (New York: Harcourt Brace, 1959).
9. Robert Glaser, "Adapting the Elementary School Curriculum to Individual Performance," *Proceedings of the 1967 Invitational Conference on Testing Problems* (Princeton, N. J.: Educational Testing Service, 1968).
10. See note 3 above.
11. Ibid.
12. See note 9 above.

13. Richard C. Atkinson, "Computerized Instruction and the Learning Process," *Technical Report No. 122* (Stanford, Calif.: Institute for Mathematical Studies in the Social Sciences, 1967).
14. Benjamin S. Bloom, *Stability and Change in Human Characteristics* (New York: Wiley & Sons, 1964).
15. Joseph M. Hunt, *Intelligence and Experience* (New York: Ronald Press, 1961).
16. See note 3 above.
17. W. J. Congreve, "Independent Learning," *North Central Association Quarterly* 40 (1965): 222–228.
18. R. H. Dave, "The Identification and Measurement of Environmental Process Variables That Are Related to Educational Achievement," Ph.D. dissertation, University of Chicago, 1963.
19. See note 14 above.
20. Torsten Husén, ed., *International Study of Educational Achievement in Mathematics: A Comparison of Twelve Countries*, vols. 1, 2 (New York: Wiley & Sons, 1967).
21. Ibid.
22. Ibid.
23. See note 8 above.
24. Robert M. Gagné, *The Conditions of Learning* (New York: Holt, Rinehart and Winston, 1965).
25. Benjamin S. Bloom, ed., *Taxonomy of Educational Objectives: Handbook 1, Cognitive Domain* (New York: David McKay, 1956).
26. See note 24 above.
27. Michael Scriven, "The Methodology of Evaluation," *Perspectives of Curriculum Evaluation*, edited by R. Stake (Chicago: Rand McNally, 1967).

Authors

"The Evaluation of Instruction: Cause-and-Effect Relations in Naturalistic Data," by M. C. Wittrock, Professor in the Graduate School of Education, University of California, Los Angeles. Dr. Wittrock was formerly editor of *Evaluation Comment,* the monthly publication of the Center for the Study of Evaluation at UCLA.

"Implications of Criterion-Referenced Measurement," by W. James Popham and T. R. Husek. Dr. Popham is a professor in the Graduate School of Education at UCLA and Director of the Instructional Objectives Exchange. The late Dr. Husek was a specialist in psychometric theory and evaluation and an associate professor in the Graduate School of Education at UCLA.

"Evaluating Tests in Terms of the Information They Provide," by Stephen Klein, Director of the Evaluation Technologies Program at the Center for the Study of Evaluation. Dr. Klein is Professor-in-Residence in the Graduate School of Education at UCLA.

"Different Kinds of Evaluation and Their Implications for Test Development," by T. R. Husek.

8 The Assessment of Student Learning

If student learning is the goal of our educational institutions, then the assessment of learning becomes an extremely important process. It is only through such assessment that we are able to determine the success of our teaching endeavors. If something is worth teaching, isn't it worth knowing whether we have succeeded in teaching it? And we must have measurable evidence that student learning has occurred before we can infer that teaching has taken place. New testing practices are evolving. Criterion-referenced evaluation is replacing traditional norm-referenced measures. This unit presents these new approaches to assessing student learning.

After completing this unit, you should be able to

1 distinguish between formal and informal evaluations (Wittrock)

2 differentiate between the four components of evaluation (Wittrock)

3 describe the principal purposes of norm-referenced testing and criterion-referenced testing (Popham and Husek)

4 contrast norm-referenced and criterion-referenced approaches to testing with respect to variability, item analysis, and reporting and interpretation (Popham and Husek)

5 classify elements of measurement—devices, operations, and situations —as norm-referenced or criterion-referenced (Popham and Husek)

6 analyze various goals of student evaluation and identify the kinds of test items needed to achieve the goals (Husek)

7 formulate a case in support of the position "tests are not efficient sources of information for the full range of educational decisions for which they are relied upon" (Klein)

8 outline Klein's four-step test construction approach and indicate how such an approach differs from present testing practices (Klein)

The evaluation of instruction has unique purposes and problems. They differ from the purposes and problems of evaluating environments, learners, or learning.

The purposes of evaluating instruction are to make judgments and decisions about instruction and instructional programs. To make these judgments and decisions from the data of evaluation studies involves new and comprehensive problems.

One of these problems is that the data of evaluation studies, and our quantitative methods for analyzing them, must enable us to relate instruction to individuals and to learning. We need data and procedures to estimate the relationships between the naturalistic environments of learning and the learner's intellectual and social processes, on the causal side, and the learning, on the effect side. That is, in evaluating instruction we are usually trying to estimate cause-and-effect relations in nonexperimental data to make judgments and decisions about the instruction. This problem in educational evaluation warrants new conceptual approaches toward its understanding and solution, and in this paper I will outline one such approach. It is the approach to evaluating instruction that underlies the organization of the UCLA Center for the Study of Evaluation, as I conceived it in the original proposal that established the Center.

In this approach, I maintain that to evaluate instruction, one must first measure at least three parts of instruction: (1) the environments of learning, (2) the intellectual and social processes of learners, and (3) the learning. Second, the relationships among these three parts of instruction must then be quantitatively estimated. New quantitative methods developed in statis-

---

The Evaluation
of Instruction

Cause-and-Effect Relations in Naturalistic Data

M. C. Wittrock

tics, econometrics, sociology, political science, and psychology are described for estimating cause-and-effect relations in nonexperimental data, although more conventional techniques of multiple regression might also serve our purposes.

In following this approach, I have also tried to show how differential and experimental psychologies can contribute to evaluating instruction. The approach is an example, I believe, of a rapprochement between differential and experimental psychologies that Lee Cronbach has been advocating for years [1].

If it proves successful, the emerging rapprochement would diminish some venerable dichotomies we overlearned in graduate school. Theory could be tested in natural settings, not only in laboratories. Cause-and-effect relations could be estimated in the nonexperimental data of evaluation studies, not only in experimental data. Differential and experimental psychologies could complement each other, not combat each other.

One purpose of evaluating instruction is to make decisions about it. Teachers, administrators, and evaluators make decisions about instruction and about the causes of learning. Their decisions involve questions such as "What were the important effects of the assignments, curricula, and experiences upon learners of different abilities and interests? In the future, what are the results of similar instructional experiences for different learners likely to be?" To answer such questions, data about the cause and effect relations existing among learners, their environments, and learning are needed by teachers, administrators, and evaluators.

Purposes and Problems of Evaluating Instruction

A second purpose for evaluating instruction is to make judgments about it. Educational researchers try to understand instruction and to make generalizations about it and about the cause and effect relations within it. Experiments and descriptive research studies are two commonly used methods for understanding instruction. But evaluation studies could also contribute to the purpose of understanding and judging instruction—if we could put together the proper conceptual and methodological tools.

Unfortunately, with the difficult decisions and judgments to be made about instruction, teachers, administrators, evaluators, and researchers have been only modestly helped by the data and methods of many evaluation studies. One reason for this lack of help is that these data and methods were designed to evaluate learners, learning, or learning environments, but not for the more comprehensive problems of relating the learner's interactions with his environment to his learning.

A second reason why some of the previous approaches to evaluation have been only modestly helpful when applied to the comprehensive problems of evaluating instruction is that they have been extrapolated far from their origins in differential or experimental psychology. In these areas there has been experience with only parts of the problems related to evaluating instruction.

In differential psychology, the central problem is the measurement of individual differences, including the writing of tests that, above all, measure differences among people. When these methods are applied to evaluating instruction, the central concern remains the measurement of individual differences among learners, not the measurement of the cause-and-effect relations among learners, instructional environments, and learning.

As a result, when teachers and administrators try to evaluate instruction with standardized tests of student achievement, they find themselves struggling with the properties of the normal curve; they find themselves unable to state in an absolute sense what their students know or what they have learned. Although they can tell how their students perform relative to other students, the teachers and administrators are not helped very much by data about differences in students' achievement to know how their students' behavior has been changed—much less to know what causal role instruction has played in determining student learning.

The methods of experimental psychology were also designed for somewhat different problems. Although experimentation is designed to determine probable causes for learning, it is not often realistic to use experiments in evaluation studies. An experiment involves treatments each applied uniformly to two or more students. It is obviously not often useful to solve the common evaluation problems of teachers and administrators, who want to evaluate the day-to-day teaching and instruction occurring in the natural contexts of their schools without resorting to techniques of random assignments and manipulated treatments.

From the above discussion, I conclude that teachers, administrators, evaluators, and researchers are interested, albeit for different reasons, in evaluating the cause-and-effect relations in instruction occurring in nonexperimental settings to make decisions and judgments about the instruction. For years, sociologists, political scientists, econometricians, and statisticians have been developing quantitative methods for estimating cause-and-effect relations in nonexperimental data. Now that these methods are being used with some success in these fields, it seems time to apply them to educational problems such as evaluation of instruction, which involves estimating these types of relations in naturalistic data.

An Approach Toward Evaluating Instruction

To introduce my approach to evaluation, which incorporates three earlier approaches and a quantitative viewpoint useful in estimating cause-and-effect relations, I must first make a distinction among conceptual approaches to evaluation by the variables and behavior they make explicit. Although explicitness is not the only basis for differentiating among approaches to evaluation, it is the best one for my purposes. Explicitness of the variables and behavior distinguishes formal from informal evaluation, and it distinguishes my approach from the three other approaches to evaluation described in this article.

Informal Evaluations.   We informally evaluate when we judge the worth of our own surroundings, our behavior, change in our behavior, and events in our lives. Informal evaluations are judgments that do not necessarily involve an explicit statement of their bases, values, experiences, variables, and data.

For example, in our daily lives we informally evaluate our environment when we say that something, such as a course in mathematics, is good. We informally evaluate our behavior when we say that we are proficient at something, such as differential calculus. And we informally evaluate learning when we say that we are more proficient at differential calculus today than we were yesterday. Finally, we informally evaluate instruction when we say that listening to a lecture about limits and functions helped us to become more proficient at calculus than we were yesterday.

These four examples are evaluations in the informal sense of the word. They are statements only of our decisions and our judgments, not of our values, experiences, nor the data basic to these decisions or judgments. In informal evaluations, our bases for making an evaluation—values, data, experience, theory, and knowledge—need not be made explicit. It is enough that the judgment is made explicit. We assume that careful and intelligent informal evaluations will be based upon experience, values, and knowledge.

Formal Evaluations.   In a formal evaluation, the judgments and decisions are again made explicit. However, we also require explicit statements and objective measures of the bases of the evaluations. In an evaluation study, the selection and objective measurement of the bases of the judgments and the decisions are the focus of most of our time and effort. Making explicit and measuring the bases of our judgments is central to the study of evaluation of instruction.

The Evaluation of Environments, Learners, and Learning.   Now I want to discuss three of the four fundamental parts of my conceptualization of evaluation of instruction. Each of these three parts has served as a conceptualization of evaluation in its own right; I regard the three components as conceptual approaches to evaluation. A comprehensive evaluation of instruction involves relating all three components to one another to obtain cause-and-effect relations from nonexperimental data.

First, if one wishes to evaluate a given course of instruction, he might look at characteristics of the instructional environment provided in the course—for example, the amount of time devoted to learning or the textbook used in the course. He might look also at the sequence of instruction, characteristics of the curriculum, of the classroom, of the school library, and of the training of the teacher of the course. In short, he would focus the study upon qualities of the student's environment; he would make them explicit and he would make decisions about them. This type of formal evaluation, which I will call *evaluation of environments*, is still commonly used in schools by teachers and administrators. It will be discussed in more detail after other types of formal evaluations are introduced.

A second way to evaluate instruction is to make explicit the students' abilities, interests, and achievements to determine student performance at the end of the instruction—usually by determining their relative standing in a group. I will call this type of study *evaluation of learners*. It is usually accomplished by measuring individual differences among students and is a popular way for professional evaluators to evaluate curricula.

Third, one might make explicit the changes in students' behavior to try to determine what had been learned during instruction. I will call this type of study *evaluation of learning*, or evaluation of relatively permanent change in behavior occurring as a result of experience. This is a relatively new approach to evaluation, a by-product of research in learning.

Fourth and last, one might measure learning (as in the third approach mentioned), quantify several of the learners' intellectual and social characteristics (as in the second approach), and also measure several of the environmental characteristics (as in the first approach above), and then try to relate the interactions of these learner and environmental characteristics to student learning. This new, uncommon, and extremely complicated type of evaluation I will call *evaluation of instruction*. Now that multivariate statistical procedures are becoming available for estimating the cause-and-effect relations in evaluation studies, this approach is feasible.

Fundamental to the above distinction among approaches to evaluation is the making explicit and quantifying of the bases for decisions and judgments about instruction. The act of judging or deciding the merits of instruction is part of evaluation, but it is not the focus of our interests here.

In elaborating the conceptual approach mentioned above, I will deliberately avoid giving examples of evaluation studies that fall into each category. My purpose in omitting examples of past work is to focus upon a new approach and to avoid implying criticism of evaluation studies quite adequately designed for their intended purposes.

The Evaluation of Environments. When our evaluation study concentrates on making explicit the physical and the human characteristics of the learners' environment, we are evaluating environments. Counting the number of books in libraries, hours spent in instruction in the classroom, school budget per pupil, intellectual merit of the teachers, college credits of a teacher in his major, or even the number of homework problems assigned to the class are examples that measure environmental characteristics commonly used by teachers and administrators to index learning.

That there may be more meaningful environmental characteristics is not the issue here. Library books and dollars invested in pupils are important to learning. But the nature and extent of the relationships among the environments, learners, and learning cannot be studied by making explicit and measuring only environmental characteristics. Obviously, measures of environmental characteristics alone are not sufficient to enable one to make objective inferences about their effects upon learners. Measures of intellectual and social processes in learners, which greatly influence the outcomes of learning, are needed, as are measures of learning.

The evaluation of student environments alone, as described above, would be a futile approach toward the evaluation of instruction. It is not well regarded among researchers in evaluation as an approach toward evaluation.

However, characteristics of instructional environments should be made explicit in evaluation studies. The teacher's primary function is to provide environments best suited to the learner to enhance his learning and development as an individual. To do this, a teacher obviously must make decisions and inferences about the educational value of environments and their probable effects upon individuals. He needs to characterize and describe those crucial qualities of environments he can manipulate; but he also needs to be able to relate them objectively to individual learners and to change in the behavior of learners. The first element of my approach to evaluating instruction has now been identified.

The Evaluation of Learners. When an evaluation study focuses upon making explicit the behavior and characteristics of learners, the term *evaluation of learners*, usually of individual differences among students, describes the procedure adequately. Many recent evaluation studies fit well into this group. Achievement tests and ability tests are the instruments often used to evaluate individual differences in student behavior for selection and placement of learners.

This prevalent approach to evaluation has grown from the study of individual differences and its psychometric problems rather than from experimentation in human learning. For a long time, some of the best work in educational evaluation has come from the study of individual differences. Probability theory, psychometrics, and differential psychology have had a substantial effect upon thinking about educational evaluation and about what should be made explicit in an evaluation study.

The student's scores on standardized tests of interests, abilities, and achievements are useful for measuring individual differences in learning to select students for more advanced study, and to place them in different treatments. With these scores we can compare a student's performance to that of other students, and we can select or place students with some success in predicting their relative standing in groups. But these tests, designed to discriminate individual differences in behavior among students, do not enable us to make rigorous inferences about what the students have learned nor about the role of environments and intellectual processes in producing the learning. In short, data on the relative achievement status of students do not tell us what, how, or why students have learned, nor the roles of antecedent learner and environmental factors in learning.

To measure what students have learned, we need to measure changes in their behavior. To answer the questions of how and why students learn, we need to quantify the salient characteristics of environments and we need to measure their relationships to intellectual and social processes, as well as to student achievement.

As a conceptualization of evaluation, the evaluation of learners is adequate for its intended purpose of obtaining data on the relative state of students' achievements, abilities, and preferences. Evaluating learners is the second essential part of an approach to evaluating instruction and its interactions with students. However, measures of individual differences among learners is only one way to measure the abilities, interests, and achievements relevant to designing and evaluating instruction for individuals. For example, to evaluate the effects of instruction designed to teach people to read French, we need to measure proactive variables, such as how well they read French at the beginning of instruction. If all of them read no French—that is, if there are no individual differences in a test of ability to read French—we are still highly interested in their scores on this test. The basic issues are the relationships between the learners' aptitudes, achievements, interests, and the instruction, not only whether there are individual differences among the learners.

The Evaluation of Learning.   One difference between measuring individual differences and evaluating learning is that, regardless of what or how well students learn, the writing of test items to discriminate among individuals does not evidence their progress directly. Common techniques of test construction and interpretation require that, regardless of how much or how little students learn, half of them are below average in achievement, most of them receive C grades, and as many of them receive D and F grades as receive B and A grades, respectively. By concentrating upon measuring *differences* among students, we tend to forget about the amounts learned by individuals—that all or many of them might learn to a mastery level, an A level, if we went about our teaching discriminatively and differently for different students. Bloom [2] has made this point quite well.

Results of Measuring Differences

It is ironic that our quest for individual differences has led us away from individualized instruction. We would do well to design different types of instruction for each individual or for each group of individuals rather than to persist in our hunt for individual differences in achievement resulting from treatments designed for all students collectively. It would be better to vary our instruction with individuals to help them learn, rather than to change the criteria until we find some differences, perhaps trivial, among their achievements. Changing the criteria of learning until we find some differences among individuals is an easy out. It avoids the basic issue of tailoring the instruction to the individual.

By retaining in our achievement test only the test items that discriminate among students, we may be omitting content-valid items that all or nearly all students have learned to answer correctly as a result of instruction. Our prevalent habits of discarding valid but nondiscriminating items to find some ways, perhaps irrelevant, in which individuals differ in achievement skirts the main issue: What instruction is best for each individual to help him learn?

These habits, involving use of the normal curve, have had a deleterious effect upon instruction and have retarded the search for improvement. Measures of individual differences among students' achievements are useful for evaluating instruction, but their measurement must not become the overriding objective of a study designed to evaluate instruction.

Measuring change in student behavior toward behaviorally defined objectives is a relatively new approach to evaluation, involving psychometric procedures which may ignore classical wisdom. This newer approach is commonly used in the study of human learning. For example, researchers with experimental backgrounds who study instruction and curriculum usually want to evaluate the effects of instruction by using criteria and test items chosen for their content validity. These researchers are not likely to discard content-valid test items to improve the ability of the test to discriminate differences among students. Their *zeitgeist* emphasizes selecting criteria and items first, and looking for individual differences later. To experimental researchers, altering the criteria of learning deliberately to produce a test that will discriminate among learners is unseemly at best if one is trying to evaluate the instruction.

A New Approach to Evaluation

During the last several years, curriculum evaluation has increasingly become viewed as the evaluation of change in behavior toward behaviorally defined goals, as described above. Unlike the evaluation of learners, learning is evaluated by taking *two* or more measures—either one measure upon each of several different groups, or two or more measures upon the same people obtained at two or more different times, usually before and after instruction.

Let us discuss this two-step process of measuring students' performance. With this model, we begin our evaluation by making explicit those changes in behavior of interest to us. Other less relevant areas of behavior change are ignored, at least for the moment.

These interesting changes of behavior must next be made explicit and defined as observable student behavior. If a student in a sixth-grade mathematics class is to learn the meaning of the Pythagorean theorem or an appreciation of mathematics, the desired changes in his behavior are defined by writing specific behavioral objectives and then by preparing tests of his behavior.

Next, a student's change in behavior is indexed, often by measuring differences in his behavior on a pretest and a post-test. These before-and-after measures are obtained to help insure that his behavior has changed during the instruction—that is, that he did not know the meaning of the Pythagorean theorem before the instruction began but that he does know its meaning after the instruction is completed. (We still cannot be certain that the instruction has been involved in his learning, but we have increased the probability that the instruction and his learning are related to each other.)

Some distinctive psychometric characteristics of evaluating learning, as different from measuring individual differences, will become more apparent by discussing them a little further. The ways of choosing items differ if we want to compare learners rather than to measure changes in their behavior. To measure learners, especially their individual differences, a test item is chosen largely by its ability to discriminate among individuals. If all or none of the students answer a particular item correctly, that item is not useful for measuring individual differences among students. Its difficulty level would not be appropriate to the job of discriminating among students, the level being either too low or too high.

On the other hand, when we measure change in behavior produced by instruction, the choice of item is determined largely by its relevance to the instruction, not by its ability to discriminate among students. To measure whether a student learned in a history class that Lincoln was President in 1861, an item that sampled that information would be included in a test of behavioral change. The fact that all, or none, of the students gave the right answer is not nearly as relevant to the measuring of learning as is the validity of the content of the item.

If all the students got a valid and reliable item wrong on a pretest, the instruction and not the test would be changed. This kind of thinking comes hard for some evaluators trained in the psychometrics of measuring individual differences.

Refining Objectives

Evaluating learning has distinctive characteristics other than its psychometric procedure. One of the more important of these characteristics is an emphasis on making explicit the behavioral objectives of the instruction. A general objective, such as "to appreciate mathematics," is an anathema. Refinement and iteration are needed to produce precisely defined, observable behaviors of students to evidence that they appreciate mathematics. Even the time limits and other conditions for the behavior need to be specified to apply this approach properly. The essence of this approach is to make explicit the changes in behavior accruing through instruction, beginning with the writing of behavioral objectives for student learning and followed by measuring the changes in behavior toward these objectives.

For evaluating learning, this approach has obvious advantages over the two approaches discussed above. The most important one is not the popular notion of writing behaviorally defined objectives before beginning to instruct learners. Instead, it is a logical result of writing these objectives—the use of an absolute rather than a relative standard for measuring learning. The objectives lead to test items written for their content validity, not for their ability to discriminate among learners. As a result of the focus on content validity, evaluators are becoming less concerned about discriminating among learners and more concerned about the individual student and his changes in behavior—his learning. And teachers are freed to conceive of mastery learning for any number of students.

Although this approach does not include explicit descriptions of educational environments or of learners, it has produced a fundamental change in our thinking about evaluation. We now think of the learning of each student, and we are less concerned about comparing him with other students.

The evaluation of learning helps us to determine what people have learned. It is the third element of my approach to evaluating instruction, and I wish to include in it changes in behavior that occur in students, teachers, and other people.

The Evaluation of Instruction. Critics of the evaluation of learning are quick to find faults in it. Some of these criticisms are justified; others are not. If one measures only behavioral changes toward preplanned objectives, he will ignore other significant changes in students resulting from instruction. Perhaps students learn the Pythagorean theorem but, in the process, also learn to dislike mathematics. Since dislike for mathematics was not an objective of instruction, according to the above approach (evaluation of learning), we might not have measured it. Not all important dimensions of change in student behavior can be foreseen. We should not ignore important criteria because they were not apparent or desired before instruction began.

Changes in behavior of people other than students—teachers, parents, etc.—are also important and should not be omitted from evaluation studies because they are different from student learning. These changes ought somehow to be incorporated into our thinking about evaluation.

Another commonly mentioned and, I believe, valid criticism is that precisely worded behavioral objectives easily tend to become narrow and trivial and to lose the essence of the instruction. In time, this narrowness could be overcome by writing hierarchical sets of more specific objectives to sample more general, imprecisely worded, but significant objectives.

The three criticisms mentioned above apply to the current use of the approach called evaluation of learning—not to the approach itself, which requires neither prespecified objectives nor a limited number of narrowly defined criteria of learning. These criticisms notwithstanding, this approach is well designed for its purposes; it is a significant concept in the evaluation of instruction.

A telling criticism of evaluation of learning is that it requires one to make explicit only the behaviors learned, not the characteristics of the environment of instruction, nor the intellectual and social characteristics of learners interacting with this environment, nor the characteristics of the school as a social system. The environment of instruction is made explicit only in gross and vague terms. The instructional package is viewed as an entity—a box marked "contents unknown." We call it a program, a curriculum, or a course of instruction; and we color the box black.

Explicitness is also lacking in the definition of the crucially important antecedent intellectual and social processes of the learners, and of the social characteristics of the school. The model is therefore not adequate for obtaining cause-and-effect relations about instruction from the data of evaluation studies. If one wants to evaluate instruction, a more comprehensive approach is logically more appropriate than the one described above for evaluating learning.

Comprehensive Approach

A comprehensive approach to evaluating instruction would require us to make explicit and to relate to each other the salient characteristics of (1) individual learners, (2) their instructional environments, and (3) their learning, as these three exist in naturalistic settings. The concept of explicitness would then be extended to include learning, antecedent student behavior, and environmental characteristics of instruction. With the appropriate multivariate statistical tools for this approach we could estimate "cause-and-effect relations" in the naturalistic data of evaluation studies.

The remaining element of such an approach can now be sketched very briefly, because three of its four components have already been introduced and discussed. The approach is based upon the assumption, discussed above, that formal evaluation includes making explicit the bases for decisions and judgments about relationships between learners and their environments—the same assumptions responsible for the progress attributable to evaluating learning. To evaluate instruction rather than environments, behavior, or learning involves a comprehensive approach, making explicit the salient characteristics of all three of the above. By making all three of these explicit, and given the multivariate statistical procedures, we should be able to relate them to each other to make conclusions and judgments about instruction not possible before.

The question is, "Do we have the fourth element to complete the approach—the methodological knowledge to estimate the cause-and-effect relations in naturalistic situations, such as instruction in schools?" In 1967–68, I was one of a group of Fellows at the Center of Advanced Study in the Behavioral Sciences at Stanford, California that met regularly to study this question. This group found (in the literature of sociology, econometrics, statistics, political science, and in the recent literature of psychology) much interest and research on this problem, ranging from attempts by political scientists to explain the causes of roll-call votes of legislators to explanations by sociologists of the causes of IQ. Some of the better papers on this subject are cited below.

An excellent discussion of the general problem of obtaining causal inferences in nonexperimental research is in a book by Blalock [3] and, from a different point of view, in one by Simon [4]. Hayward Alker, a political scientist, has written many papers on causal relationships in nonexperimental data, but two are of special interest to evaluators [5].

Because the methodology of obtaining causal relations from nonexperimental data is of obvious relevance to evaluating instruction, several articles on this methodology are worthy of mention. The first two, by Wold [6], introduce the basic concepts and limitations of these approaches; the third, a paper by Duncan [7], discusses path analysis as used in sociology; and of the currently available articles, a paper by Yee and Gage [8] is the most relevant to the problems of evaluating instruction. Also of interest are papers by Boudon [9], Goldberg [10], Simon and Rescher [11], and the earlier work by Lazarsfeld [12], Kempthorne [13], and, of course, Sewall Wright [14].

The above-mentioned approaches to causal explanations from nonexperimental data are too complex to discuss in detail here. However, the article by Duncan [15] explains one approach, path analysis, pioneered by Sewall Wright, with special potential for educational evaluation and for educational research. By using path analysis, one can compute path coefficients for each chain or network of variables hypothesized to be influencing one another in a causal way. The path coefficients, each representing a different prediction from a different theory, provide one empirical way to compare theoretical predictions about causation in nonexperimental data. Path coefficients do not "prove" causation (neither does anything else), but they can help to reduce the error variance in our statements about causes and effects.

These comments about methodological analyses complete my introduction of an approach to the evaluation of instruction. If the approach proves useful in evaluation research, we should be able to relate learning to the environments and individuals "causing" it. We should be able to evaluate instruction rather than learners or learning. It may become possible to learn how social and other characteristics of the environments of instruction interact with students to mediate changes in their behavior. At the UCLA Center for the Study of Evaluation, work is currently in progress applying this approach to evaluating instruction.

Summary

In summary, I view the study of evaluation of instruction to be the study of the relationships between naturalistic learning environments and learners on the one hand, and the criteria of learning on the other. From my point of view, evaluation studies should contribute not only to decisions about the specific instruction measured in each study but also to judgments, knowledge, and understanding of teaching and instruction. For too long we have compartmentalized theory and laboratory research from practice and naturalistic research. Because we now have useful methodological tools, in evaluation studies we should try to examine the cause-and-effect relations in instruction in schools, and we should try to obtain estimates of the probability of our explanations being wrong. My approach brings together educators, experimental psychologists, differential psychologists, sociologists, and statisticians to work on a significant problem of common interest —the evaluation of instruction.

This approach to evaluating instruction is obviously in its infancy. It is too early to know its usefulness and its limitations. It does offer the hope of reducing the error variance in quantifying and explicating some of the relations which exist in instruction. This approach should enable us to analyze teaching and instruction, to study theoretical and practical issues in naturalistic settings, and to evaluate instruction.

If it does none of these things, it will, I hope, still have stimulated the underlying purpose for developing it. That purpose is to find new and comprehensive approaches to studying problems of education. These approaches must go beyond our habits of routinely applying disciplines or other methods to problems when intellectual effort at the conceptual level is needed before these applications and extrapolations can have much meaning. Without implying that education is a discipline, we can be disciplined in our study of its problems. And we need to devise comprehensive research approaches appropriate to studying its complex problems.

Notes

1. Lee J. Cronbach, "The Two Disciplines of Scientific Psychology," *American Psychologist* 12 (1957): 671–684.
2. Benjamin S. Bloom, "Learning for Mastery." See pp. 94–113 of this book.
3. Hubert M. Blalock, Jr., *Causal Inferences in Nonexperimental Research* (Chapel Hill, N. C.: University of North Carolina Press, 1964).
4. H. A. Simon, *Models of Man: Social and Rational* (New York: Wiley & Sons, 1957).
5. Hayward R. Alker, Jr. "Causal Inference and Political Analysis," in *Mathematical Applications in Political Science*, edited by Joseph L. Bernd, vol. 2 (Dallas, Tex.: Arnold Foundation, Southern Methodist University, 1968). *See also* "Statistics and Politics: The Need for Causal Data Analysis," paper presented at the annual meeting of the American Political Science Association in Chicago, September 1967.
6. Herman O. Wold, "Causal Inference from Observational Data: A Review of Ends and Means," *Journal of the Royal Statistical Society* (London) 119 (1956): 28–50. *See also* "La technique des modèles dans les sciences humaines," in *Sciences Humaines* (Rue de Millo, Monaco: Centre International d'Etude des Problèmes Humains, 1966).
7. Otis D. Duncan, "Path Analysis: Sociological Examples," *American Journal of Sociology* 72 (1957): 671–684.
8. A. H. Yee and N. L. Gage, "Techniques for Estimating the Source and Direction of Causal Influence in Panel Data," *Psychological Bulletin* 70 (1968): 115–126.
9. Raymond Boudon, "Methodes d'analyse causale," *Revue française de sociologie* 6 (1965): 24–43.
10. A. S. Goldberg, "Discerning a Causal Pattern among Data on Voting Behavior," *American Political Science Review* 60 (1966): 913–922.

11. H. A. Simon and N. Rescher, "Cause and Counterfactual," *Philosophy of Science* 33 (1966).

12. Paul F. Lazarsfeld, ed., *Mathematical Thinking in the Social Sciences* (Glencoe, Ill.: Free Press, 1954).

13. Oscar Kempthorne, et al., *Statistics and Mathematics in Biology* (Ames, Ia.: Iowa State College Press, 1954).

14. Sewall Wright, "The Method of Path Coefficients," *Annals of Mathematical Statistics* 5 (1934): 161–215.

15. See note 7 above.

During the past several years measurement and instructional specialists have distinguished between norm-referenced *and* criterion-referenced *approaches to measurement. More traditional, a norm-referenced measure is used to identify an individual's performance in relation to the performance of others on the same measure. A criterion-referenced test is used to identify an individual's status with respect to an established standard of performance. This discussion examines the implications of these two approaches to measurement, particularly criterion-referenced measurement, with respect to variability, item construction, reliability, validity, item analysis, reporting, and interpretation.*

The question of what score to use as the most meaningful index of a student's performance on a test has been the subject of many discussions over the years. Percentile scores, raw scores, and standard scores of various kinds have been advocated. The arguments have almost always begun with the premise that the test is a given and that the issue is how to obtain the meaningful score. That is, there has been general acceptance of how the test should be constructed and judged. Test theory as explicated in most elementary testing texts has been assumed to represent a commonly held set of values. In recent years some writers (e.g., Cronbach and Gleser, [1]) have begun to question the usefulness of classical test theory for all testing problems. This broadens and complicates the question above; the problem is now not only how to summarize a student's performance on a test, but also how to insure that a test is constructed (and judged) in a manner appropriate to its use, even if its use is not in the classical framework.

One facet of this issue has particular relevance to tests based on instructional objectives. For several years now, particularly since the appearance of Glaser's article [2] on the subject, measurement and instructional specialists have been drawing distinctions between *norm-referenced* and *criterion-referenced* approaches to measurement. But it appears that, other than adding new terms to the technical lexicon, the two constructs have made little

Implications of Criterion-Referenced Measurement

W. James Popham and T. R. Husek

difference in measurement practice. Perhaps the reason for this is that few analyses have been made of the practical implications of using criterion-referenced measures. Most of us are familiar with concepts associated with norm-referenced measurement. We grew up with them. A criterion-referenced approach, however, is another matter. What differences, if any, does a criterion-referenced framework make with respect to such operations as test construction and revision and to such concepts as reliability and validity? This article will examine some of these implications by contrasting criterion-referenced and norm-referenced approaches with respect to such central measurement notions.

It is not possible to tell a *norm-referenced* test from a *criterion-referenced* **The Basic Distinction** test by looking at it. In fact, a *criterion-referenced* test could also be used as a *norm-referenced* test—although the reverse is not so easy to imagine. However, this truth should not be allowed to obscure the extremely important differences between these two approaches to testing.

At the most elementary level, norm-referenced measures are those used to ascertain an individual's performance in relationship to the performance of other individuals on the same measuring device. The meaningfulness of the individual score emerges from the comparison. It is because the individual is compared with some normative group that such measures are described as norm-referenced. Most standardized tests of achievement or intellectual ability can be classified as norm-referenced measures.

Criterion-referenced measures are those used to ascertain an individual's status with respect to some criterion, i.e., performance standard. It is because the individual is compared with some established criterion, rather than other individuals, that these measures are described as criterion-referenced. The meaningfulness of an individual score is not dependent on comparison with other testees. We want to know what the individual can do, not how he stands in comparison to others. For example, the dog owner who wants to keep his dog in the backyard may give his dog a fence-jumping test. The owner wants to find out how high the dog can jump so that the owner can build a fence high enough to keep the dog in the yard. How the dog compares with other dogs is irrelevant. Another example of a criterion-referenced test would be the Red Cross Senior Lifesaving Test, where an individual must display certain swimming skills to pass the examination regardless of how well others perform on the test.

Since norm-referenced measures are devised to facilitate comparisons among individuals, it is not surprising that their primary purpose is to make decisions about *individuals*. Which pupils should be counseled to pursue higher education? Which pupils should be advised to attain vocational skills? These are the kinds of questions one seeks to answer through the use of norm-referenced measures, for many decisions regarding an individual can best be made by knowing more about the "competition," that is, by knowing how other, comparable individuals perform.

Criterion-referenced tests are devised to make decisions both about *individuals and treatments,* e.g., instructional programs. In the case of decisions regarding individuals, one might use a criterion-referenced test to determine whether a learner had mastered a criterion skill considered prerequisite to his commencing a new training program. In the case of decisions regarding treatments, one might design a criterion-referenced measure that reflected a set of instructional objectives supposedly achieved by a replicable instructional sequence. By administering the criterion-referenced measure to appropriate learners after they had completed the instructional sequence, one could reach a decision regarding the efficacy of the sequence (treatment).

Although both norm-referenced and criterion-referenced tests are used to make decisions about individuals, there is usually a difference in the two contexts in which such decisions are made. Generally, a norm-referenced measure is employed where a degree of *selectivity* is required by the situation. For example, when there are only limited openings in a company's executive-training program, the company is anxious to identify the *best* potential trainees. It is critical in such situations, therefore, that the measure permit *relative* comparisons among individuals. On the other hand, in situations where one is only interested in whether an individual possesses a particular competence, and there are no constraints regarding how many individuals can possess that skill, criterion-referenced measures are suitable. Theoretically, at the close of many instructional programs we might hope that *all* learners would display *maximum* proficiency on measures reflecting the instructional objectives. In this sense, of course, criterion-referenced measures may be considered *absolute* indicators. Thus, both norm-referenced and criterion-referenced tests can be focused on decisions regarding individuals—it is the context within which these decisions are made that really produces the distinction.

Now one could, of course, use norm-referenced measures as well as criterion-referenced measures to make decisions regarding the merits of instructional programs. Certainly, this has been a common practice through the years as educators have evaluated their curriculum efforts on the basis of pupil performance on standardized examinations. But norm-referenced measures were really designed to "spread people out" and, as we shall see, are best suited to that purpose.

With this initial distinction in mind, we shall now examine the implications of the two approaches to measurement, particularly with respect to criterion-referenced measures, for the following topics: variability, item construction, reliability, validity, item analysis, reporting, and interpretation.

Variability

The issue of variability is at the core of the difference between norm-referenced and criterion-referenced tests. Since the meaningfulness of a norm-referenced score is basically dependent on the relative position of the score in comparison with other scores, the more variability in the scores the better. With a norm-referenced test, we want to be able to tell Jamie from Joey from Frank, and we feel more secure about telling them apart if their scores are very different.

With criterion-referenced tests, variability is irrelevant. The meaning of the score is not dependent on comparison with other scores; it flows directly from the connection between the items and the criterion. It is, of course, true that one almost always gets variant scores on any psychological test; but that variability is not a necessary condition for a good criterion-referenced test.

The subtle and not-so-subtle implications of this central difference in the relevance of variability must permeate any discussion of the two approaches to testing. For example, we all have been told that a test should be reliable and valid. We have all read about test construction and item analysis. The procedures may not always be simple, the formulas may not be trivial, but there are hundreds of books and thousands of articles to guide us. Unfortunately, most of what these "helpmates" outline as "good" things to do are not only irrelevant to criterion-referenced tests, but are actually injurious to their proper development and use. This is true because the treatments of validity, the suggestions about reliability, and the formulas for item analysis are all based on the desirability of variability among scores. The connection may not be obvious but it is always there.

Item Construction

The basic difference between item construction in norm-referenced and criterion-referenced frameworks is a matter of "set" on the part of the item writer. Until we reach that automated era when computers can cough forth many items per minute, someone is going to have to construct them. The primary differences in purposes of norm-referenced and criterion-referenced measurement will usually influence the item writer to a considerable degree in at least one very significant way and, possibly to a lesser extent, in a second way as well.

Most important, when a writer constructs items for a norm-referenced test, he wants variability and, as a consequence, makes all sorts of concessions—sometimes subtle, sometimes obvious—to promote variant scores. He disdains items that are "too easy" or "too hard." He tries to increase the allure of wrong-answer options. All of this he does to produce variability. Occasionally this overriding criterion may reduce the adequacy of the instrument, for even spurious factors may be incorporated in items just to produce variance.

The criterion-referenced item writer is guided by another goal. His chief rule is to make sure the item is an accurate reflection of the criterion behavior. Difficult or easy, discriminating or indiscriminate, the important thing is to make the item represent the class of behaviors delimited by the criterion. Those who write criterion-referenced items are usually far more attentive to defining the domain of relevant test responses and the situations in which they should be required. This rather fundamental difference in "set" on the part of criterion-referenced and norm-referenced item writers can clearly contribute to differences in the resulting items.

A second difference associated with test construction is that although norm-referenced and criterion-referenced measures used to make decisions regarding individuals require that the same test (or an equivalent form) be used with different individuals, criterion-referenced tests used for evaluating programs need not. The concept of item sampling (Cronbach [3]; Husek and Sirotnik, [4]) in which different people complete different items (thereby permitting the sampling of more behavior with shorter tests) is highly appropriate for evaluating the adequacy of treatments. Thus, for such situations a number of different test forms, each containing different criterion-referenced items, could be constructed. Individuals nurtured on the concept of "everybody gets the same items" will often overlook this economical, yet powerful shortcut. . . .

Once the test is originally devised, we would like to have procedures available for improving it. In a norm-referenced context we have available the time-honored devices such as item-analysis techniques and reliability estimates that can guide us in test-refinement operations. With criterion-referenced measures, however, some of these classical constructs must be used differently. The next few sections of this paper will describe the nature of these differences.

Reliability

We all should know that for a single number to be used to describe the performance of a person on a test, the items on that test should all "measure the same thing" to some minimal extent. That is, the test should be internally consistent. This matter is treated in measurement texts in the chapter on reliability.

Now it is obvious that a criterion-referenced test should be internally consistent. If we argue that the items are tied to a criterion, then certainly the items should be quite similar in terms of what they are measuring. But although it may be obvious that a criterion-referenced test should be internally consistent, it is not obvious how to assess the internal consistency. The classical procedures are not appropriate. This is true because they are dependent on score variability. A criterion-referenced test should not be faulted if, when administered after instruction, everyone obtained a perfect score. Yet, that would lead to a zero internal consistency estimate, something measurement books do not recommend.

In fact, even stranger things can happen in practice. It is possible for a criterion-referenced test to have a *negative* internal consistency index and still be a good test. (See Husek and Sirotnik [5] for a more extensive treatment of this possibility.)

Thus, the typical indices of internal consistency are not appropriate for criterion-referenced tests. It is not clear what should replace them. Perhaps we need estimates, comparable to the standard internal consistency formulas, which can take larger temporal units into consideration, for example, by considering both a preinstruction test administration and a postinstruction test administration as part of the same extended phenomenon. Perhaps ingenious indices can be developed that reflect the ability of a test to produce variation from preinstruction to postinstruction testing and, in these terms, internal consistency—despite score-range restrictions. But until that time, those wishing to improve criterion-referenced tests should not be dismayed if the test, because of little score variance, yields a low internal consistency estimate. It is really unwise to apply such estimates.

The foregoing discussion applies only to situations where the test is used to assess a single dimension, such as one instructional objective, as opposed to several dimensions, such as three very disparate objectives. If the objectives are substantially different, the items measuring them should be considered as different tests, not a single all-encompassing measure.

Other aspects of reliability are equally cloudy. Stability might certainly be important for a criterion-referenced test, but in that case, a test–retest correlation coefficient, dependent as it is on variability, is not necessarily the way to assess it. Some kind of confidence interval around the individual score is perhaps a partial solution to this problem.

The reader should not misinterpret the above statements. If a criterion-referenced test has a high average inter-item correlation, this is fine. If the test has a high test–retest correlation, that is also fine. The point is *not* that these indices cannot be used to support the consistency of the test. The point is that a criterion-referenced test could be highly consistent, either internally or temporarily, and yet indices dependent on variability might not reflect that consistency.

Validity

Many of the procedures for assessing the validity of norm-referenced tests are based on correlations and thus on variability. Hence, with validity as with reliability, the results of the procedures are useful if they are positive, but not necessarily devastating if they are negative.

Criterion-referenced measures are validated primarily in terms of the adequacy with which they represent the criterion. Therefore, content-validity approaches are more suited to such tests. A carefully made judgment, based on the test's apparent relevance to the behaviors legitimately inferable from those delimited by the criterion, is the general procedure for validating criterion-referenced measures.

Certainly, for both norm-referenced and criterion-referenced measures a test specialist might employ construct-validity strategies to support the confidence he can give to his instruments. For example, we might wish to augment our confidence in a measure we were using as a proximate predictor (e.g., administered at the close of instruction) of some more distant criterion (e.g., occurring many years hence). If positive intercorrelations occur among several proximate predictors (of the same distant criterion), we could add to our understanding of whether a given proximate predictor was doing its job.

Item Analysis

Item-analysis procedures have traditionally been used with norm-referenced tests to identify items that were not properly discriminating among individuals taking the test. For instance, in an achievement test an unsatisfactory item would be one that could not properly discriminate between the more and less knowledgeable learners (as reflected by total test performance). Nondiscriminating items are usually those that are (*a*) too easy, (*b*) too hard, and/or (*c*) ambiguous.

For criterion-referenced tests the use of discrimination indices must be modified. An item that doesn't discriminate need not be eliminated. If it reflects an important attribute of the criterion, such an item should remain in the test. We might be interested in a "nondiscriminating" item's ability to discriminate among *anyone,* e.g., its ability to discriminate between those individuals who have and those who haven't been exposed to instruction. But, as in the case of reliability estimates, such indices are not currently available.

A positively discriminating item is just as respectable in a criterion-referenced test as it is in a norm-referenced test, but certainly not more so. In fact, the positively discriminating item may point to areas of instruction (if the criterion measure is assessing the effects of instruction) where the program is not succeeding well enough.

However, negatively discriminating items are treated exactly the same way in a criterion-referenced approach as they are in a norm-referenced approach. An item that discriminates negatively is, in an instructional context, answered correctly more often by the less knowledgeable than by the more knowledgeable students. When one discovers a negative discriminator in his pool of criterion-referenced items, he should be suspicious of it and after more careful analysis can usually detect flaws in such an item.

Of course, discrimination indices are little more than warning flags, and one must still use common sense in weighing the worth of an item identified as a negative discriminator. It might be that some deficiencies in the instruction caused the result rather than any fault of the item. Yet, it is more likely that the item is deficient. For example, suppose that the negatively discriminating item was originally generated, along with 19 other items, as a measure of a particular type of criterion behavior. Now, in order for the item to yield a negative discrimination index, there would first have to be variable subject performance. But in addition, more of those individuals who scored well on the total 20-item test would have to miss the suspect item more frequently than those who scored badly on the total test. Under such circumstances it seems more likely that it is an item deficiency rather than instructional deficiency, although the latter possibility should be kept in mind.

Is it worth the trouble? Since we are only concerned with the identification of negative discriminators, not nondiscriminators, should criterion-referenced measures be subjected to item-analysis operations? This would seem to depend on the ease with which one can conduct the necessary analyses. As data processing becomes increasingly automated and less expensive, such analyses would seem warranted in situations where the effort is not immense.

We use norm-referenced and criterion-referenced tests to make decisions about both individuals and treatments. We need, therefore, to interpret test results properly in order to make the best possible decisions. With respect to norm-referenced measurement, the methods of interpreting the results of an individual's test performance are well known. Since we are interested in an individual's performance with respect to the performance of other individuals, we use such group-relative descriptors as percentile rankings or standard scores. Such indices allow us to tell, from a single score, how well the individual performed in relation to the group.

When interpreting an individual's performance on a criterion-referenced test, however, such group-relative indices are not appropriate. Some criterion-referenced tests yield scores that are essentially "on–off" in nature; that is, either the individual has mastered the criterion or he hasn't. For example, certain examinations in the chemistry laboratory may require a pupil to combine and treat chemical compounds in such a way that they produce hydrogen. In such tests it is sufficient to report whether or not the learner has displayed the desired criterion behavior.

More commonly, however, a range of acceptable performances exists. For example, suppose that an instructional objective had been devised that required a learner to multiply correctly pairs of three-digit numbers. We could prepare 20 items composed of randomly selected digits to measure this skill. Because of possible computation errors, the required proficiency level for each successful student might be set at 90 percent or better, thereby allowing errors on two of the 20 items. In reporting an individual's performance on a test such as this, one alternative is to once more use an "on–off" approach, namely, either the 90 percent minimum has been achieved or it hasn't.

Whether we wish to report the degree of less-than criterion performance should depend *exclusively* on the use we can make of the data. For example, if there are only two courses of action available to the individual, depending on his success or failure with respect to the criterion, then we need only report it as that—success or failure. However, if some differential experiences are to be provided on the basis of the degree of his less-than-criterion performance, then one would be interested in how far away he was from the criterion. For instance, if there were two remedial multiplication programs available, one for those very close to criterion and one for those who scored 60 percent or below on the 20-item examination, then we would report the degree of his performance. The point is that such gradations in reporting are only a function of the alternative courses of action available to the individual after the measurement has been made.

With respect to the evaluation of treatments, it has already been pointed out that norm-referenced measures are not the most suitable devices for such purposes since their emphasis on producing heterogeneous performance sometimes diverts them from adequately reflecting the treatment's intended objectives. In using criterion-referenced measures for purposes of treatment assessment—e.g., testing the merits of a new set of programmed mathematics materials—we have several alternatives. We could simply report the number of individuals who achieve the preestablished criterion. Although such a procedure seems to supply scant data, it has the advantage of making graphically clear the proportion of learners who did not achieve criterion-level proficiency. Too often this result is masked through the use of statistical averages.

We could also use traditional descriptive statistics such as means and standard deviations. Because one is often interested in the average performance produced by a treatment as well as its variability, such statistics are useful. An average "percentage correct," however, is a helpful addition. Sometimes, if the criterion level for an individual has been set as a particular level, it is useful to report the proportion of the group that reached that level. For instance, using 80 percent as a criterion level, then one might describe a group's performance as 92–80, indicating that 92 percent of the group had achieved 80 percent or better on the test. Such reporting, however, overlooks the proportion and degree of the better-than-criterion performance. It would seem, then, that in using criterion-referenced measures to make decisions about treatments, the best course of action would be to employ a number of these schemes to report the group's performance in order to permit more enlightened interpretations.

Different Kinds of Criterion-Referenced Tests

Up to this point we have discussed criterion-referenced tests as if there were *one* such animal. Actually, there are *two*. One could be said to be the ideal case and the other the more typical case.

In the ideal case the items are not only tied to the criterion but, in addition, the test is homogeneous in a very special sense. Everyone who gets the same score on the test has obtained the score in essentially the same manner. The meaning of a score is thus altogether unambiguous. If we know a person's score, we know his response pattern; we know within error limits exactly what he can and cannot do. This would be an ideal criterion-referenced test, since it not only eliminates the need for a reference group but also immediately tells us the behavior repertoire of the student for that criterion. This kind of test has been discussed for some time. Guttman mentioned it as early as 1944 [6] and Tucker elaborated on the concept in 1952 [7].

Unfortunately, this kind of test is still mostly a dream for educational testers. Since we need to know an immense amount about the subject matter of the test, and perhaps even about the reasons why students make certain kinds of responses, these tests at the present time are found only in relatively restricted and formal areas such as mathematics.

The other type of criterion-referenced test is more typical. The items on the test can be thought of as a sample from a potentially large group that might be generated from a criterion. The score on the test is not completely unambiguous; if we know that a student earned a score of 90 percent correct, we do not know which items he missed. However, we do know—if we have constructed our test properly—that of the items defining the criterion behavior, the student missed only 10 percent. And if the test is homogeneous, this tells us a great deal about what the student can do.

The purpose of the foregoing discussion has been to draw distinctions between norm-referenced and criterion-referenced measurement with respect to several key measurement constructs. Because of the recency of its introduction into the field, criterion-referenced measurement received most attention. This should not imply any superiority of one approach over the other. Each has its relatively distinct role to play. The roles are only relatively distinct because one can usually employ a test developed for one purpose in another situation and still derive useful information from it. It seems, however, that there are some psychometric properties of these two types of measurement that render them most appropriate for the purposes for which they were originally designed.

Notes

1. Lee J. Cronbach and G. C. Gleser, *Psychological Tests and Personnel Decisions,* 2d ed. (Urbana, Ill.: University of Illinois Press, 1965).
2. Robert Glaser, "Instructional Technology and the Measurement of Learning Outcomes: Some Questions," *American Psychology* 18 (1963): 519–521.
3. Lee J. Cronbach, "Evaluation for Course Improvement," *Teachers College Record* 64 (1963): 672–683.
4. T. R. Husek and K. Sirotnik, "Item Sampling in Educational Research: An Empirical Investigation," paper presented at the national meeting of the American Educational Research Association in Chicago, February 1968.
5. Ibid.
6. L. Guttman, "A Basis for Scaling Qualitative Ideas," *American Sociological Review* 9 (1944): 139–150.
7. L. Tucker, "Scales Minimizing the Importance of Reference Groups," in *Proceedings, Invitational Conference on Testing Problems* (Princeton, N. J.: Educational Testing Service, 1952), pp. 22–28.

The decision to give a student a grade in a course, to admit him to college, to assign him to a particular educational curriculum, or to promote him is based almost entirely on his performance on ability and achievement tests. Such tests, also, are relied upon to provide information about the quality of educational programs and systems. For example, whether Project Headstart or a program for the gifted will be continued depends in large part on how well the students in the programs perform on the tests used in evaluating them. Thus, test results wield enormous power in educational decisions that determine the kinds of educational programs a student receives and the level and direction of his educational career. These, in turn, greatly influence his place in society.

Reliance upon and faith in the efficacy of testing have resulted mainly from the relative *efficiency* of tests as vehicles for providing *information for decisions* about students and the educational programs they receive. In other words, tests are almost always cheaper, quicker, fairer, and more valid and reliable information sources than are other assessment techniques, such as interviews. By following this line of reasoning one step further, it becomes apparent that the value of a test is determined by the quantity, quality, and cost of the information it provides for educational decisions.

The two major points of this paper are: (*a*) current ability and achievement tests, whether constructed by test experts or teachers, are not especially *efficient* sources of information for the range of educational decisions for which they are relied upon; and (*b*) tests *can* be constructed that will be efficient for making such decisions. Before discussing these points, however, it is necessary to consider two aspects of tests: their *purpose,* i.e., how the information they provide will be used, and the *philosophy* underlying the manner in which they are constructed.

Any good educational measurement text describes the varied purposes of tests, such as selection, placement, etc. For the present discussion, however, we shall examine only two major types of uses. These are: (*a*) *student evaluation,* i.e., tests used in making decisions about individual students;

Evaluating Tests in Terms of the Information They Provide

Stephen Klein

and (b) *program evaluation,* i.e., tests used with groups or samples of students to provide information for decisions concerning educational programs that students might receive or are receiving.

Tests used in the first category, student evaluation, provide information about such things as whether a student has learned what he was supposed to have learned from a course or whether he has the prerequisite knowledge and ability needed for college. Tests used in program evaluation, on the other hand, are supposed to provide information about how well a program achieved or is achieving its objectives.

A second way of classifying tests is in terms of the *philosophy* underlying the manner in which they are constructed—which, in turn, is reflected in how scores are reported. Here again, two major types of tests should be considered—norm-referenced versus criterion-referenced tests (Glaser [1]). Popham and Husek [2] have noted the following differences between these kinds of measures: "Norm-referenced measures are ... used to ascertain an individual's performance in relationship to the performance of other individuals on the same measuring device.... Criterion-referenced measures ... are used to ascertain an individual's status with respect to some criterion, i.e., performance standard."

In the college-selection situation, for example, the admissions officer has traditionally been concerned primarily with each applicant's *relative* likelihood of success. Norm-referenced data, such as high-school grades and test scores on college-admissions tests, have been the most successful predictors for this purpose. Criterion-referenced data, on the other hand, are very useful in determining whether an educational program achieved its objectives. The differential utility of these two kinds of data for various kinds of evaluation problems has led to developing norm-referenced measures for student evaluations and criterion-referenced tests for program evaluations.

Problems with Tests

This doubling of test-development costs in order to handle different kinds of evaluation problems results in duplication of effort (such as developing essentially the same items twice where one really could serve for both purposes). It is also misleading to the typical test user, who would expect that after such specialization the final products would meet his student- or program-evaluation needs. The reason he is deceived is that neither the existing norm- nor criterion-referenced measures are adequate for student or program evaluation. In other words, they do not provide all the necessary information for making either kind of evaluation decision.

Norm-referenced measures, for example, are very effective in ranking students (or groups of students) in terms of their ability, knowledge, or other salient characteristics. When constructed and standardized properly, they also provide a good basis of comparison between students or groups at different schools through the use of norm and percentile tables. Normative test data would be very useful for selection and promotion decisions and even for program-evaluation decisions if one knew what a score on such measures really meant. Unfortunately, score conversions such as percentiles and stanines do not indicate either what the student has learned or at what level he will perform if promoted or admitted to college. This problem has led to applying criterion-referenced interpretations to norm-referenced data via the use of grade norms and predicted grade-point averages (GPA). Despite the many difficulties associated with such "scores," they do contribute to the test user's understanding of the general level at which the student can perform. Predicted GPA's and grade norms fail, however, in describing precisely what the student has and has not learned. One implication of this situation is that some very different admissions decisions might be made if it were disclosed that even students with scores below the 25th percentile had the skills actually needed to be able to perform college work.

A second type of problem with standardized norm-referenced tests is that they are likely to measure a somewhat different set of objectives than those stated for a specific educational program. For example, a score on a published science test may represent overall performance on ten objectives; however, a given science program may be concerned with only four objectives, and just two of these may be included in the standardized test. Thus, the single total score on the science test, whether converted to grade norms or not, would not be an appropriate measure for evaluating the success of the science program. In brief, norm-referenced measures have been very useful in providing data about general performance levels needed for many student and program evaluation decisions, but very weak in contributing information regarding specific skill and knowledge development.

Criterion-referenced measures, on the other hand, complement their normative counterparts. They do this by adequately describing the specifics and what a test score means. They do not, however, provide the often-needed normative base for comparisons and interpretations. The relative strengths of criterion-referenced measures have led to their being relied upon for many program evaluation decisions. Some school districts even require independent educational firms supplying special training to specify in the contractual agreement the criterion levels at which the students are to perform.

The foregoing use of criterion-referenced measurement would be a laudable practice if one knew how to determine what criterion objectives to specify, or what level of performance constitutes their attainment, or how to interpret the results if the objectives are or are not achieved. To illustrate this point, let us suppose that a new course unit in tenth-grade biology led to 30 percent of the students attaining all of the unit's 20 objectives, 50 percent of the students attaining 15 objectives, and only 20 percent of the students achieving less than ten objectives. These results look very impressive, and a school official might be very pleased with the effectiveness of the program. But would he still be happy if he discovered that most students could achieve ten of these objectives before taking the unit, or that the criterion of attainment was one out of five items correct per objective, or that the items used to measure an objective were not truly representative of the range of items that might have been employed, or that 80 percent of the students at other schools (having students of comparable ability) attained all 20 objectives using a criterion of four out of five items correct per objective? One expects that the school official would make a rather different evaluative decision regarding the program's worth had this latter information been available to him. Clearly, grade norms or other kinds of normative-based data would help clarify the actual utility and significance of the program in achieving its objectives.

Criterion-referenced measures, further, typically suffer from their being limited to the program's specific objectives. This may seem like a correct approach unless one asked such questions as: "If the student (or program) failed to meet an objective, did he (it) miss by an inch or a mile?" or "If two students achieved an objective, could one of them attain more advanced objectives?" The answers to these questions would certainly have a bearing on evaluation decisions dealing with the relative effectiveness of different programs and what subsequent educational treatments should be instituted (i.e., remedial or advanced). It should be noted, however, that these latter problems are not limitations of criterion-referenced measures per se, but of the way most of these measures are developed, scored, and interpreted.

To summarize, norm-referenced measures often provide useful information in evaluating the *relative* performance of students and programs with respect to general performance criteria. Their weakness mainly has been in failing to provide specific information about particular skill development and needs. Such information is necessary in making decisions regarding subsequent educational treatments and the effectiveness of a given program in achieving its limited set of objectives. Criterion-referenced measures, on the other hand, have the advantage of being able to provide the latter kinds of specific information. What they fail to do is provide a basis for interpreting fully what the attainment of an objective really means—whether it is significant and important, or trivial and unnecessary.

A New Combination

The foregoing discussion is the basis for the first major point of this paper, namely: despite their comparative advantages over other assessment techniques, typical tests are still not especially efficient sources of information for the full range of educational decisions for which they are used and relied upon. Let us now turn to the second point, namely: tests can be constructed, and the results they provide can be reported in a way that will facilitate making such decisions. The basis for this new path is the obvious but generally untried technique of combining the better components of the norm- and criterion-referenced approaches. The essential characteristic of this approach is that it includes the concepts of item-difficulty and normative-score reporting in the development and interpretation of criterion-based measures. This would entail the following steps:

1. *Specify the objectives.* The objective(s) each test is supposed to measure should be stated clearly. Popham [3] and others have prepared excellent guides as to how objectives should be written. The decision as to which objective(s) to measure may be a difficult one, but literature reviews, research studies, professional judgments, and related sources of information should help clarify just what kinds and levels of performance should be assessed. Sample objective:

> The student can add two numbers, each of which is more than 9 but less than 100.

The level of generality at which an objective is stated is, of course, an important consideration. Some guidelines that may help in determining this level are as follows: (1) It usually is a good idea to have at least three items per objective; thus, one certainly should not have more objectives than the number of items on which he can collect adequate data. To achieve this end, one can either reduce the number of objectives measured during a testing session or broaden the statements of the objectives so that they include subobjectives. (2) Write the objectives at a level of generality that will be interpretable to the person who has to use the test results. It helps the test constructor to be specific, but too many specifics may make the data uninterpretable to the user unless he is at least provided with more general statements.

2. *Develop test items for each objective.* A clear statement of the objective will provide a very good guide to both the type of item and performance level(s) (i.e., item difficulties) needed to measure that objective. Guides for developing test items are readily available (e.g., Ebel, [4]; Wood, [5]) and should be followed to assure that items measure the objective, are appropriate for the students to be tested, and are feasible to administer in a cost-effective manner. It is especially important, however, that the items selected for an objective be a good, representative sample of the total population of items that might be used to measure that objective. This sampling should cover both the range of formats that might be used and the range of item difficulties. Sample items:

$$10 + 20 =$$
$$\begin{array}{r} 38 \\ +97 \\ \hline \end{array}$$

Thus, if the objective was that the student could add two numbers, each of which was less than 100, it would not be a good idea just to use items involving the addition of one-digit numbers. The primary reason for including items that span the difficulty levels within an objective is that differences between students and programs could be assessed more accurately. This would occur because a student's score on an objective would reflect the degree to which he attained it; and it is a well-known fact that students do differ in their performance even with the same instruction, because they differ in their ability to profit from it. Including items, then, that span the range of difficulties would eliminate the practice of setting arbitrary cutoff points to assess whether a student (or program) did or did not achieve an objective, since the percentage of items correct on the objective would provide an indication of the degree of attainment.

3. *Develop test items to measure related objectives.* In the case of a series of en-route objectives, it is important to include items that measure performances that come before and after the one(s) being studied. By the same logic, it is equally important to assess performance both on objectives that are easier and more difficult to master than just the one(s) of major interest. Sample items:

$$24 + 36 + 89 =$$
$$8$$
$$+ 25$$
$$\overline{}$$

The reasons for measuring these kinds of related objectives are that they (*a*) provide information about the unanticipated outcomes of educational programs, (*b*) indicate how close a program (or student) came to meeting or surpassing the objective(s), and (*c*) show the level at which subsequent educational treatments should be pitched. For example, the students' improvement in addition may have surpassed the stated objectives of an experimental mathematics program, but on further inspection it might be revealed that this performance was obtained at the expense of proficiency in subtraction. Thus, even though the experimental program may not have been concerned with subtraction per se, it was important to assess it if one wished to evaluate fully the quality of this program.

One by-product of this approach is the information gained regarding the actual difficulty or learning sequence of various objectives. For example, if students perform better on items measuring a supposedly advanced or terminal objective than they do on the ones presumed to lead up to it, assumptions regarding the ordering of objectives might merit reappraisal.

4. *Provide a score and score interpretation for each objective.* This information should reflect both criterion- and norm-referenced performance on the items designed to measure the objective. A sample interpretation might read as follows: "Donald Jones (or Program 3) got four of the six items correct on objective number 7 (addition of whole numbers less than 100). Approximately 80 percent of the other students in Donald's class did this well. Students of equal ability in other classes (or programs) only got one-third of the items correct, which is typical of the second-graders in this

state (i.e., the median score statewide on this objective is 33 percent correct)." This type of interpretation allows the reader to know what the student can and cannot do and also provides him with a frame of reference for interpreting this level of performance.

Before discussing this approach further, it is important to clarify what is meant by an educational "objective" and how its level of generality influences the way it is measured. An "objective" describes the type and level of performance a student might achieve. Very explicit statements of objectives, such as "the student can add two numbers each of which is less than 100," are termed "behavioral" [6] and refer to a relatively narrow range of performance levels. On the other hand, global objectives or goals, such as "the student can perform basic arithmetic computations," are less precise and encompass a wider range of performance levels (e.g., "1 + 1 = ?" vs. "39 ÷ 17 = ?").

It is apparent, therefore, that the broader the objective to be assessed, the more items are needed to cover its full range of performances. The major implication of this situation for test construction is that the measurement of a global objective involves the assessment of several subobjectives. Since information about both types of objectives is often needed, scores should be reported for both. For example, "Joe's score in arithmetic computations was 18, which he obtained by scores of 6 in addition, 5 in subtraction..." The interpretation of these scores would, of course, require clear statements of the objectives along with the criterion- and norm-referenced information described in Step 4.

Difference from Present Practice

And now let us examine how the suggested four-step test construction approach differs from present practices. An inspection of current tests and manuals indicates that most publishers of standardized achievement tests usually claim to go through the first two steps of specifying objectives and writing items to measure them. However, they rarely provide scores on each of the objectives or content areas that their tests (or subtests) purport to measure. For example, the 55 items in the mathematics achievement test of the Cooperative Primary Tests [7] are supposed to assess the following eight concepts: Number, Symbolism, Operation, Function and Relation, Approximation, Measurement, Estimation, and Geometry. [8] However, only one score is provided for the 55 items. This problem is demonstrated in the table below, where it can be seen that two objectives (Number and Geometry) account for 42 percent of the test's items and have a mean item difficulty of .74; and another two objectives (Operation and Measurement) account for 38 percent of the items but have a mean item difficulty of .55. Dispersion of scores on the test, therefore, is obtained by having different difficulty levels for different objectives rather than by building in a broad range of difficulties within each objective. The implication of this test-construction technique is that students who get high scores can achieve different kinds of objectives rather than just perform better than low-scoring students on the same objectives. The test manual, on the other hand, implies that the student's score reflects his ability to master the eight objectives. Supplying the norm- and criterion-referenced information described in Step 4 above for each objective would indicate when tests are constructed in this manner. It would also be a major step toward helping to individualize instruction by showing the strengths and weaknesses of each student or program and clarifying what a test is really measuring and how it is measuring it.

Analysis of the Mathematics Achievement Test (Form 12a) of the Cooperative Tests of Primary Mental Abilities

Content Area	Number of Items	Mean Item Difficulty
Number	17	.73
Symbolism	6	.66
Operation	13	.55
Function and Relation	3	.59
Approximation	1	.32
Measurement	8	.54
Estimation	1	.65
Geometry	6	.75

At this point one wonders why the field of educational measurement has been so slow to incorporate the better characteristics of norm- and criterion-referenced tests and score reporting into a single package. One reason might be interdisciplinary rivalry ("lack of professional communication") between psychologists, who tend to develop norm-referenced tests, and certain educationists, who prefer constructing criterion-referenced tests. A second reason may be the unwarranted fear of the usual criticisms of subscores on tests. In other words, many existing tests providing subscores fall victim to one or the other of the following two problems: high subtest score intercorrelation (i.e., the subtest scores are so highly related to each other as to make them indistinguishable); or unreliability due to the brevity of the subtest (i.e., the number of items in it).

The latter two criticisms can be dismissed by applying the principle that the utility of a test (or test score) should be evaluated in terms of the information it provides. For example, if the first situation occurred—i.e., high interscore correlation—it would mean that either the items going into each score were providing essentially the same information because they were measuring the same thing (and thus should be combined into a single score), or performance on two objectives was similar because the students had equivalently good or poor training in both areas. In most instances, a simple

The Problems of a Single Package

experiment in which training is given on only one objective would clarify whether the subtest scores were really measuring different objectives. In other words, if the scores on all objectives improved equally after instruction, it is probably safe to assume that the subtests are measuring the same rather than different objectives [9]. Thus, high interscore correlations should disappear with differential learning if the subscores really provide information about what was and was not learned.

The second criticism, unreliability due to brevity of the subtests, is even less tenable. In the case of program evaluation, for example, a subtest can be lengthened easily by using item-sampling techniques [10], thereby improving a test's reliability (the formula for this increase as a function of length may be found in any measurement text, e.g., Cronbach [11]). In other words, a given student need only take a few items, while other students receive a different set. Such item-sampling procedures keep test length the same for a given student but substantially increase the total number of items providing reliable information about how well a program is meeting its objectives. In the case of student evaluation, however, there is no substitute for highly reliable and valid information if one has to use that data in making a decision about a student's performance. But even relatively unreliable subscores are still valuable, since they could be used diagnostically to locate possible problem areas for further testing.

Another potential criticism of the proposed four-step approach is that teachers cannot use it in constructing their own tests. Teachers do not have the time or expertise to write clear, relevant objectives and/or good items to measure them [12]. While this is true, it is also true that teachers can be relieved almost entirely of this chore by test experts. This idea may at first seem heretical to many educators, but on further reflection they will realize that experienced and trained item writers can do this job better than teachers. What is needed, therefore, is an atlas of objectives with sets of items (short tests) for each objective. This atlas should organize the objectives and their levels by such things as difficulty and the type of cognitive functioning required (e.g., Bloom [13]; Guilford [14]) and, where possible, include norm- and criterion-referenced interpretations of scores. With this tool, the teacher could select objectives he wished to measure along with the necessary related objectives and the short tests needed to assess student performance on them. Teachers would, of course, have to help in this test development as well as construct items for objectives not included in the atlas. In fact, frequent use of the atlas for course tests and quizzes may even eliminate the need for the classical standardized achievement test since all the information (and more) would have been collected via the course examinations. Such atlases can be a reality and their development is already underway [15,16,17].

As noted in the beginning of this paper, tests should be evaluated in terms of the quantity, quality, and cost of the information they provide. It is the premise of this paper that the test-construction and score-reporting procedures outlined above will provide far more information than is being supplied by most currently available tests. The cost of developing these new procedures would be somewhat greater initially than current methods. There would be a savings, however, deriving from the use of a single set of tests for a variety of purposes and from reduced testing time and teacher involvement in test construction. It seems likely, therefore, that any additional development costs would be offset by the substantially greater quality and quantity of relevant information provided. As test publishers try this route, we can easily observe its merits by measuring the depth of the path beaten to their doors by people who use test data in making decisions.

Notes

1. Robert Glaser, "Instructional Technology and the Measurement of Learning Outcomes," *American Psychology* 18 (1963): 514–521.
2. T. R. Husek and W. James Popham, "Implications of Criterion-Referenced Measurement." See pp. 131–139 in this book.
3. W. James Popham, *The Teacher-Empiricist* (Los Angeles: Tinnon-Brown, 1970).
4. R. L. Ebel, *Measuring Educational Achievement* (Englewood Cliffs, N. J.: Prentice-Hall, 1965).
5. A. D. Wood, *Test Construction* (Columbus, Ohio: Merrill, 1961).
6. See note 2 above.
7. *Handbook: Cooperative Primary Tests* (Princeton, N. J.: Educational Testing Service, 1967).
8. The ETS test was chosen for analysis because it exemplified a common problem with most standardized achievement tests and the data were readily available in the test manual.
9. T. R. Husek, "Different Kinds of Evaluation and Their Implications for Test Development." See pp. 150–155 in this book.
10. F. M. Lord and M. R. Novick, *Statistical Theories of Mental Test Scores* (Reading, Mass.: Addison-Wesley, 1968).
11. Lee J. Cronbach, *Essentials of Psychological Testing*, 2d ed. (New York: Harper, 1960).
12. R. L. Thorndike, "Helping Teachers Use Tests," *Measurement in Education* 1 (1969).
13. Benjamin S. Bloom, ed., *Taxonomy of Educational Objectives: Handbook I: Cognitive Domain* (New York: David McKay, 1956).
14. J. P. Guilford, *The Nature of Human Intelligence* (New York: McGraw-Hill, 1967).
15. PROBE, *Instructional Objectives and Items Exchange* (Los Angeles: University of California Center for the Study of Evaluation).
16. *Reading Experience and Development Series Tests* (New York: American Book Company, 1969).
17. CTB/McGraw-Hill, Del Monte Research Park, Monterey, California.

Psychometric theory, as it developed during the early decades of the 20th century, was based on the conception of a test as a measuring instrument. Psychological theory in general, just as physical theory had been for many years, was based on the idea of concepts that existed independently of our knowledge of them. A psychological test was an attempt to obtain a measure of one of these qualities—such as "intelligence." Early definitions of the criteria for judging the worth of a test flowed from that conception of the nature of a test. A test should be valid, and it was valid to the extent to which it measured what it was supposed to measure; a test should be reliable, and it was reliable to the extent to which it measured whatever it was measuring.

Test theory has become more sophisticated since the early part of the century, and the concepts of validity and reliability have changed. We no longer treat validity and reliability as if they were intrinsic characteristics of a test in the manner that weight and mass are characteristics of a rock or a stick; rather, we view validity and reliability as generic terms that define a class of questions that might be asked about the use of a test. Since different tests may be used for different purposes, and some tests for more than one purpose, different conceptualizations of how to judge a test have developed, and a number of different kinds of validity and reliability have been introduced.

At the present time it is relatively easy to find texts on testing and on measurement that attempt to demonstrate to students that a test may be valid for one purpose and not for others [1]. When teaching a course, it is not difficult to find textual support that a test does not have to have *a* validity coefficient and *a* reliability coefficient, but rather that validity and reliability evidence should be appropriate to the use to which the test is put. I could also cite a measurement test with a 1968 copyright, which

Different Kinds of Evaluation and Their Implications for Test Development

T. R. Husek

defines validity and reliability in the old way, but I like to think that the problem is just that dinosaurs do not die easily.

However, the changes in the manner in which a test is judged have not been matched by changes in the suggested procedures for developing tests, at least at the point of application, in courses on testing for teachers and counsellors. We have become much more sophisticated in discussing validity and reliability, but we still face many obstacles in our treatments of evaluation problems. Most education students are still told to develop tests as if there were only one purpose for the test, a purpose I feel can be defined fairly as that of providing maximum discrimination among the scores of the students who take the test. That is, we tell students to construct tests that have maximum variances, and we give students formulae for item analyses that produce homogeneous tests—homogeneous in content and homogeneous in difficulty level.

At this point I should further define what I mean by *evaluation* and set some limits on the context of my argument.

Evaluation Defined

By *evaluation* I mean a subjective decision made by one or more people. A teacher giving a grade is an example of an evaluation, just as is the decision of a dean not to grant tenure to a member of his faculty. There are many different kinds of evaluation tasks, but I am going to limit myself to a discussion of just a few of them. First, I will restrict myself to treating evaluation in the public-school setting. Second, I will talk about just two sets of evaluation tasks in the schools; namely, the evaluation of students and the evaluation of instructional treatments. Although limited, this area still includes an awesome chunk of material.

Although I view evaluation as an essentially subjective decision, I believe that the more information relevant to his decision that a decision maker has, the better the decision will be. I also believe that tests are valuable techniques for providing evaluators with information that can be useful in helping them make sensible decisions.

In the context of using a test to help the evaluator make better decisions, what kinds of information might be useful to a teacher who is asked to evaluate students in the school? Unfortunately, there is not a simple answer to this question. However, several different decision problems can be posed with respect to the teacher, who might want to tell the students apart most easily with respect to their scores on achievement tests; to evaluate the students in terms of how well they have learned the stated objectives in the course; to evaluate the students in terms of how much they had learned during the course; to be able to tell the A students from the rest of the class; or to be able to tell the F students from the rest of the class.

Each one of these student-evaluation concerns of the teacher could be said to constitute a purpose for which a test could be constructed. Unfortunately, there is no evidence to demonstrate that items most useful for one purpose are very useful for another purpose.

An examination of the types of items that would satisfy the criteria implied by the various teacher goals would be useful here. The first student-evaluation goal mentioned was that of maximally discriminating among students in terms of their performances on an achievement test. This is the goal that is usually treated in evaluation texts. But what happens to the teacher who follows the usual procedures? Let us examine a hypothetical, good social-studies teacher. Our teacher has been taught to try to specify his teaching goals in terms of behavioral objectives, and he also agrees that his best hope of evaluating his students is in terms of objective tests. So he constructs a test to give to his students and over a period of several years discards some items and rewrites others in line with the results of item analyses that he faithfully performs. It does not make too much difference what kind of item analysis he performs, but let us assume that he uses something that tells him how well his items discriminate between the high scorers and the low scorers on the total test. Let us also assume that our teacher is a good one and actually gets across much of what he hopes he is teaching.

With these assumptions, what kind of test is developed? The item-analysis procedure, first of all, eliminates items that everyone completes correctly or that everyone misses. This will mean that in the long run, especially if the teacher is a good one, most items directly related to the teacher's objectives will be dropped from the test because they do not discriminate among the students. This should not be surprising, and it is certainly not new. Thirty years ago Lindquist was telling test constructors that the objectives of a course would not be good sources for discriminating items. The developing test will also tend to become more homogeneous: isolated items will tend to be dropped, and items picking up similar information will tend to be selected.

In fact, over a period of years, I think that our hypothetical social-studies teacher is developing a good, general mental-abilities test with items focused on the social studies. This kind of test may not be the kind of test the teacher thinks he wants, but it is certainly the kind that will produce variability in the student test scores.

Now let us go back to the second possible student-evaluation goal that the teacher might have. The second goal I mentioned had to do with evaluating the students in terms of how well they had achieved the objectives as defined by the teacher. It is obvious that the items useful here might not be discriminating items, although, if grades must be assigned, discriminating items are needed. Item-analysis information concerning these items might be useful, but the judgment of the teacher is more important.

The third student-evaluation goal I mentioned for the teacher–evaluator was the goal of evaluating the students in terms of how much they had learned during the course. This goal implies that the teacher is interested in changes in the students that have occurred during the course, not just final performance. The items that are good for assessing the changes should pass several screens, including that they be relevant to the course, that they be missed by almost all of the students before the course, and that at least some of the students pass the items at the end of the course.... This collection of items may overlap, with the good items for student-evaluation goals one and two, but the overlap could be very slight. There is no necessary reason for a test that maximally discriminates among students at the end of a course to have many of the same items as a test that has maximum change-score variance, and there are many arguments that would conclude that the tests be very different.

My suggested student-evaluation goals four and five are variants on the same point. For each of these goals the teacher's aim is to discriminate among students at a given achievement level. I believe that, for most cases, this problem reduces to the selection question where there are a certain number of applicants for a position and a given selection ratio. That is, if a teacher knows how many students he has and how many A's he wants to give, then the qualities of the optimal test have been investigated at length by the personnel psychologists, and I believe that with respect to difficulty level the items should be concentrated at the point where the decision is to be made....

Now I turn to the evaluation of instructional treatments. This is, of course, the problem of curriculum evaluation, which is rather murky territory. I will largely avoid this area, which could—and does—fill books [2]. I restrict myself to the situation where a teacher or a school is trying to evaluate a course. I will also largely ignore aspects of the situation where one section of the course is compared with another, or one instructor with another. **Evaluation of Instruction**

In the situation as I restrict it, the primary question is how well the course produces changes that the evaluator feels are desirable; i.e., the course is to be evaluated in terms of whether or not it meets its own objectives—learning objectives, at that. In this way I hope to avoid discussion of the value of the course's objectives as opposed to other objectives, the implications of this course for other courses and for other student and family activity in and out of school.

The questions as I have posed them would lead the evaluator to use some sort of pretest/post-test difference in order to obtain useful information. An achievement test given at the end of the course might tell the teacher how much the student knows at the end of the course, but it obviously would not inform the teacher whether or not the course was related to the scores that the students obtained.

However, although I think that this kind of evaluation could best be served by pretest/post-test differences of one form or another, I do not suggest that the better items would necessarily be those that reflect large changes during the course. It is certainly possible for items few students pass before the course and few pass after the course to be good items, which should alert the teachers to inadequacies in the course. It is also possible that items no student passes at the beginning of the course and almost all students pass at the end of the course could be bad items. These last, spectacularly strange items are related to a course that is not aimed at teaching terminology but in which, nevertheless, the items contain terms to which the student is introduced during the course. These items could be answered by some students before the course, if they only knew the language.

How does one obtain a good test for evaluating a course? The answer is that it is certainly not easy, but that the items should possess the following characteristics: they should be related to the objectives of the course; they should be items that few, if any, students answer correctly at the beginning of the course; and they should be items that are not dependent on special language obtained in the course unless the learning of the language is part of the objectives of the course. The items that meet the criteria I have outlined come closest of all the classes of items I have discussed to the learning objectives of the teacher.

Up to this point, I have treated, in a very superficial manner, some five different student-evaluation goals and one general course-evaluation goal. I have suggested that tests most useful for one of the evaluation tasks would not necessarily be similar to good tests for other of the tasks. I have ignored most of the field of curriculum evaluation and many other aspects of evaluation. I have passed over issues of the nature of the items, whether in terms of the two published taxonomies (Bloom, [3]; Krathwohl, [4]) or in terms of Guttman's more recent thinking in the field of ability items [5] or in terms of Glaser's suggestions about criterion-referenced tests [6,7]. I am going to mention only in passing the idea that, for some purposes, perhaps the items that predict some future behavior might be the best items to use for evaluation purposes. For example, a teacher program that attempts to produce a certain kind of teacher might want to try to develop items that predict whether a student will or will not be that kind of teacher and use those items for evaluation purposes.

A Pool of Items

The other general suggestions I have are based on a recommendation that larger and better item pools be developed for various subject matters. The vast effort in the national assessment program and current research at the Instructional Objectives Exchange [at UCLA], which is a major phase of the Project for Research on Objective-Based Evaluation (PROBE), will probably lead to the writing of many good items that will become available to the schools, but one way or another the pools should be developed. If pools of items are available, then it is possible for some schools to use matrix sampling [8,9] and two-stage testing, at least for the larger courses that have several sections. By this I mean that the following kind of test might be used: the first part of the test is taken by all the students, who turn in their answer sheets while keeping a record of their answers. Then the answers to the questions are given to the students, who score their own tests. Depending on their scores on the first part of the examination, the students take different second parts of the examination. There are a number of different ways in which the branching could occur, based on the content and/or the difficulty of the items. But in general, the second part of the examination would be used to obtain information focused on areas the first part of the examination pointed out. These first two parts of the examination are used for student evaluation and perhaps even diagnosis; that is, the items are chosen to be useful in discriminating among the students. Recently there has been a growing interest in this type of sequential testing, notably that of Linn and Rock [10].

There is also a third part to this examination—the section that makes most use of matrix-sampling procedures. In the third section of the examination, each student answers only a few questions, but not all the students answer the same questions. A number of different items are each answered by a few students. For example, with a class of 100 students and multiple-choice questions, the last five questions for each student could be this third section of the test. The last page of each student's test booklet could contain five questions, but there might be ten different last pages, each of which is given to ten different students. In this way, data on 50 questions, each answered by ten students, could be obtained. This last part of the examination could be used to evaluate the course, and it could also be used to try out new items for other purposes.

I should mention that the student-evaluation part of the examination of the future—the first two sections—does not really have to be in two stages for most current evaluation, especially if the branching is based on difficulty. But perhaps some of us will still be alive when tests are also used for diagnostic purposes, and for those purposes several stages would be quite useful.

Notes

1. J. C. Nunnaly, *Psychometric Theory* (New York: McGraw-Hill, 1967).
2. Ralph W. Tyler et al., *Perspectives in Curriculum Evaluation* (Chicago: Rand McNally, 1967).
3. Benjamin S. Bloom et al., *Taxonomy of Educational Objectives: The Classification of Education Goals, Handbook I: Cognitive Domain* (New York: David McKay, 1956).
4. D. A. Krathwohl, *Taxonomy of Educational Objectives: The Classification of Educational Goals, Handbook II: Affective Domain* (New York: David McKay, 1964).
5. L. Guttman, "Structure of Interrelationships among Intelligence Tests," *Proceedings of the 1964 Invitational Conference on Testing Problems* (Princeton, N. J.: Educational Testing Service, 1965), pp. 25–36.
6. Robert Glaser, "Instructional Technology and the Measurement of Learning Outcomes," *American Psychology* 18 (1963): 519–522.
7. W. James Popham and T. R. Husek, "Implications of Criterion-Referenced Measurement." See pp. 131–139 in this book.
8. T. R. Husek and K. Sirotnik, *Item Sampling in Educational Research* (Los Angeles: Center for the Study of Evaluation, 1967).
9. K. Sirotnik, *An Analysis of Variance Framework for Matrix Sampling*, CSE Report No. 52 (Los Angeles: Center for the Study of Evaluation, 1969).
10. R. L. Linn and D. A. Rock, "An Exploratory Study of Programmed Tests," *Educational and Psychological Measurement* 28 (1968): 345–360.

Authors

"Evaluation for the Improvement of Instructional Programs: Some Practical Steps," by Garth Sorenson, Professor at the Graduate School of Education, University of California, Los Angeles. The evaluation checklist presented in the article emerged from a series of projects aimed at developing effective and reproducible instructional programs.

"Antidote to a School Scandal," by John D. McNeil, Professor at the Graduate College of Education, University of California, Los Angeles.

"A New Role in Education: The Evaluator," by Garth Sorenson.

"Teacher Evaluation: Toward Improving Instruction," by Marcia A. Boyer, Assistant Director of the ERIC Clearinghouse for Junior Colleges.

9 Evaluating Instructional Programs

In higher education, there is emerging an approach to faculty evaluation that stresses teacher accountability for student learning. Members of the faculty and the instructional programs they devise are being judged not by the means employed, but by the ends achieved. If students have not learned (changed), then it can be assumed that the teacher and/or his instructional program have been unsuccessful. This unit focuses on the newly developing approaches to evaluating instructional programs.

After completing this unit, you should be able to

1 present a rationale for undertaking a program of faculty evaluation, and list the three general categories of evaluation criteria (Boyer)

2 formulate a set of assumptions underlying instructional evaluation (Sorenson, 1968)

3 present a case for or against student evaluations as an important measure of instructional quality (Boyer)

4 explain the concept of "the effects of the instructional process" as important criteria in faculty evaluation (Boyer)

5 develop a set of faculty evaluation criteria, each supported on at least two bases, including relevance to good teaching and measurability (Boyer)

6 outline the basic approach to faculty evaluation known as "supervision by objectives," including its two basic underlying assumptions, its form and process, its feasibility, and an assessment of its value (McNeil)

7 state the rationale for the professional evaluator and describe the main functions he should perform (Sorenson, 1968)

8 differentiate between summative evaluation of outcome and formative evaluation (of progress and/or implementation) (Sorenson, 1971)

9 list and explain the eight principles of formative evaluation (Sorenson, 1971)

During the past decade a movement has been developing that, if properly supported, could contribute greatly to the improvement of education. In general, the movement is an attempt to develop a sound and cumulative knowledge base for instruction together with an adequate educational technology. It is hoped that these practices will enable each new generation of teachers to acquire from the previous generation a repertoire of effective instructional tools, instead of each teacher's having to develop his own instructional skills and techniques.

One of the most important aspects of the movement toward improving instructional procedures is an emerging concept that has been called "evaluation of learning experiences" by Tyler [1], "evaluation for course improvement" by Cronbach [2], "formative evaluation" by Scriven [3], and "implementation and progress evaluation" by Alkin [4]. Some have likened it to the idea of quality control in industry. This concept holds that part of the effort and resources ordinarily expended in developing and using any instructional program—whether lecture series, syllabus, textbook, workshop, or training film—should be devoted to testing out and improving that program, particularly during the course of its development, to ensure that the program will work with a particular group of students. Sophisticated program developers do not expect a program to work very well the first time it is tried, and therefore they see it as part of their task in developing any program to take steps to find out why it is not working, to change it, to try it again, and to continue the process until the finished program is effective for those for whom it was intended.

The concept of formative evaluation has evolved in consonance with the gradual shift in the definition of the "good" teacher. In the traditional concept of the teacher's role, the focus of evaluation made good classroom performance an end in itself. The current concern, however, is with the

---

Evaluation for the Improvement of Instructional Programs

Some Practical Steps

Garth Sorenson

effect of the teacher's methods upon pupil performance as evidenced not merely by academic achievement tests but even more by "criterion-referenced" tests and unobtrusive measures that provide scores on a number of specific objectives rather than a single global score. Contemporary educators may still want students to learn what is in the textbook, but they have begun to reconsider what is meant by such terms as *to learn* and *to know,* and they are trying to develop ways to estimate the kind and amount of learning that has occurred in line with these definitions [5]. The assumption here is that all students, given proper directions and incentives, can learn a great deal more than they presently do, regardless of IQ or aptitude. Further, if a student does not learn in the class, it does not automatically follow that the failure to learn is because of some defect in the student—or in the teacher, for that matter. The defect is likely to be in the instructional procedures that were used.

The process of finding out at the *end* of a period of time whether or not an instructional procedure has worked with a particular group of students has been called "summative" or "outcome evaluation." Outcome evaluation is a fairly complex and time-consuming process and borrows a number of concepts and procedures from educational measurement and experimental design. As Cronbach [6] has pointed out, it often requires a great deal of effort just to show that something did not work. (A director of one large education laboratory has described the evaluator as the person "who brings the bad news to the program developer that he has failed again.") It was for such reasons that Cronbach argued that, given the resources and effort required for evaluation, it would be more useful to direct that effort to improving a particular instructional program—that is, to take the "formative evaluation" tack—rather than merely to answer the question whether or not the program produced statistically significant differences in amounts of learning between students taught by that particular method and those who received either no teaching or were taught by another method.

But how to do formative evaluation? It is one thing to insist that evaluation is needed and another to develop workable procedures. This paper outlines a partial model of formative (or implementation-progress) evaluation consistent with new concepts emerging over the past two decades as a result of various R & D efforts. A number of general principles are proposed, a specific illustration presented, and a checklist provided to serve as a guide for evaluators.

Principle 1. The purpose of any instructional program is to produce measurable changes in the students for whom it was designed; if these changes do not take place, something may be wrong with the program or how it was implemented.

A Summary of Formative Evaluation Principles

The kinds of changes to be produced by instructional programs include changes in knowledge, feelings, attitudes, etc. For example, some instructional programs are designed to teach people to speak a foreign language, others to play the piano, others to solve problems in calculus, others to understand philosophical concepts. Or instructional programs might be designed to increase a student's feeling of self-confidence, particularly in relation to his school work, or to reduce that form of fear and anxiety sometimes called "school phobia." Still others might have the goal of increasing social responsibility or reducing racial prejudice—if anyone knows how to do that.

Principle 2. For any instructional program, it is essential that the goals of the program—whether they involve knowledge, feelings, or attitudes—be defined in terms of performance, behavior, or actions.

No one ever observes "knowledge," "feelings," "sense of responsibility," or "self-confidence" directly. We infer each of these characteristics from what a person does, that is, from his performance or the products of his performance—for example, from something he writes. Therefore, in designing a program aimed at increasing a person's ability to read, to understand, or perhaps to create, it is essential that we specify what actions on the part of the learner are to be observed and who will observe them, in order to make a judgment as to when learning has occurred. We must devise a set of procedures for getting an accurate record of the learner's performance, or at least a reasonable sample of his performance. For these purposes we will sometimes use achievement tests and sometimes other methods of making observations. Husek [7] has suggested that the tests or other measures should meet three criteria: first, they should be related to the objectives of the instructional program; second, they should consist of items that few, if any, of the students answer correctly at the beginning of the course; third, the items should not depend on special language learned in the course, unless the learning of the language is part of the objectives.

It should be emphasized that while the developer of the program should give considerable attention to the kinds of performances he is trying to produce, he should by no means limit his methods of observation to traditional tests. The concept of unobtrusive measures has received attention for a variety of reasons, and in their book, Webb et al. [8] suggest a number of alternative directions in which to look.

Principle 3. Instructional procedures should be designed to fit the prestated goals—to teach the students the kinds of performance specified.

Obviously, this principle is not to be understood as recommending that students be coached in the answers to standardized achievement-test questions, but it does mean that procedures be included that enable the students to learn the kinds of skills which the test will measure. One way *not* to devise an instructional procedure is to select a training film or textbook or to plan a class discussion without first asking, "What do I want the students to learn from this procedure?"

Principle 4. The program developer should follow a theory or model of instruction.

By a theory of instruction is meant a set of propositions about how people can most effectively be taught, together with specific rules based on these propositions to serve as guidelines in such program development activities as preparing instructions to students, arranging sequences of learning tasks, providing for and properly timing the use of incentives, giving students information about their own performance, etc. One purpose of the instructional theory is to reduce the randomness of program planning—the amount of trial and error spent in program writing—and in its place, to develop a set of rules that will enable us to create new and more effective "generations" of programs with less effort. Useful propositions about instruction are to be found in a number of places. Bruner [9] has described some of the conditions for "discovery" learning. Ausubel [10] has made suggestions about the use of "advance organizers." Gagné [11] has presented ideas about task analysis and learning hierarchies. Examples of specific rules are provided by Popham [12], Stolurow [13], and others.

As program developers engage in formative evaluation, they should do so with an eye to revising their instructional model as well as the particular program on which they are working.

Principle 5. Instructional programs should be repeatable.

If someone invents an unusually effective method of teaching Russian, or calculus, or the writing of poetry, it is desirable that the operations constituting that method be described in sufficient detail that other teachers, willing to put forth a reasonable effort to learn those operations, will be able to apply the method with reasonable accuracy. However, to make an instructional program repeatable, it is usually insufficient merely to provide a precise description of the operations. It is also necessary to train other users to conduct those operations in the way that they were planned.

It follows that for each instructional program the developers should provide a set of training procedures for teaching others to use the program as it was intended to be used.

Principle 6. Instructional programs should be pretested. In developing any program, steps should be taken to guarantee that the program will produce hoped-for changes in members of the target population. To be effective, evaluation should not be delayed until the program has been completed, but should, as Cronbach [14] has argued, be a part of the developmental operations so as to avoid waste of time, effort, and money.

It is difficult, if not impossible, to evaluate an entire instructional program at once. But it is feasible to evaluate a program one component at a time. For example, a course of study may consist of a number of lessons, each lesson consisting of several parts, and each part requiring, say, from 5 to

50 minutes of student time. The evaluation plan should be designed to take each part in turn.

Essential in the process of formative evaluation is that both the program itself and the procedures for training others to use the program undergo the "tryout cycle." As used here, the term *tryout cycle* refers to the following steps:

1. The component is presented to a small sample—say, six students—of the target population.
2. Its effects on the students are assessed by means of pre- and post-tests and other observations. Cronbach reminds us that at this stage it is more important to focus on student responses to individual items than on total test scores.
3. The component is revised.
4. It is tried on a new sample.
5. The cycle is repeated until the component has become demonstrably effective.

Principle 7. Since any given instructional program will work more effectively with some students than with others, the formative evaluation plan should be designed to obtain information about the characteristics of the students, especially those who did not learn from the program.

Instructional programs should be developed for particular target groups —persons about whom certain kinds of information are available or can be obtained—rather than for people in general. Two major categories of student characteristics are obviously important: their previous learnings, and their patterns of motivation. To illustrate: a lesson in advanced calculus would not be appropriate for people who had not already learned beginning calculus. An instructional program in mathematics to be used with students who do not like mathematics would have to be designed to attract, hold, and teach these unmotivated students and would probably be different from one designed for groups of students eager to learn mathematics. It follows that for any instructional program it may be necessary to develop alternative components for particular categories of students.

Principle 8. Formative evaluation requires a particular array of roles, skills, and tools that have not been traditionally employed in developing instructional programs.

Evaluation should not be confused with the more traditional practice of accreditation, which relies on the impressions of experts. Evaluation requires empirically derived information about the effects, both good and bad, expected and unexpected, of the program on the students. For the gathering of these data, a deliberate and continuing program must be planned and a staff must be made available and trained to carry out the necessary procedures.

It is easy to point to examples of effective programs, for example in remedial reading, that teachers for some reason have failed to use, even when the use has been approved by school administrators, school boards, etc. It is easy to find examples of programs that teachers use incorrectly, and it is easy to find examples of programs that work well with some students but not with others. Developing programs tailored for acceptance by particular teachers who use them effectively, and designing these programs with sufficient flexibility and discrimination so as to fit the particular students being taught, calls for a special development team equipped with special skills and using special tools. The need for these development team roles and skills has not been recognized by program developers in general.

In developing an instructional program, it is obvious that questions regarding the "content validity" of the programs be answered. For example, are the concepts presented in this program sound, up-to-date, etc.? It is less obvious that other technical questions must also be answered:

1. What could go wrong during the instructional process? At what points in the program is failure most likely to occur?
2. Who is in a position or can be placed in a position to pick up and feed back clues as to the nature of that failure, if it does occur?
3. What procedures are needed to obtain information systematically from the observers about the nature of the difficulties encountered by the users in learning to apply the program, and by the students in learning what the program intends for them to learn?

For such questions to be answered, a formative evaluation approach would take into account considerations like these in setting up a program-development team:

1. The users must be trained, so someone needs to play the trainer role.
2. During the tryout cycle, the users should be monitored to see if they are using each component as planned. It follows that the program-development team must prepare monitoring schedules and include someone to play the monitor role.
3. The students should be pretested and post-tested. Someone must choose or build instruments and administer them.
4. The trainer, the users, the monitor, and the students should be asked routinely and systematically to note where difficulties occur and should be invited to suggest possible solutions to these difficulties. It follows that someone should be assigned the task of asking questions and recording answers. Someone, perhaps the team as a whole, will need to review these answers and make revisions in the program accordingly.

At the risk of stating what to some will be obvious, I would like to give an example to illustrate how the principles of formative evaluation might be applied by someone developing a course in educational psychology for **An Example from Teacher Education** teacher candidates. It is assumed that such a person will not be developing the course in isolation, but will be a member of a team of instructors who are planning a unified and comprehensive teacher-training program and who are working together to evaluate the effectiveness of one another's courses.

One of the most useful and most generally taught concepts in American psychology is the concept of reinforcement. Let us suppose the instructor wanted his students to be able to use this concept. Following the line of reasoning outlined here, some of the early questions to be asked by the team of instructors would include, "What do we want teacher candidates to know about reinforcement? Since this course is part of a professional curriculum, what do we want the candidates to be able to do as a result of having learned the concept? What observations would we make in order to determine whether or not a given candidate had achieved a knowledge of this concept?"

In a traditional course in educational psychology, a student might be judged to have learned the concept of reinforcement when he could define the term as it was defined by a particular psychologist, or perhaps when, on a multiple-choice test, he could correctly identify which of several definitions of various psychological concepts fitted the term *reinforcement*. Such a performance on the part of the student would indicate that some degree of learning had indeed occurred, but whether it would have been enough to enable the student to make profitable use of the concept in teaching is questionable.

A professor of educational psychology who tried to follow the suggestions implicit in this paper and who began with the question, "What kinds of behavior on the part of the student would signify that he has learned what we want him to know about the concept of reinforcement?" might postulate a sequence of performances something like those described below. The professor could then infer that a teacher candidate had learned the concept of reinforcement if he were able to:

1. write a correct paraphrase of the definition given in the textbook, using words other than those used by the author or the instructor. Ability to paraphrase would indicate that more than sheer rote learning had occurred.
2. distinguish between correct and incorrect examples of the concept presented, let us say, in written form, perhaps on a multiple-choice test.
3. give new and correct illustrations of the concept—examples other than those given by the textbook or the instructor.
4. identify logical implications of the concept for teacher behavior.
5. observe a teacher instructing a class and later describe in writing the actions taken by the teacher that might reasonably be expected to act as reinforcements to a particular student.
6. describe the steps to be taken in order to determine whether a particular set of teacher actions had been reinforcing.

7. write a lesson plan that prescribed actions to be taken by a teacher in order to reinforce particular kinds of student behavior, such as behavior patterns that constitute good study skills.
8. describe in writing a strategy for testing the lesson plan—for determining whether or not the planned teacher actions were reinforcing, specifying what observations would be required, who would make them, etc.

Having decided upon the hierarchy of performances he wanted to teach in his course, the psychology instructor—or preferably the team of instructors—would proceed concurrently to do three things:

1. The team would develop a set of performance tests, which would then constitute an operational definition of each of the course goals.
2. The team would develop a plan for instructing teacher candidates in the course concepts in such a way that they could be expected to pass the performance tests. In developing the instructional plan, they would presumably follow a theory of instructions such as that exemplified by Popham [15].
3. The team would devise a strategy for evaluating their instructional plan. In developing the evaluation strategy, they might use a checklist [16] such as the following:

Formative Evaluation Checklist
This checklist is for use by developers of instructional programs that are implemented by teachers, counselors, school administrators, etc. Examples of instructional programs might include lectures, remedial classes, workshops, sensitivity-training sessions, counseling interviews, etc.

A. Evaluation Plans: Do project plans specify a strategy for formative evaluation, together with a time schedule?
1. Have outcome measures been developed prior to or concurrently with program materials? Are there plans for improving outcome measures?
2. Does the plan provide for a schedule of tryout cycles for each component?
3. Does the plan include provision for getting feedback from each member of the evaluation team about observed difficulties and potential solutions to problems?
B. Development Team: Have the following evaluation roles been defined? Who will play each of these roles? Will different persons play the roles of developer and monitor?
1. Program or materials developer(s)
2. Trainer(s) of such potential users as teachers, counselors, school administrators, etc.
3. Monitors of the activities of the users during training

4. "Experimental" users, e.g., the teachers who try out the program during its developmental stage and help to improve it

5. Data gatherers and processors, e.g., clerks, programmers, coders of tape-recorded protocols, etc.

6. Small samples of the target population(s), e.g., students who serve as subjects and who provide reactions to the program, as well as taking pre- and post-tests

7. External observers of members of the target population(s). Sometimes outcome measures will involve performances on measures other than standardized achievement tests. For example, performance tests for student teachers would probably require trained raters.

C. Outcome Measures
1. Have outcome measures been developed for each component of the program? What evidence is available regarding the validity and reliability of these measures?

2. Do the outcome measures provide information about possible side effects—unexpected outcomes, both positive and negative, e.g., changes in interests and attitudes—as well as attainment of knowledge and skills?

3. Do the outcome measures satisfy conventions of validity and reliability? For example, since the outcome measures are the operational definitions of the goals of an instructional program, are they indeed viewed by the developer(s) as fully appropriate? If not, are their limitations explicated?

D. Instructional Program
1. Is the program repeatable? Are the steps to be taken—by the user/teacher, counselor, administrator, sensitivity trainer, workshop director, etc.,—clearly spelled out, in unambiguous language, and in sufficient detail that they can be understood and followed? Have the instructions been pretested?

2. Is the instructional program organized into testable units—components requiring 50 minutes or less of student time?

E. Formative Evaluation Materials: In addition to the instructional program, have the following materials been developed, or are they in the process of being developed?
1. Trainers' manuals, which outline specific steps to be taken in training users

2. Users' manuals, which outline specific steps to be taken in conducting a particular instructional program

3. Users' performance tests, by which to estimate the degree of competence of a user

4. Monitors' manuals, including observation schedules that enable the monitor to compare users' performance with a criterion model and to provide information about the number and kind of errors made by a user during a specified period of time. The schedule should enable the monitor to report whether a user is able to follow directions and to inhibit his tendency to improvise; it should also enable the monitor to note the kinds of difficulties the user encounters so that the directions can be rewritten to anticipate these difficulties.

5. Questionnaires consisting of open-ended questions such as "What kind of difficulties were encountered in trying to make the program work?" "What suggestions do you have for changes in the outcome measures, the program, the training procedures, the monitoring?" etc. These questionnaires should be directed by the developers to all other members of the evaluation team, including (a) trainers, (b) monitors, (c) users, (d) members of target population, (e) observers.

F. Measures of Individual Differences among Members of the Target Population

1. Are data being systematically gathered about those individual differences that are likely to make the program more effective with some students than with others? Data should include measures of the following:

    a. previous learning
    b. study skills—ability to attend, read, listen, take notes, follow directions, "psych out" teachers, prepare for examinations, etc.
    c. attitudes and beliefs—the feeling that one can learn, can cope, that it is one's responsibility to try, etc.

2. Are users, monitors, and observers encouraged to "intuit" crucial differences in students not measured by existing tests in order to provide clues as to the kinds of measures that need to be developed?

G. Administrative Arrangements

1. Funds: Has a part of the program budget been earmarked specifically for formative evaluation?
2. Personnel: Is there a full evaluation team assigned to each program being developed? From the beginning of the project?
3. Job descriptions: Is there a complete job description for each of the roles listed under B above?
4. Working relationships

    a. Do developers and other members of the evaluation team work cooperatively, or do they see themselves in competition with one another?

b. Do developers and other members of the evaluation team see themselves as having a common goal, i.e., the development of a replicable and demonstrably effective instructional program?

c. Is each person responsible to one and only one super-ordinate?

d. Does each person know to whom he is responsible?

Conclusion

The major emphasis of this paper is that one of the most important services to be performed by evaluation is the improvement of instructional procedures and programs. To achieve this end, the evaluation should focus upon how well the program's components achieve their objectives within the realistic settings for which they were designed. This emphasis will help ensure that the program will work effectively with the particular group of students for whom it was intended.

The advantages to be accrued from formative (i.e., implementation-progress) evaluation seem clear. Rather than waiting to find out at the end of a program whether it has been successful by running an outcome evaluation, it is more useful to direct that effort toward improving the program by testing and refining it while it is still under development. In addition to the greater economy of effort and time offered by this approach is the increased quality and effectiveness of the instructional program. The outline of principles and the checklist in this paper present guidelines to facilitate these kinds of evaluations.

Notes

1. Ralph W. Tyler, *Basic Principles of Curriculum and Instruction* (Chicago: University of Chicago Press, 1950).
2. Lee J. Cronbach, "Evaluation for Course Improvement," *Teachers College Record* 64 (1963).
3. M. Scriven, "The Methodology of Evaluation," *Perspective of Curriculum Evaluation* (Chicago: Rand McNally, 1967).
4. Marvin C. Alkin, "Products for Improving Educational Evaluation," *Evaluation Comment* (1970).
5. Stephen P. Klein, "Evaluating Tests in Terms of the Information They Provide." See pages 140–149 in this book.
6. See note 2 above.
7. T. R. Husek, "Different Kinds of Evaluation and Their Implications for Test Development." See pp. 150–155 in this book.
8. Eugene J. Webb et al., *Unobtrusive Measures: Nonreactive Research in the Social Sciences* (Chicago: Rand McNally, 1966).
9. Jerome S. Bruner, *The Process of Education* (Cambridge, Mass.: Harvard University Press, 1961).
10. David P. Ausubel, *Educational Psychology: A Cognitive View* (New York: Holt, Rinehart and Winston, 1968).
11. Robert M. Gagné, *The Conditions of Learning* (New York: Holt, Rinehart and Winston, 1965).
12. W. James Popham, *The Teacher-Empiricist* (Los Angeles: Tinnon-Brown, 1970).
13. L. M. Stolurow, *Teaching by Machine*, Cooperative Research Monograph No. 6. U.S. Department of Health, Education, and Welfare (Washington, D.C.: U.S. Government Printing Office, 1961).
14. See note 2 above.

15. See note 12 above.
16. This checklist was not derived primarily by a deductive process; it emerged out of a series of projects aimed at developing effective and reproducible instructional programs. Some of the projects were conducted by doctoral candidates at UCLA who were attempting to develop instructional models in counseling. These include Hawkins [17], Broadbent [18], Anderson [19], and Quinn [20]. One project, headed by Hildebrand of the Colorado State Department of Education, was devoted to the development of an effective strategy for the diffusion of improved educational practices to the small rural schools.
17. R. K. Hawkins, "Comparison of Three Experimental Modes of Counseling," Ph.D. dissertation, University of California, Los Angeles, 1967.
18. L. A. Broadbent, "The Effects of Two Different Belief Systems on the Perceptions of Two Experimental Modes of Counseling," Ph.D. dissertation, University of California, Los Angeles, 1968.
19. E. C. Anderson, "Promoting Career Information-Seeking Through Group Counselor's Cues and Reinforcements," Ph.D. dissertation, University of California, Los Angeles, 1970.
20. J. B. Quinn, "The Influence of Interpersonal Perception on the Process of Change in Two Experimental Modes of Counseling," Ph.D. dissertation, University of California, Los Angeles, 1970.

A recent survey by the National Education Association regarding the evaluation of teachers warns of an approaching school scandal. [1] More than one-half of the nation's teachers report no confidence in their school system's program of teacher evaluation. This scandal can be avoided. There is a way to improve our procedures for evaluating teachers and at the same time increase the learning of pupils. The suggested approach is labeled "supervision by objectives."

Objectives in Teacher Evaluation

Briefly, supervision by objectives is a process by which a supervisor and a teacher agree in advance as to what they will accept as evidence that the teacher has or has not been successful in changing the behavior of his students. An agreement is drawn up before the teacher acts and is designed to counter the prevailing practice of trying to make an *ex post facto* judgment of ends. The contract is tentative to the extent that at any time the two parties can renegotiate. For example, the original target is modified if the teacher finds during the course of instruction that he has overestimated the changes possible, or if he subsequently determines more important changes for his students. This will happen frequently, and the supervisor has to agree that the modification is warranted and to accept the alternate criterion measures.

The period of time during which the contract functions is variable. A contract can be used for guiding the observation of a single lesson. In this case, the supervisor and teacher confer in advance as to what they will accept as indicators that pupils have learned from the lesson. A contract may also be written to cover a year's course of instruction. Evidence of effectiveness then is matched at the end of the year against criteria agreed upon at the beginning of the year.

Learning theory and empirical data support the view that when there are clear statements of objectives, learning is more efficient and objectives are attained more readily. Differences in objectives between supervisor and teacher are resolved *before* instruction under the contract plan. This is

Antidote to a School Scandal

John D. McNeil

in contrast to those situations where teachers have been successful in producing changes in learners (i.e., have been successful teachers) but have failed on their ratings as teachers because the supervisor did not concur in the desirability of the results produced. Furthermore, once there is agreement on the ends of instruction, the teacher and supervisor become partners in the enterprise. The teacher will want all the help he can get from the supervisor. Advice and suggestions are valued by the teacher because they are seen as related to the teacher's own desired changes in learners. When there is no agreement on goals, suggestions from supervisors tend to be viewed as irrelevant, as the supervisor's personal impositions upon the teacher.

Basic to supervision by objectives are two assumptions. First, learning is evidenced by a change in behavior. For example, a child is given a problem such as $9 + \square = 11$ and is asked to respond by completing the equation. If the child is unable to make the correct response, instruction follows, and, subsequently, the child is presented with the same problem or new problems involving inverse relationships of addition and subtraction. If he is now able to make the correct response, we say he has learned. Learning is shown when one responds to particular situations or classes of situations in new ways. There is no way of knowing whether a change has occurred without observing a behavior or a consequence of behavior, such as a product, composition, or other tangible work.

Two Basic Assumptions

Second, teaching is successful only when the instructor's predetermined and intentional changes sought in the learner actually occur. If the desired responses do not occur in the learner, teaching is ineffective.

The criterion problem in teacher evaluation arises because of differences in interpretation of ideals and the failure to distinguish means from ends. Historically, teaching encompasses more than the ability to produce a behavioral change. We speak of the importance of appearance, the value of a teacher whose voice is of high quality and whose conduct in the community is exemplary. The qualities associated with the good teacher are unlimited. One of the difficulties with our attempts at evaluation of teaching has been that we have not agreed as to how ideals shall be manifested in specific behavior. Is good citizenship better manifested by a protest or by conformity? Further, we have too frequently made the means of instruction the criterion rather than testing to see if the means we employ really produce more important instructional outcomes.

Supervision by objectives is an attempt to secure initial agreement on the part of the supervisor and teacher as to the specific changes to be wrought in learners, thereby clarifying the meaning of ideals and insuring that the intents of instruction are present to guide the selection of means. If there is no agreement on the ends of instruction, then there can be no meeting of minds regarding the appropriate procedures to follow in the classroom and no fair assessment of teacher effectiveness. A teacher cannot accept suggestions from a supervisor regarding teaching practice if that practice is inconsistent with the behavioral changes deliberately planned by that teacher. Many arguments as to whether or not a teacher is following sound principles of learning are in fact arguments over differences in outcomes sought from instruction. There is, for instance, no particular value in the frequently recommended practice of pupil participation in classroom discussions if the objective is the ability to recall information from printed sources. In fact, silent reading of a textbook might be more appropriate for the latter objective because of economy of time.

Supervision by objectives requires a shift from judging a teacher's competency by the procedures followed in the classroom to judgment of the teacher in terms of the results he is producing in students. We are now saying that we do not know with certainty which methods will produce the desired results but that we are willing to find out. There is a tendency to conceive of the teacher as an inquirer or hypothesis maker and not as one who has arrived in his craft. The principal of a school and a teacher must not regard an instructional practice as an end in itself, e.g., whether children raise their hands or not before speaking; whether seats are in one direction; whether the teacher talks most, all, or some of the time. The questions to be asked are: "How are these things related to the changes we are trying to effect in boys and girls?" "How will a specific procedure bring about the results we seek?"

What the pupil is asked to do and to know as a result of a single lesson, a semester, or a year's course of study can be specified. *We cannot teach what we cannot specify.*

Judging Teacher Performance

In those situations where teachers distrust evaluation, the most flagrant criticism of supervisors is that they observe a teacher's performance without knowing what that teacher is trying to accomplish. The principal who visits a room without knowing the objective of the lesson is forced to attend to room environment—e.g., the blinds aren't even—or to make some inane comment about the nice children. In a sense, judging the teacher independently from the consequences sought and attained is like judging the ballplayer on the basis of his form rather than observing where the ball goes. More than that, we sometimes judge performance of the teacher without first finding out what game he is playing. If there is agreement initially by the supervisor and the teacher upon the desired ends of instruction—whether they be with respect to subject-matter attainments, changed attitudes towards civic problems, or personal problems met—then the teacher has a chance to succeed and an opportunity to profit from supervisory assistance when the objectives are not being met.

Instruments for evaluation have fostered narrowness of instructional objectives and have served particular interests. What we think is important is what we look for in observation. Observation of instruction was formerly based heavily on the belief that the teacher should be an exemplar of an ideal in the mind of the supervisor. Early instruments for observing instruction called attention to the personal qualities of the teacher, such as appearance, a factor that is still noted. Just a short time ago, a young teacher came into the UCLA Office of Supervised Teaching in tears. She had been downgraded because her skirts were too short, and because she used too much eye makeup. The hairstyles, beards, and clothes of male teachers also invite criticism. Emerson's comment belongs here: "You are trying to make that man another you. One's enough."

Later a number of observational instruments were developed by people with particular axes to grind. Sociologists and mental hygienists provided a set of glasses for educators to use in viewing instruction. They never made it clear that when one put on these glasses, he automatically bought the objectives of the donors. For instance, there were observational schedules prepared by sociologists. What do sociologists view as the purpose of the school? Socialization of the child. What did they ask observers to look for? Peer-group interactions. "Use your sociogram to find out who speaks to whom, under what conditions, and with what effect." "Who are the isolates and who are the stars?"

Bias in Observation Scales

Also there were observation schedules prepared by the mental hygienists. What do they conceive as the most important function of the school? Mental hygiene. As a consequence, we have the study of Wickman, [2] who asked psychologists to rate as most serious to least serious behaviors like cheating, swearing, masturbating, remaining silent in the classroom. Then teachers were asked to list what they thought were the most serious behaviors. Sure enough, teachers thought cheating, swearing, and masturbating to be serious problems but with respect to quiet in the classroom as a problem, teachers asked, "Are you kidding?" So psychologists went to work and established child-study centers that taught teachers to identify the quiet child and regard him with suspicion. Subsequently, it was announced that teachers and psychologists were more nearly agreed in their view of serious behavior in terms of the framework—the framework of the psychologists.

Use of the analytical tools of specialized fields have a place, but schools have functions other than socialization and mental health. The acquisition of the disciplines, problem-solving abilities, and cultural values are also important. Therefore, we must have observation systems that are more value neutral and focus on variables that will be relevant to the attainment of a wide range of objectives, not just serve the objectives of the sociologist and the analyst.

However, not only the sociologists and the psychologists are masqueraders. Many educators, too, have developed observational instruments that reflect a particular value and bias. For instance, Marie Hughes [3] looks at a teacher in terms of whether or not the teacher exercises a controlling, a content, or an encouraging function. The so-called encouraging behavior is the end upon which favorable judgment rests for Dr. Hughes.

Under the Hughes system, if the teacher had a different end, such as content mastery, she would be judged weak regardless of her success in obtaining the objective. In other words, we must have agreement on the ends first and then judge the effectiveness of teaching—not judge the teaching without agreement on the ends.

The Task of the Observer

What should we look for when we observe? Let us remember that by our definition the good teacher is the one who is able to effect desired changes in the learner. Let us also admit that we don't have certain knowledge of how to produce these changes. There is no unequivocal interpretation about the desirability of any given educational practice. That is why it is so important to view each teaching situation as an experiment in which one says: "If I do these things, the learners will be able to make these responses" and to have the courage to see whether or not the predicted results occur. When the desired consequences do not follow, one must try to reason why and try an altered approach, again noting consequences.

The observer of instruction must do two things: record factual descriptions of what took place during the lesson and collect evidence of the extent to which the desired results have occurred. Together, the facts noted during the lesson and the evidence of results serve to generate modified approaches or modified objectives. Among the kinds of incidents to be noted are opportunities to practice the desired behavior, the number of times each child had an opportunity to respond, and the confirmation or additional information given the learner following his responses. It is particularly important that the supervisor record actual events, not inferences. The supervisor can confront the teacher with a record of observable behavior; he cannot confront the teacher with inferences without facts to support them and expect anything more than resistance. One might record that the red-headed boy continually hit his partner on the head with a pencil but should not merely record that the red-headed boy was not paying attention. The latter is an inference; the former is a fact. As an observer, I once wanted to say that a boy who hit with the pencil was not paying attention, but my inference was wrong. The boy's subsequent responses to problems posed by the teacher showed he was "tuned in." I don't know about the boy he was hitting.

Social psychological variables and their indicators, such as the seating patterns of children and the frequency of correction given by the teacher, are useful analytical tools for guiding the observer; however, I repeat that the observed practice itself is to be tested. For example, we are told to look for instances of warmth in a teacher. There may be behaviors that one would classify as warm and friendly, but warmth and friendliness as *you* define them might not be universal qualities to be sought in teachers. Warmth and friendliness are often in the eyes of the pupils rather than in the teacher or supervisor. It is difficult to find any teacher who is not seen as warm and friendly by at least one pupil or cold by another. We have teachers who are viewed by middle-class pupils as just or fair because these teachers keep their distance and show impartiality. Yet some children interpret this impartiality as coldness. By way of example, there was a lad who was unhappy with his teachers until he met one many of us would classify as nagging and chastising. This boy responded by saying "At last I've found a teacher who cares about me." This boy, a Mexican-American, might have been responding to his cultural norm, which says children should heed specific instructions from adults and not lead independent lives. I would be surprised, however, if the pronouncing of one's name correctly, consulting the interests of learners, and interacting with their parents produced undesirable consequences. Nevertheless, we must regard our procedures as something to be tested and challenge our pet assumptions about what will work.

The behavioral model presented so far for the evaluation of instruction is narrow in that it focuses upon the teacher's ability to formulate and attain accepted educational objectives. Only those teaching practices that are found to be directly related to the attainment of the objectives are legitimate in accordance with this model. This system of supervision attempts to control the particular bias of the supervisor or pressure groups. As an instance of such bias, a novice teacher was subject to removal because she didn't put the paints back in the right place and was, therefore, disorderly and unfit for teaching. We must distinguish judgments that rest upon professional knowledge from judgments that represent parochial preferences. The fact that a community or board of education says it wants its teachers to be hard-shelled Baptists or Caucasians is an example of parochial values, not professional ones. The list of parochial expectations is unlimited. I am suggesting, however, that we give more attention to the professional qualifications of the teacher independent of parochial expectations and pressures. The professional supervisor must deal with the distinctive feature of teaching. This distinctive feature of teaching is the competency to select appropriate changes to be sought in learners and the ability to produce these changes. Our problem in supervision is to make explicit the behavioral changes we are attempting to effect in our learners. To the extent that there is agreement on these changes as being desirable, we can plan effective programs and collect evidence that certain procedures are valid.

Developing a New Framework

Advocating that the teacher be judged by the changes he produced in pupils is but half the coin of supervision, for if the results are not favorable one has to know what to modify in his instructional procedures. Impressions of teaching are not enough. Factual observations are required to describe teaching. An analysis that will tell one what to vary in order to improve teaching effectiveness requires a description of the teaching act. What, then, shall be the basis for developing a framework for observation? So far we have indicated the existence of frameworks that are quite appropriate when the instructional outcomes are socialization, mental health, and objectives associated with progressive education of the 1940s. Our problem now is to develop analytical tools that can serve a wider range of instructional outcomes. Learning theory and principles offer wider generalization; theory is not tied to specific outcomes. The principle of overlearning, for instance, is held to increase retention of all behaviors, not just those associated with mental, physical, or moral considerations. However, the very fact that a principle of learning does not bear a one-to-one correspondence with a given classroom practice makes it difficult to agree whether or not the principle is being followed. For example, it is commonly accepted that one can modify the behavior of a learner by providing him with reinforcers or rewards following efforts that approximate the desired changes. But this principle requires specific agreement as to how the principle will be manifested in a given classroom before it is useful to supervisor and teacher. What will be accepted as evidence that reinforcement is present? Praise by the teacher? Special privileges? Opportunity to choose one's own task? Reinforcement, opportunity to practice the behavior desired, and knowledge of results are factors or principles that guide our observation. But these factors are not facts; they merely serve to elucidate the gathering of facts. Principles and theory are of little value in supervision unless they lead to collecting specific facts during the observation.

Supervision by Objectives

The outline [on page 177] illustrates two requirements for rating and observing a teacher. You will note that the first requirement is that the teacher and supervisor agree on the objectives of the lesson(s) and the kinds of evidence that will be collected indicating whether objectives were reached or not. The second requirement is that the supervisor collect descriptive facts observed during the lesson(s). The selection of facts may be guided by a learning principle or other variable or framework that one finds helpful in calling attention to observations that might otherwise be ignored. It must be emphasized, however, that the principle has no absolute validity; a principle is not a fact. A teacher becomes furious when a supervisor cannot give factual instances to back up charges that the teacher did not follow principles of learning, such as failure to individualize. Also the documented failure itself must be checked against its consequences.

Following the teaching and collecting of evidence, the supervisor and teacher contrast intended outcomes with evidence of actual outcomes. Where insufficient progress is made by learners, supervisor and teacher together examine observations made during instruction. Review of the facts may lead to suggestions to be tested in subsequent lessons. Observed lessons will reveal more appropriate objectives or ways to vary practice.

Summary

In this paper a procedure for evaluation of teachers has been proposed. The proposal is called *supervision by objectives*. It places emphasis upon the consequences of instruction in terms of pupil gain. Gain can be changes

Rating and Observation Form

1. Agreement upon tentative objectives of instruction
   a. List below the measures, observations, or indicators of quality in a pupil's product (e.g., theme) that will be accepted as evidence that the teacher is to receive a rating of outstanding, good, or poor. (What must pupils accomplish in order for the teacher to get a grade of outstanding? What have the supervisor and teacher agreed upon as evidence that pupils have or have not made desired progress?)
   b. Indicate the kinds of situations to which pupils will be expected to respond differently from that response presently in their repertoire. (E.g., given any Spanish word ending in *ar*, pupils will correctly conjugate the verb in the present tense.)
2. Facts that will be collected for describing the teacher's instructional procedures.

Principle	*Facts to be collected*
a. Reinforcement (reward system)	Percentage of pupils whose papers receive positive comments for correct performance
b. Individualization	Number of alternative assignments available to class
c. Opportunity to practice the behavior desired	Number of times each pupil was called upon for oral response
d. Prompting	Examples presented before requiring learners to generate the rule
	Number of responses demanded from learners without teacher prompting

   e. Other: The supervisor may use any principle or theoretical framework that will direct attention to factual observation in the classroom. The utility of the principle is validated when it leads to the teacher's subsequent changing of specific aspects of instruction and to the consequence of greater pupil gain in desired directions.

in attitude and self-concept as well as mastery of subject matter. The procedure does not throw out analytical schemes in the observation of instruction but relegates the use of such schemes to guiding one in the making of a descriptive record of teaching, not judgment. The point is stressed that principles of learning and instruction in the abstract are not sufficient and that indicators of the presence or absence of principles must be operationally defined. In the proposed behavioral model, principles and theory are seen as sources for generating new approaches and modifications in teaching method. The model demands, however, that proposed departures be empirically tested, that evidence of the effect of the innovation be collected. The proposal is a timely one. The American public expects results from schooling. As public support of education increases, there will be increasing insistence on a factual basis for educational decisions. In the past, no one has taken such a basis very seriously, especially in respect to decisions regarding teacher effectiveness. The rising dissatisfaction of teachers regarding evaluation procedures is a case in point. If administrators and teachers are ready to negotiate on criteria for effectiveness that stress results in terms of the desired behavioral changes in learners rather than to rely upon personal impressions of the teacher and his procedures as criteria for evaluation, we can avoid a national scandal and at the same time improve the quality of learning for all pupils.

Notes

1. *Evaluation of Classroom Teachers,* Research Report 1964–R14 (Washington, D.C.: National Education Association, Research Division, October 1964).
2. E. K. Wickman, *Children's Behavior and Teachers' Attitudes* (New York: Commonwealth Fund, Division of Publications, 1928).
3. Marie M. Hughes, *A Research Report—Assessment of the Quality of Teaching in Elementary Schools* (Salt Lake City: University of Utah, 1959).

With the increase of federal funds for education, a new professional is emerging—the evaluator. He is somewhat different from the expert in tests and measurements and in research design usually found working on a college faculty. Rather, he is a person who spends part or all of his working hours at research and development activities, thinking about and planning the evaluation of educational processes. Because his role is a new one on the educational scene, his functions and his relationship to other educational experts need to be more clearly defined. It is the aim of this article to present some ideas about that role.

Two papers on evaluation, one by Scriven [1] and one by Stake [2], contain a number of assertions and implicit assumptions about the evaluator's role which deserve examination. Among them are the following:

1. Scriven would assign evaluators the task of determining the effectiveness of instructional programs. But more than that, he would have them evaluate the goals of these programs as well. It is not enough for the evaluator to find out whether the teacher of mathematics or English or physical education has taught the students what he intended to teach them. The evaluator must also decide, Scriven believes, whether the specific course content was appropriate and worthwhile; for, as Scriven sees it, the evaluator is the person best qualified to judge.

2. Scriven holds that the relative goodness of different educational goals is to be determined by applying a set of absolute standards that will somehow be obvious to the evaluator. Apparently, Scriven doubts that it is possible for intelligent, informed, and well-intentioned people seriously to disagree about what should be taught, for he asserts that arguments over criteria turn out to be mainly "disputes about what is to be counted as good, rather than arguments about the straightforward 'facts of the situation,' i.e., about what is in fact good."

3. Continuing his argument, Scriven implies that without absolute standards, evaluation is in fact probably impossible. "The process of relativism has not only led to overtolerance for overrestrictive goals, it has led to incompetent evaluation of the extent to which these have been achieved...."

A New Role in Education

The Evaluator

Garth Sorenson

4. Stake seems to imply that since absolute standards exist, it is not necessary to take the individual teacher's nor the individual school's goals into account. He seems to believe that such standards should be applied even if they relate only slightly or not at all to the local school's resources and goals. "It should be noted that it is not the educator's privilege to rule out the study of a variable merely by saying, 'That is not one of our objectives.' "

5. Both Scriven and Stake believe that it is possible and perhaps desirable to appraise teaching and other instructional programs independent of their effects on the students. Stake says, "The educational evaluator should not list goals only in terms of anticipated student behavior. To evaluate an educational program, emphasis must be given to what teaching as well as what learning is intended...." And, "It is not wrong to teach a willing educator about behavioral objectives—they may facilitate his work. It is wrong to insist on them...." Scriven further comments that "pressure on a writer (curriculum maker) to formulate his goals, to keep to them, and to express them in testable terms may enormously alter his product in ways that are certainly not always desirable."

6. It may be inferred that Scriven believes that teachers who feel threatened by evaluators holding such absolute values should be ignored or at least discounted. "A little toughening of the moral fibre is required if we are not to shirk the social responsibilities of the educational branch of our culture."

7. While it appears that he endorses most of Scriven's assertions, Stake would qualify at least one of them. If an individual evaluator were less than fully qualified, Stake would substitute a team of specialists as the appropriate determiners of educational goals and practices. The team would consist of experts in "instructional technology... psychometric testing and scaling... research design and analysis... the dissemination of information... (and perhaps) a social anthropologist." He does not include historians, philosophers, businessmen, labor leaders, legal experts, or even nonbehavioral scientists.

To be sure, the assertions listed above do not constitute a summary of what Scriven and Stake have said in their papers. Nevertheless, it appears that they represent, at least roughly, some of the beliefs of Scriven and Stake and a point of view resembling that of a number of writers on public education.

Inherent Problems

In spite of the fact that a number of brilliant and famous men support a position similar to that just described, I believe that if evaluators generally were to take an absolutist position, a number of unfortunate consequences would follow.

For one thing, teachers would be unwilling to cooperate and work with these evaluators. An evaluator who insists on evaluating in terms of his own goals while ignoring what the school people are trying to do, an evaluator who criticizes them and the school for failing to do what they had not intended to do in the first place, would certainly be viewed as threatening. It can be safely predicted that teachers who feel threatened will resist and will devote their time and energies to defending old practices rather than to examining and improving them.

A second unfortunate consequence would be that evaluators would not get the support they need from powerful groups in the community who have a legitimate interest in what goes on in the school. Evaluation requires large amounts of time, money, and other commodities that evaluators cannot get without a good deal of public support—especially if they already have alienated the teachers and school administrators. Many of the individuals and groups in this country whose support is needed believe that the schools were invented to serve the needs of society and ultimately are answerable to the taxpayers, or at least to someone other than professional evaluators.

These individuals and groups do not always agree with one another about how the schools can best serve society, but they do agree that the schools are not autonomous. Many of these individuals—for example, Paul Goodman, Robert Hutchins, Sidney Hook, James Conant, John Goodlad, Roald Campbell, Ralph Tyler, Clark Kerr, Admiral Rickover, Harold Taylor, Paul Woodring, Jerome Bruner, David Ausubel, Myron Lieberman, Lawrence Cremin, Benjamin Bloom, to name only a few—as well as many groups have given a good deal of thought and study to questions about the goals and methods of education. They are likely to regard individuals whose main qualification for the prescribing of educational goals is that they are experts in psychometry, research design, or social anthropology, but who are ignorant of the philosophical and political issues in education, as naive, arrogant, parochial, and, therefore, unworthy of assistance.

A third possible consequence—an evaluation program based upon the absolutistic assumption that "good" educational programs exist independently of persons and their preferences and independently of what students learn—is bound to fail. Its results are certain to be both inconclusive and meaningless.

An analogy can be found in the attempts to evaluate teacher effectiveness. After surveying the results of half a century of research, investigators like Anderson and Hunka [3] and [other educators] have concluded that research in this area has been unproductive and has reached a dead end because of problems encountered in developing suitable criterion variables. In statistical terms, the variables lack reliability. It is my contention that the reason for the failure to develop usable criterion variables is a basic error in the way in which the researchers conceptualized the problem—more specifically, in their reliance on an absolute model of teacher effectiveness. Virtually all the investigators assumed either implicitly or explicitly the existence of sets of behaviors that objectively define the teacher—behaviors that exist as an absolute, independent of any particular observer and would be recognized by an experienced educator when he encountered them, even though he might not be able to verbalize them in advance. Those researchers were failing to recognize and take into account the fact that any two observers are likely to differ in their beliefs about the ideal traits of the good teacher.

Ryans [4] found that even when two observers were simultaneously watching the same teacher, they did not agree about him in their independent ratings unless they had had considerable training in Ryans' rating system—and sometimes not even then. It was probably his observers' differing notions about the ideal teacher they were observing. Analogously, any two evaluators are likely to disagree about the goals of education and can, therefore, be expected to disagree about the "goodness" of whatever actual method or program they may at a specific time be seeking to evaluate. The point is, there never has been and never will be general agreement on the goals of education any more than there is agreement on the qualifications and characteristics of the ideal teacher. Though particular groups of people will agree on particular goals, we must live with the fact that there is a welter of conflicting ideas on the subject in the society as a whole.

Alternative Assumptions

Following is a set of assumptions that may provide a reasonable alternative to those selected from Scriven and Stake.

1. Educational institutions should serve the needs of society and of the individuals who comprise society; these needs are both complementary and interdependent.

2. A society's needs can best be defined by the members of that society through discussion, persuasion, and, ultimately, through voting. To insure that the goals of education will correspond with the citizens' views of their needs, the goals should be defined in a process of interaction between professionals and representatives of the society.

3. Every society changes; its needs and values are in a constant state of flux. Because of increases in population, knowledge, and technology, our society is very different from what it was even a decade ago. We now need new classes of workers, e.g., technicians who can build and operate computers. And because, as Gerard Piel [5] has pointed out, we are no longer a society characterized by scarcity of goods, values based on dearth, such as hard work, thrift, etc., are less salient. As our needs and values change, we must expect our educational goals to change.

4. Even though many of our values seem to be changing, we continue to prize diversity. Ours is a pluralistic society with different religions, political viewpoints, subcultures, and values. We believe that our heterogeneity makes our society richer, more interesting, and stimulating. What is even more critical, we believe that heterogeneity makes our society viable. To accommodate such a diverse population, we must expect our educational goals and practices to be varied.

5. The goals of our educational institutions are not and never have been limited to purely academic objectives. Most people want the schools to

do more than to teach the traditional academic subjects: they want individual and societal objectives included. For example, a century ago, the McGuffey Readers attempted to inculcate moral principles. More recently, James B. Conant [6] said that the schools should provide a basis for the growth of mutual understanding between the different cultural, religious, and occupational groups in our country. "If the Battle of Waterloo was won on the playing fields of Eton, it may well be that the ideological struggle with communism in the next 50 years will be won on the playing fields of the public high schools of the United States."

6. We can tell if an educational program or teaching method is working only by observing whether hoped-for changes are occurring in the students —at the same time making certain that damaging changes are *not* occurring, e.g., learning to hate a particular subject or learning to believe one cannot learn arithmetic even if he works at it. We cannot properly evaluate an instructor or a program without assessing the effects, wanted and unwanted, on students. To evaluate a schedule of events within a school, or a series of teacher activities, or any array of teacher characteristics while neglecting the product is to examine intentions without considering consequences.

7. Educational goals must be stated in descriptive rather than in interpretive language. We have learned that it is not useful to define educational goals in the terms formerly used by professional educators and still used by their critics. We know that instead of such high-sounding slogans as "transmitting the cultural heritage," "educating citizens for democracy," and "developing the individual's potential," we must develop objectives defined in terms of changes in pupils' behavior or in the products of student behaviors. We must also be careful that, in rigorously setting behavioral goals, we do not slip into triviality. We must be prepared to defend each behavioral goal in terms of value assumptions and to answer the question why one particular behavioral goal is better than another. These points do not represent new thinking. They describe a trend which, according to Ralph Tyler [7] began about 1935—a trend of which many public school teachers still are unaware. Tyler stated that it is more important to evaluate the educational process than the structure of the school and that it is more important to evaluate the product than the process. I would rephrase this point: the proper way to evaluate both the educational process and the structure of the schools is to find out whether they are in fact producing the hoped-for product.

T he function of the professional evaluator should be to help teachers and administrators in a given school to do such things as the following:

The Function of the Evaluator

1. *Define their goals in terms of pupil performance*. John McNeil [8], Director of Supervised Teaching at UCLA, and I both have found that many experienced teachers are not able to define their objectives in language that describes observable changes in pupil behavior. It is easy to be critical of such teachers, and it is easy to state educational goals behaviorally—if

we limit ourselves to rote learning. For example, "students will be able to name the bones of the body" is a goal stated in behavioral terms. While this goal may be important in some contexts, it is a very limited one. The behavioral definition of higher-order goals is much more difficult. At the end of a course, teachers want their students to perform in such a manner as to warrant the inference that the students have learned to "know," "understand," "appreciate," and "think" about what the teacher has tried to teach. Merely to tell teachers that they should state these goals behaviorally is far from sufficient. What would be more helpful would be to show them how, and to invent more sophisticated instruments for them to use.

2. *Learn how systematically to discover differences among pupils that require particular kinds of instruction.* Teachers need appraisal devices that will do more than reveal differences in what students already have learned. They need instruments that will also reveal barriers to, or interferences with, learning, among them, (*a*) misconceptions; (*b*) particular habits, such as failure to pay attention; (*c*) certain needs that the child is satisfying at the expense of learning, e.g., need for group approval or sensitivity to peer pressures; and (*d*) attitudes deriving from class and ethnic background, etc. Some important differences among students are so subtle that, without sophisticated instruments, the child who has not learned to attend to the teacher's instructions may be mistaken for a dull child, or an angry one, or perhaps one with a constitutional impairment.

3. *Design and administer evaluation programs.* More importantly, professional evaluators should help individual teachers to find out which of their instructional procedures are paying off and which are not. With guidance, it is possible for the teachers themselves to try out and to evaluate alternative instructional methods on the job. For example, Bartlett [9] demonstrated that when an instructor spent part of his time in an algebra class teaching study habits, the students learned more than when he spent the entire time teaching algebra.

P ublic school people do not need more critics—critics abound. What these educators *do* need is someone to help them find and test alternative solutions to the complex problems they face daily. For the most part, university personnel who have the knowledge to perform the kinds of evaluation functions described above have not been taking their knowledge to the schools. They have been publishing their findings in professional journals, but they have failed to make explicit to teachers the relevance of those findings for the teachers' work. Hopefully, the R & D evaluator will bridge the gap between the laboratory and the field.

Notes

1. M. Scriven, "The Methodology of Evaluation," (Bloomington, Ind.: Indiana University, 1965). Mimeographed.
2. R. E. Stake, "The Countenance of Educational Evaluation," (Urbana, Ill.: University of Illinois, Center for Instructional Research and Curriculum Evaluation, 1966). Mimeographed.

3. C. C. Anderson and S. M. Hunka, "Teacher Evaluation: Some Problems and a Proposal," *Harvard Education Review* 33 (1963): 74–96.
4. David G. Ryans, *Characteristics of Teachers* (Washington, D.C.: American Council on Education, 1960).
5. Gerard Piel, *Science in the Cause of Man* (New York: Random House, 1961).
6. James B. Conant, *Education and Liberty* (Cambridge, Mass.: Harvard University Press, 1953).
7. Ralph W. Tyler, "Modern Aspects of Evaluation," *California Journal of Secondary Education* 29 (1954): 410–412; *see also* "The Curriculum: Then and Now," *Proceedings of the 1956 Invitational Conference on Testing Problems* (Princeton, N. J.: Educational Testing Service, 1957).
8. John McNeil, "Antidote to a School Scandal." See pp. 170–178 in this book.
9. W. H. Bartlett, "The Practical Application of Psychological Facts in the Classroom As Demonstrated by Teaching a Specific Study Method to Elementary Algebra Students of the Junior College Level," master's thesis, University of California, Los Angeles, 1960.

E valuation of the teaching faculty of community and junior colleges may be undertaken for a number of reasons, including (1) assessment for promotions or merit pay increases, (2) administrative curiosity about the quality of instruction, and (3) the improvement of teaching quality. The last is the most frequently cited reason for instructor evaluation, based on the view of junior colleges as "teaching institutions."

Problems confronting those who want to undertake instructor evaluation include establishing guiding principles, designating appropriate criteria for judging instructor effectiveness, selecting suitable evaluators, and administering effective methods of evaluation.

This article addresses these problems associated with instructor evaluation. Documents included in this review were selected from materials received and processed by the ERIC Clearinghouse. Particular emphasis is placed on documents relating to evaluation for the purpose of improving instruction. All documents cited in the Notes [pp. 190–191] have been announced in *Research in Education*.

Principles

Regardless of who designs the evaluation procedure and regardless of the techniques employed, certain principles should be followed. Morin [1] suggests that

1. evaluation is a complex and vital process and thus it must not be treated casually ...
2. the evaluator must employ "scientific" procedures in an effort to collect objective data
3. evaluation of individual instructors should focus primarily on definable segments of observable behavior—both of the teacher and of the students
4. to determine the desirability of changes in student behavior, some prior descriptions must be prepared in operational terms of the type of performance desired
5. both instructor and evaluator must be cognizant of, and accept as legitimate, the stated objectives of the instructional procedures
6. the evaluative procedure must be inherent in the total scheme for instructional development in the college

---

Teacher Evaluation
Toward Improving Instruction

Marcia Boyer

Although some apply to certain evaluation techniques more than to others, these or similar principles should be carefully considered as the first step in any evaluation procedure.

There appears to be no consensus regarding the specific criteria for judging effective teaching. Bannister [2] states that there are three general categories of criteria an evaluator should consider when either constructing or selecting an evaluation instrument:

Criteria

1. Classroom atmosphere—a "climate" conducive to student ease, where students feel they have the respect of their instructor and classmates, where they are challenged by their work, where they are confident they can succeed, and where they experience gratifying success
2. Instructor—a person who is tolerant, reasonable, approachable, who possesses mastery of field and understanding, interest, and enthusiasm for the subject, who is thoroughly prepared for each class, and who conducts each class efficiently without annoyances or mannerisms which divert attention
3. Course—one that has clearly defined objectives and standards that must be attained, that utilizes methods and material adapted to specific needs of the student but allows for individual differences, in which there is student participation, reviews at regular intervals, fair tests returned promptly, in which the interrelatedness of knowledge and relation to daily life are stressed, and in which students are apprised periodically of the quality of the progress

Not all of these criteria necessarily apply to all methods of evaluation; the evaluator must select the criteria most appropriate for his particular purposes.

Despite the fact that instructors sometimes deny the reliability and value of student ratings, this method is receiving increased attention. One source [3] notes that student evaluations, when carefully and properly handled, provide the best criterion of quality of instruction. Research conducted by Rayder [4] demonstrates that student ratings of instructors are not substantially related to the student's sex, age, grade-point average, or grade(s) previously received from the instructor being rated. Moreover, students, unlike administrators or even teaching colleagues, have the opportunity to view the instructor in his day-to-day teaching activities and therefore should not be ignored as evaluators.

Evaluation by Students

The most common method employed in student ratings is the opinionnaire. Several documents provide samples of student rating forms [5, 6, 7, 8, 9, 10, 11]. Most require the student simply to rate his instructor on various attributes relevant to teaching ability; several, however, include open-ended questions or invite suggestions and comments.

The possible value of student evaluations is demonstrated in a study conducted at St. Johns River College [12]. The evaluation form required students to rate their instructors on a scale of one to five, on scholarship, skill of presentation, positive personal traits, and accuracy in evaluating students. Students were invited to supplement their ratings with written comments. A comparison of scores achieved by the full-time teaching faculty for the two years 1964–65 and 1965–66 yielded the following results:

1. Of the full-time instructors rated the first year, 14 did not return in the fall of 1965. Ten of these were in the lower half of the rating, thus reducing the spread of returning faculty by nearly one-third.
2. Fifteen instructors who rated in the lower half did return; all but one of these instructors improved on the next rating.

It was further reported that faculty members who made significant improvement had taken the students' ratings seriously, particularly their written comments.

Instructor Self-Appraisal

An example of self-evaluation is presented by Anderson [13]. Each instructor rated himself on a seven-point scale for the following attributes: speaking voice; mannerisms or pleonasms; knowledge of subject matter; personal enthusiasm; enthusiasm engendered in students; digressions; handling of questions; and general atmosphere created in the classroom. The instructor then made audiotapes of two one-hour class periods. After listening to the tapes, he completed another rating sheet and compared the two ratings. Although no statistically significant differences were found between the "before" and "after" ratings, more than half the faculty appeared sensitive to the information obtained from the tapes. Of the 19 instructors involved, five rated themselves more favorably the second time, six rated themselves less favorably, and eight did not change their ratings. The instructors concluded that the exercise was of value to them. Anderson lists the advantages of this technique as follows:

1. evidencing interest in the teaching process itself by the administration
2. indicating confidence by the administration in the faculty's ability to evaluate themselves as professionals and to make their self-indicated improvements
3. giving the faculty a workable and frequently interesting method whereby they may improve themselves
4. preserving the anonymity of the faculty, thus forestalling feelings of "Big Brother" watching
5. establishing essentially a self-operating and perpetuating system not calling for a great amount of time
6. placing the dean in the position of being called in for aid by a motivated faculty member, rather than being looked upon as an instructor with unwanted advice

7. providing specific and concrete examples (preserved on tape) of problems that can be referred to on replay, without having to rely on notes or faulty memory

This technique, with additional experimentation (preferably using videotape), could be a valuable tool in producing increasingly better instructors.

In their monograph "Measuring Faculty Performance" [14], Cohen and Brawer present a comprehensive treatment of the objectives, techniques, and concomitant problems of faculty evaluation. They contend that, although evaluation is often stated to be for the purpose of improving instruction, the methods seldom relate to instructional practices and even less to the results of instruction. They propose that evaluation would be more meaningful if it were related to instruction as a discipline rather than to the person of the instructor. If the instructor is to be observed as one force in the learning environment, methods other than those now typical must be employed. More important, the effects of the instructional process must be included in the evaluation design. They suggest that student achievement of learning objectives is the main criterion on which studies of faculty and of instructional effect should be based. The use of student gain on short-range objectives as a measure of teacher effectiveness is generally acknowledged as being more valid than the use of such criteria as, for example, the teacher's effort expended or the various perceptions of observers.

One scheme for evaluating instructors by student attainment is proposed by Israel [15]. This technique is based on the premise that the ends of instruction must be agreed on before evaluation procedures can be established and teacher effectiveness assessed. The essence of this technique is the development of a carefully selected set of objectives for the student to accomplish and an assessment of the skills, attitudes, and uses of knowledge exhibited by the teacher. The objectives should be developed cooperatively by the teacher and the administrator, for a necessary factor is mutual agreement on what would be accepted as evidence of student attainment of the specified objectives. One distinct advantage of this technique is that, in addition to providing a framework for evaluating instruction, it facilitates instruction; when there are clear statements of objectives, learning is more effective and objectives are attained more readily.

Three alternative methods for implementing this technique are provided by the author. The first calls for the instructor and administrator jointly to determine objectives, to establish criteria for judging attainment of these objectives, and subsequently to evaluate how well students achieved the objectives. If the objectives were not met, necessary modifications to the original objectives could be made and the teaching techniques of the instructor could be altered. The second alternative is similar to the first except that it calls for a classroom visitation by the administrator, thus providing more frequent and rapid feedback to the instructor. The third alternative differs from the second in that it calls for pre- and post-tests to be administered to the students for the purpose of measuring the attainment of objectives. One advantage of the last alternative is that it assures the same type of evaluation for all instructors.

Cohen and Brawer [16] note that faculty evaluation may eventually prove effective in promoting the development of instructional specialists. Currently, a junior and community college instructor must be competent in all aspects of the instructional process. Through instructor specialization, an institution may be staffed by a core of people who collectively, but not necessarily individually, display excellence in all matters relating to teaching. Instructional specialization suggests team teaching, a practice becoming widespread among institutions at all levels of education. Team members who do not function effectively hinder their immediate colleagues, who can apply necessary sanctions to force them to change or to eliminate them from the team. Evaluation then becomes a process by which colleagues influence each other's activities and eventually it becomes an integral part of the instructional development of the college.

Summary

Junior and community colleges, emphasizing the teaching function, must provide their students with the most effective instructors and teaching methods possible. Therefore, instructor evaluation must be an integral part of the overall developmental plan of the college.

Presented in this review are three different approaches to instructor evaluation: student evaluation by opinionnaire, instructor self-appraisal, and team evaluation involving both the instructor and his administrator. While the first two techniques have demonstrated merit as means of improving instruction, the last, based on student attainment of learning objectives, is more directly relevant to the purpose of evaluation. It appears that the benefits to be derived from this approach more than compensate for the time and energy required to implement it.

Notes

1. Lloyd H. Morin, "A Feasible Scheme for the Evaluation of Instructors," seminar paper, University of California, Los Angeles, 1968. (ED 024 361)
2. John Bannister et al., "Evaluating College Teaching," *Curriculum Reporter Supplement* (December 1961). (ED 022 450)
3. See note 2 above.
4. Nicholas F. Rayder, *College Student Ratings of Instructors* (Lansing, Mich.: Office of Educational Services, Michigan State University, 1968). (ED 021 527)
5. C. L. Overturf, *Student Rating of Faculty at St. Johns River Junior College, with Addendum for Albany Junior College* (Palatka, Fla.: St. Johns River Junior College, 1966). (ED 013 066)
6. Naomi Fitch, *Evaluation of Instructors in California Junior Colleges* (Berkeley, Calif.: University of California, 1965). (ED 014 959)
7. Gordon Kilpatrick, *Another Look at Teacher Evaluation in American Junior Colleges* (Torrance, Calif.: El Camino College, 1967). (ED 020 720)
8. See note 4 above.
9. See note 2 above.

10. Rita Schmidt, ed., *Insight: A View of the Faculty Through the Eyes of Their Students* (San Marcos, Calif.: Palomar College, 1968). (ED 023 405)

11. *Instructor Rating Scale Study, Orange Coast College, Fall Semester, 1968* (Costa Mesa, Calif.: Orange Coast Junior College, 1968). (ED 028 775)

12. See note 5 above.

13. John E. Anderson, "The Auto-Critique Method of Instructional Evaluation," *Proceedings of the Fourth Junior College Administrative Teams Institute* (Pensacola, Florida, July 1964). (ED 013 634)

14. Arthur M. Cohen and Florence B. Brawer, *Measuring Faculty Performance*, Monograph No. 4 (Washington, D.C.: American Association of Junior Colleges, 1969). (ED 031 222)

15. Jack W. Israel, "Innovation in Evaluation: Teacher Assessment by Objectives," seminar paper, Los Angeles, University of California, 1969. (ED 029 625)

16. See note 14 above.

EDRS supplies copies of ERIC REPORTS in two forms:

1. Microfiche—4″ × 6″ sheet of microfilm on which up to 70 pages of text are reproduced
2. Hard copy—reproduction of the document on paper at the original size

To facilitate rapid turn-around for priority requests, a "walk-in" order service is available at the EDRS facility:

Leasco Information Products, Inc.
4827 Rugby Avenue
Bethesda, Maryland 20014

Authors

"Accountability Defined," by Marvin C. Alkin, Associate Professor at the Graduate School of Education, UCLA. Dr. Alkin is Director of the Center for the Study of Evaluation.

"Accountability for Student Learning," by John E. Roueche, Professor of Junior College Education at the University of Texas at Austin, where he is Director of the Community College Leadership Program.

10 Accountability

During the 1970s, accountability has rapidly become the "in" word in education. Students have always been accountable. Now that some colleges are agreeing to share with students the responsibility for student learning, decisions must be made in regard to different aspects of accountability—goals, program, and outcome. If colleges are to be judged not by what they promise, but by how students perform, answers must be found to the question, "Who is accountable to whom and for what?"

After completing this unit, you should be able to

1 construct, by drawing on the several definitions of accountability suggested, your own definition of educational accountability (Alkin)

2 state the three types of educational accountability outlined and for each type discuss who is accountable, to whom, and for what (Alkin)

3 relate various accountability schemes (e.g., voucher plan, external performance contracting, internal performance contracting) to the accountability types to which they are addressed (Alkin)

4 define accountability and describe its application to education (Alkin, Roueche)

5 discuss necessary ingredients of individualized learning that make professional accountability possible (Roueche)

6 justify the need for accountability as a means of fulfilling the promise of the open-door college (Roueche)

It is oversimplistic to say that schools are accountable or they are not. Different areas of participation and negotiated responsibility suggest the need to consider different accountability "types." In this article we propose to view accountability as composed of three types: goal accountability, program accountability, and outcome accountability. These derive from an attempt to answer the question "Who is accountable to whom and for what?"

Introduction

The public has lost faith in educational institutions. Traditional acceptance of educational programs on the basis of their past performance and apparent but unsubstantiated worth is no longer the rule. The public has demanded that schools demonstrate that resources are being utilized "properly." But this has meant far more than mere financial accounting to ensure that funds have not been illegally spent or embezzled. What is demanded instead is that schools demonstrate that the outcomes they are producing are worth the dollar investment provided by communities. In short, what has been called for is a system of "educational accountability."

But educational accountability is very much like other abstract virtues such as patriotism and truthfulness which are universally acknowledged but not amenable to facile description. Lack of adequate description has been one of the major shortcomings of accountability. The reader investigating the subject for the first time becomes immediately inundated with a plethora of views, schemes, mechanisms—and, for that matter, a multitude of definitions.

To say that discussion of accountability has been confusing and that definitions of accountability have been amorphous and imprecise is to understate the problem. Barro [1] says that the basic premise of accountability is that "professional education should be held responsible for educational outcomes—for what children learn." Many teachers and teacher organizations have a negative connotation such as "it is for punishment." Some school administrators feel accountability can be used to eliminate some of the "deadwood" in teaching. Boards of trustees frequently feel the same way about eliminating the "deadwood" and "overstaffing" in administration. Some economists view accountability as a panacean information system that will cure educational ills by ensuring the wisest allocation of scarce resources. To many people, then, *accountability* is the answer. It is "in," however, in a variety of ways for different kinds of proponents.

Accountability Defined

Marvin C. Alkin

Popham [2] asserts that "educational accountability means that the instructional system designer takes responsibility for achieving the kinds of instructional objectives previously explicated." Lopez [3] casts the definition in a social context: "Accountability refers to the process of expecting each member of an organization to answer to someone for doing specific things according to specific plans and against certain timetables to accomplish tangible performance results." Lieberman [4] asserts that the objective of accountability is to relate results to resources and efforts in ways useful for policy making, resource allocation, or compensation.

Smith [5] suggests three kinds of accountability: program accountability, process accountability, and fiscal accountability. *Program* accountability is concerned with the quality of the work carried on and whether or not it met the goals set for it. *Process* accountability asks whether the procedures used to perform the research (teaching) were adequate in terms of the time and effort spent on the work, and whether the experiments (lessons) were carried out as promised. *Fiscal* accountability has to do with whether items purchased were used for the project, program, etc.

Lessinger [6] has said, "Accountability is the product of a process; at its most basic level, it means that an agent, public or private, entering into a contractual agreement to perform a service will be answerable for performing according to agreed-upon terms, within an established time period, and with a stipulated use of resources and performance standards."

In this paper we will tentatively settle on a definition of accountability: **Definition** Accountability is a negotiated relationship in which the participants agree in advance to accept specified rewards and costs on the basis of evaluation findings as to the attainment of specified ends.

The essence of this definition is that a negotiated relationship exists in which each of the participants agree in advance as to the criteria (evaluation findings) that will be used to determine acceptability. Furthermore, the level of attainment on these criteria in order to achieve acceptability is pre-specified. Finally, the negotiants stipulate a set of rewards and penalties that will attach to compliance/noncompliance.

At the heart of all of the above elements is the concept of "negotiation." Negotiation, for example, is suggested in the kind of dialog that leads to mutual acceptance of a position, or in the acceptance of a negotiated, specified end. Negotiation frequently involves the allowable constraints, such as the students to be worked with and the instructional materials to be utilized. One major form of negotiated relationship, although not the only one, is the written contract. A contractual agreement will specify the locus of problem solving and areas of responsibility between the negotiants. To establish these relationships, a contract will provide with utmost explicitness and clarity, a set of stated constraints; the negotiated ends in light of the constraints; designation of responsibility in terms of who is responsible for what, to whom, and when; criteria for judging attainment of ends;

specification of the rewards and costs to include payment and penalty schedules.

Before such contractual explicitness can be achieved in terms of relationships between negotiants in a system of accountability, we must first address some contextual considerations and discuss the major segments within that context. Without such specification it is virtually impossible to adequately address the locus of problem solving and areas of responsibility in any manageable form.

We view the three major segments of the accountability context as (1) goals and objectives, (2) programs, (3) program outcomes. A system of accountability can be functional only in educational institutions that have clearly defined goals and objectives. These goals and objectives derive from interactions with various constituencies whose views are thought to be relevant and whose priorities are reflected in the specified outcomes. For these objectives, which in turn are related to the broader goals, there are specific, clearly defined, and validated instructional programs or strategies. The instructional programs or strategies have been validated to the extent that there are specific product specifications demonstrating the success of the programs relative to the stated objectives of the program for various kinds of population groups, one of whom is the group for which it will be employed. A further element of this context is a specific procedure for measuring the program's outcome in terms of the stipulated objectives. To the extent that the school context approaches such a rational effort, it is possible to have an accountability system.

Three Types of Accountability

Part of the differing conceptions of accountability undoubtedly stem from our insistence that accountability is unidimensional. It is oversimplistic to say that schools are accountable or they are not. For each area of the context there can be different role participants. Different areas of participation and responsibility suggest the need to consider different accountability "types;" the three components outlined above suggest that there are perhaps three types of accountability.

We propose to designate the three types of accountability as *goal accountability, program accountability,* and *outcome accountability.* These three accountability types derive from an attempt to answer the question "Who is accountable to whom and for what?" When this question is considered with respect to the context areas listed above, we note that different participants are involved on various occasions.

Goal Accountability

The first area to be considered is *goal accountability.* School boards are accountable (or should be) to the public for everything that they do. But the foundation of this accountability relationship is in educational goals. School boards are accountable to the public for the proper selection of goals. After all, school boards are legally supposed to function as the lay group expressing the desires and wishes of a broader constituency as to what should be the goals and objectives of the educational program. This determination is clearly within the domain of the public's review responsibility. In goal accountability, school boards are accountable to the public for ensuring that the proper goals and objectives are being pursued.

After goals and objectives are selected, responsibility rests somewhere for the selection of instructional strategies deemed most effective for achieving the stipulated goals and objectives. This responsibility for *program accountability* rests generally with the school administration and other school personnel designated by administration. If we conceive of the teachers as being program operators and intend to hold them accountable for the outcomes of their activities, then clearly they may only be held accountable within the constraints of the programs with which they have been provided. The responsibility for program accountability rests with administrators and other members of the professional staff engaged in the process of program selection, modification, and adoption.

Program Accountability

In program accountability, these administrators and other district personnel—though again ultimately responsible to the public—are specifically accountable to the school board for maintaining a program that is appropriate for meeting a set of stipulated objectives. We cannot hold a machine operator responsible for his products until we have demonstrated that the machine he has been provided with has the capability for producing that outcome. We cannot expect a printing-press operator to produce 100 copies a minute on a machine whose maximum output is 50 copies per minute. We cannot expect a racetrack driver to push 300 miles an hour out of an automobile whose limit is far below that standard.

If we are to follow this line of argument to its logical conclusion, then clearly producers of program components (let us refer to these as instructional products) must be held accountable for the products they produce. This is an area of accountability about which we have heard very little. While there is considerable demand that the classroom teacher be accountable, where is the outcry for accountability on the part of textbook producers? Who demands that producers of filmstrips, films, and supplemental materials present the specifications of their products in terms of outcomes that may be anticipated?

As part of the standards implied in program accountability, a demand should be placed on those to be held accountable for instructional programs that the producible program outcomes be stipulated in terms of the various sets of constraints and the varying inputs that might be encountered. That is, one cannot merely stipulate, without a considerable loss of accuracy in description, that a given product will produce objectives A, B, and C at a given level of achievement. It is also necessary to indicate what the expectations would be for different characteristics of student inputs (for different student groups). This is similar to the example previously discussed in which a printing-press operator might be expected to produce 100 copies a minute on a given machine. It is important in that example to consider such things as the quality and weight of the paper to be used, color of the ink, type of master plate, etc. In the race car example it is necessary to be aware of the performance standards for different kinds of roads and weather conditions. Similarly, in educational accountability it is important to have an indication of the performance standards for each program in terms of a variety of input constraints.

With respect to program accountability a difficult and confused area is the role of teachers in, and as a part of, instructional programs. The confusion is amply demonstrated by the diverse views as to what is meant by "teacher accountability." For example, there are those who maintain that teacher accountability is determined on the basis of input standards for teachers. That is, a teacher is accountable if he demonstrates that he is an able teacher in terms of his ability to teach and by satisfactory application of his skills in terms of the amount of effort put forth on his job. This view of the teacher's role basically considers the teacher as a program component, a part of the instructional program. Under such a definition of teacher accountability one merely looks at teachers as a potential input or program component. Here teacher accountability is judged in the same way that a textbook, film, or a filmstrip is considered; the accountability task under such a viewpoint is to ensure the quality of the teacher input. Thus, we may use teacher-performance tests as a basis for determining whether teachers participating in the program meet a standard of accountability in terms of their ability to teach.

Within this same definition of the role of teachers, but beyond certification of teacher-input quality, there is a further consideration of the accountability task. This area of accountability responsibility relates to the proper utilization of teacher input. That is, accountability requirements demand that there be an assurance that the inputs (teachers) are working an appropriate number of hours using those skills considered to be appropriate. The notion of teachers *as part of* instructional programs requires accountability examination in terms of input and process evaluation.

Outcome Accountability
A second view of teacher accountability is one in which the teacher is urged to be responsible for the quality of student outputs. In this view the teacher is considered as an instructional manager utilizing a program whose capabilities have already been determined. Here the teacher is held responsible for the outcomes of his management of that program. This type of accountability we will refer to as *outcome accountability*....

In outcome accountability, an instructional leader (usually a teacher) is accountable to administration for specified pupil outcomes thought to be a function of teacher management of the instructional program. That is, a teacher manages an instructional program which has certain product capabilities; the job is to determine whether the teacher has managed the program in such a way as to achieve standards or criteria that might be expected from the program.

We have previously said, however, that teachers may only be held accountable within the constraints of the program with which they have been provided. There are those who would maintain, however, that the accountability concern should not focus upon these constraints since the teacher, to a great extent, *is* the program. In this light, in terms of financial outlay for program operation, those costs incurred directly by the teacher amount to the major portion of the available budget. Further, there is sufficient evidence that program constraints have minimal impact upon student outcomes. One would not deny that the teacher incurs the greatest amount of cost in program operation or that program constraints have only a small effect. Yet teachers do work with constraints, such as type of students, kind of text, size of classroom, etc. Though the effects of these constraints may be small, they do, to varying degrees, affect the management of the program and to that extent must be considered in outcome accountability.

We have already discussed three major accountability types (goal, program, and outcome) and have indicated a response for each relative to the question, "Who is accountable to whom and for what?" A summary description of each of these types, along with three sets of factors, is presented in the chart: (1) who is accountable—the specific individual or group bearing the responsibility; (2) to whom—the individual or group demanding accountability, (3) for what—specific tasks required.

Accountability Types: Summary

Accountability Types

	Who Is Accountable	To Whom (Primary Responsibility)	For What
Goal Accountability	School Board	Public	Goal and Objective Selection
Program Accountability	School District Management	School Board	Development and/or Selection of Instructional Programs Appropriate for Stated Objectives
Outcome Accountability	Instructional Manager (i.e., Teacher)	School District Management	Producing Program Outcomes Consistent with Preselected Objectives at a Performance Standard Appropriate for the Instructional Program

**Implications of
Various Accountability
Schemes**

A number of schemes have been noted in the literature for achieving greater accountability in schools. Many of these, such as the voucher plan or performance contracting, have been thought of as almost synonymous with accountability. It is important to recognize, however, that these accountability schemes cannot be understood properly without considering to which accountability types they are addressed (e.g., goal accountability, program accountability, outcome accountability) and how they fit within the accountability context previously described.

We will consider three accountability schemes that are fairly exemplary of the kinds of proposals presently made and which cover a broad range of accountability types. These three schemes are the voucher plan, performance contracting with an external contractor, and performance contracting with a teacher.

Under the voucher plan the school passes on the responsibility for all three kinds of accountability. By giving fund grants directly to parents for their expenditure on a program of their own choosing, the school is in essence relieving itself of the full accountability responsibility. No longer must schools be accountable for goals, because parents with funds in hand will choose educational institutions or programs having goals compatible with their preferences. By such a choice parents and not public schools will be holding their own contractor responsible for both program and outcome accountability. Thus the voucher plan represents a complete irresponsibility on the part of public schools in terms of accountability.

Under performance contracting with an external contractor, while the school retains the responsibility for goal accountability the contractor becomes responsible for program and outcome accountability. In essence, appropriate goals have been decided upon for a program; the school has consulted with various constituencies about the relevance of various goal areas and has selected a goal or set of goals most worthy of consideration. The external performance contractor is held responsible for the creation of a program to meet these goals as well as for the implementation and management of that program. That is, the external contractor must show both program and outcome accountability. If the community complains about the program and feels that the schools have not achieved the desired outcomes, it is the responsibility of the external contractor; he has obviously failed to do his job. The only way the school can be held accountable is if there is criticism that the goals pursued are incorrect or inappropriate.

In a system of performance contracting in which the teacher rather than the external contractor is the instructional manager, the school delegates the responsibility only of outcome accountability. That is, the goals have been determined within the school; the program has been determined within the school, including a specification of its capabilities, and the teacher as an instructional manager is to be held accountable for program outcomes. If the teacher is unable to attain educational outcomes equal to a prespecified standard, and that standard is considered appropriate for the given program and students, then it is the teacher who is held accountable. On the other hand, if there is a question about the adequacy of the program itself for achieving the specified goals and objectives, then the school itself (or the school administration) is found short on the accountability criteria.

What we have demonstrated is that there are three types of accountability and there are various schemes that have been presented whereby different agencies or individuals take the responsibility for various types of accountability. In developing a total accountability program, apparently the first decision to be made is the locus of the responsibility for each of the three accountability types.

Notes

1. S. M. Barro, "An Approach to Developing Accountability Measures for the Public Schools," *Phi Delta Kappan* 52 (1970): 196–205.
2. W. J. Popham, "Instructional Objectives Exchange, 1960–1970." CSE Reprint No. 19 (Los Angeles: University of California, Center for the Study of Evaluation, 1970).
3. F. M. Lopez, "Accountability in Education," *Phi Delta Kappan* 52 (1970): 231–235.
4. M. Lieberman, "An Overview of Accountability," *Phi Delta Kappan* 52 (1970): 194–195.
5. Bruce L. R. Smith, "Accountability and Independence in the Contract State," in *The Dilemma of Accountability in Modern Government: Independence vs. Control,* edited by Bruce L. R. Smith and D. C. Hague. (New York: St. Martin's Press, 1971).
6. L. Lessinger, "Engineering Accountability for Results in Public Education," *Phi Delta Kappan* 52 (1970): 217–225.

**Definition of
Accountability**

The word *accountability* embraces several degrees and kinds of meaning depending upon the area where attention is focused within the educational spectrum. Innovators are likely to consider it a promising idea with profound implications for the academic world. It may seem threatening and unreasonable to other educators who are reluctant to accept responsibility for academically inept and poorly motivated students. Disillusioned clients of education might view it as just another platitude because they have been conditioned to judge promises by the harsh reality of results.

Accountability is certainly far more than a glib term that elicits strong feelings in teachers. It is an operational concept grounded in the belief that public educational institutions exist to serve the communities that support them and must therefore shoulder responsibility for their students.

We should avoid the simplistic view of thinking about accountability in only one possible form, whether it be performance contracting, voucher plans, teachers' merit salaries, or what-have-you. The core meaning, or common dimension, in all manifestations of accountability is an emphasis upon the educational results achieved for the resources used. Accountability aims squarely at what comes out of an education system. It requires clear definitions of objectives in terms so operational and definite that it is possible to evaluate or measure the extent to which they are being achieved. If educational institutions exist primarily to cause learning, then educators should scrutinize the results of their efforts by determining how well students are being taught. Accountability suggests that educators at all levels be held functionally responsible for those educational outputs they are able to effect. In a broad sense accountability means that the entire institutional body, including the board, the president, the administration, and the teachers are responsible for the performance of their students.

**Forces Bringing
Accountability About**

The contention that accountability is an idea whose time has come is substantiated by the fact that the 1971 annual convention of the American Association of Junior Colleges selected accountability as its theme. Federal

Accountability
for Student Learning

John E. Roueche

emphasis on accountability can be seen in the requirement that projects funded under Titles VII and VIII of the Elementary and Secondary Education Act produce predictable and measurable results that can be certified by independent audit. The public education systems' accelerating costs and declining performance levels have generated serious misgivings and led to demands that expenses be linked to results. Disenchanted taxpayers throughout the nation have rejected numerous school-bond issues, while elected officials at all government levels have responded to voter pressures by adopting a hard line in questioning education's effectiveness.

Although billions of dollars have been spent on compensatory education, the poor academic performance of disadvantaged students enrolled in these programs evidences education's apparent inability to meet the needs of increasingly large numbers of citizens. There has been a growing realization that equality cannot be achieved educationally by exposing students from widely disparate cultural and socioeconomic backgrounds to identical schooling. Equal opportunity can be realized only by obtaining equity of results. Each student must be seen as a unique individual and accepted at whatever academic level he may have reached. He then requires individual attention, rather than common exposure, if he is ever to have an equal opportunity to attain specified educational results. The fact that equal opportunity can be judged only by results means that educational institutions must be held accountable and evaluated by how well they perform in causing equality of student learning, rather than by what they promise to do and how they use their resources.

Public education's failure to respond to society's needs contributed to the performance-contract phenomenon. The idea is simple. A private company (presumably free to be more innovative than a public institution) contracts with a school system to run a learning program. The company guarantees that students will reach certain objectives in a specified time period. The fee the company receives is based upon how well the students are able to perform. Private industry's penetration in Texarkana of the multibillion-dollar public education system started a nationwide trend as major cities seeking low-cost dropout prevention followed the performance-contract example. More than 30 performance contracts were federally funded in 1970. Last year the OEO invested over $5½ million to test performance contracting in 18 different districts.

Today the public education system is experiencing the most prolonged and profound challenge ever to confront it. Current national conditions have created forces that virtually demand the application of accountability to education.

The National Need for Accountability

Who can deny that the failures of the education system contribute to social discord and violence?

Every year, more than one million of this nation's young people are condemned to live nonproductive lives because they either drop out of school or graduate without the knowledge and skills necessary to participate effectively in a complex and competitive society. In poverty-stricken urban areas, dropout rates reach 70 percent. While governmental education expenditures exceed $65 billion a year and dollar costs per student year have nearly doubled in the past decade, there are an estimated 15 million functionally illiterate students in this country. In one year, one-third of the youth who failed the Armed Forces Qualification Test had high-school diplomas; yet, that test is based upon fifth- and sixth-grade levels of reading and mathematics.

Educational opportunity is too often limited to that class of students who view higher education as a normal part of growing up. Vital human talents are wasted because of geographic and financial barriers to postsecondary education as well as elitist attitudes that brand academically deficient and nontraditional students "undesirables," even though they need education desperately. Although junior/community colleges should be conceiving more imaginative programs to extend educational opportunity to all citizens, their performance generally falls far short of expectations. Most junior colleges advocate an "open door" policy, yet few are faithful to that promise. Equal opportunity in the community college is more often slogan than fact. The large majority of students who enroll in remedial courses fail to complete those courses satisfactorily and are doomed to failure or even forced to terminate their education. Typically alarming attrition rates are not sterile statistics. They reflect the extinguished hopes of disadvantaged young people who believed that the "open door" offered them a chance.

Associate Commissioner for Education Don Davies expressed these thoughts with the words:

Every citizen pays a price in money, in uncertainty, in fear, and in social problems for the school failures, the dropouts, the undereducated. The price we pay as a nation is so heavy that we are forced to move or to face disaster. [1]

Accountability and Individualized Instruction

The contemporary junior/community college is a multiphase institution with a unique potential for meeting national education requirements. Its reason to exist originated in, and continues to hinge upon, societal demands to fulfill broad educational needs that have been ignored by narrowly oriented traditional institutions. The two-year college movement is marked by a positive philosophy, a social thrust, and a practical style. It is committed to the ideals that universal higher education rightfully should be available to anyone who can profit from it and that educational accessibility should be extended to all people through "open door" admissions.

Two-year colleges, situated within commuting distance of potential students, charging modest fees, and offering a multidimensional curriculum remove many barriers to higher education. Their philosophy of equal educational opportunity for all abilities, classes, interests, and ages results in a nontraditional student body drawn largely from the lower two-thirds of the socioeconomic spectrum. Many students are disadvantaged to the degree that their backgrounds have failed to provide cultural experiences generally found in young people that colleges are accustomed to teaching.

Accountability is particularly applicable to open-door two-year colleges because they contain a variety of students from diverse educational backgrounds. Equal opportunity for these groups will never be realized without drastic changes in traditional methods of instruction.

Recently, we have begun to question many long-accepted instructional procedures (the lecture methods; the predetermined amount of material to be covered in a given period of time; the excessive reliance upon books as a learning resource, to the neglect of other media; the organization of learning activities into academic years; semester-hours' credits, and grade-point averages). It has become apparent that all of these constitute a restrictive approach to the learning process. Many commonly accepted instructional methods must be changed if the concern for student learning implicit in the promise of the open door is to be realized. Assigning a grade of F to an academically inept student will not cause him to learn. Traditional procedures, such as norm-referenced testing and curve-based grading, cannot be used as relevant measures of academic performance in an open-door college because these procedures assume that all will not succeed.

Learning-oriented instruction must become the hallmark of junior colleges. Teachers' lectures cannot be considered synonymous with student learning if the needs of typically heterogeneous student bodies are to be accommodated. Individualized approaches must allow for students who learn best by seeing and doing rather than by hearing and reading. Since junior colleges are primarily teaching institutions, they should adopt approaches to instruction that stress student learning. They should try new programs and methods that allow for the fact that some students learn faster than others. Given the diversity of student capabilities in the typical junior-college classroom, it makes little sense to establish verbal learning in rigid time frames as the standard against which all must be measured. The lecture and textbook approach requires a high level of verbal ability and reading comprehension that is lacking in academically disadvantaged students.

Equal opportunity is fundamentally a commitment to equity of results according to individual capabilities and interests. This implies that junior college faculties must be held accountable for individually prescribed and measured student learning.

Research has shown that specifying learning objectives in precise terms and using well-organized, self-paced instructional sequences to reach those objectives can guarantee learning for up to 95 percent of all students. When specific objectives are established, teachers can be held accountable for students who are able to show learning by functioning in ways that were not possible before teaching took place. Learning is the only valid indication of teaching and can be construed further as a change in behavior. Instructional accountability is based on specifically defined objectives, measurement techniques that determine precisely what the teacher intends to accomplish, and instructional systems that insure that most students will achieve the objectives. The basic ingredients to this approach include:

1. individual examination and diagnosis in order to make allowances for individual learning rates
2. student participation in selecting course objectives, content, and instructional methods in order to increase student interest and motivation, and to insure that content is relevant to student needs
3. giving students specific, measurable course objectives describing how each goal is to be reached, the student action required, the conditions of performance, and the minimum-performance criterion
4. flexible time frames to allow each student to progress at his own rate
5. nonpunitive grading because research has shown that 95 percent of all students may achieve mastery (noncompetitive, because students compete only against themselves)
6. utilization of audiovisuals and other media selected on the basis of their potential to cause learning

This scientific, individualized approach to learning provides teachers with an opportunity to be the true professional—to become accountable for achieving equity of educational results.

Will Accountability Work in Two-Year Colleges?

The ideals of accountability and equal opportunity require drastic changes in traditional educational attitudes. Quite honestly, many instructors believe that students who fail simply cannot learn because they are hopelessly below any significant level of academic achievement. They place the major blame for failure on the student without questioning their own methods, philosophy, and criteria.

Faculty members in junior colleges sometimes are not prepared to teach in accordance with the unique philosophy of that institution. They may be academically inclined subject-matter specialists who think in terms of their own graduate-school experience. Some prefer dispensing specialized knowledge to advanced students rather than teaching remedial courses. Other teachers may not agree with the philosophy or the open-admissions policy of the two-year college movement. These misplaced faculty members fail to understand that an instructor is worth only as much as he contributes to the purposes of the institution.

Self-serving, elitist attitudes do not belong in a junior-college movement that has been blessed with a democratic heritage expressed in the philosophy of the open door. The primary function of a junior-college instructor is to teach. He must be committed to that role and specialize in instructional processes.

Students have traditionally been held responsible through tests and recitations for whatever they may or may not have learned. Accountability shifts the emphasis of that responsibility from the student to the faculty, the administrators, and the governing officials of the college.

Active efforts to seek, enroll, and retain every possible student in the community are necessary if the two-year college movement is to extend greater educational opportunity to all citizens. But whatever is done to recruit the nontraditional student and provide him with a supportive environment is fruitless unless individual teachers become accountable for producing equal educational results. Instructors must understand the unique nature of the junior-college environment and become convinced that the disadvantaged are capable of learning.

The faculty may be the key element in effecting change, but teachers cannot be held accountable unless the total institution is dedicated to that end. A sincere endorsement of accountability must pervade all sectors of the college. Thus, while accountability is in one sense a primary responsibility of the junior-college teacher, in another sense the total institution is involved. Drastic changes in the attitudes of instructors, administrators, and governance officials are required if the "open door" is to become a fact rather than a slogan.

The effectiveness of any organization depends directly upon the quality of leadership exercised therein. Junior-college administrators must become educational leaders, not only by establishing policies and procedures that encourage and reward successful teachers, but by creating a climate where all college members are willing to be accountable. The college leadership must take upon itself responsibility for establishing institutional styles that make the college accountable externally to the community and internally to the students from the community.

Educational Leadership and Accountability

The strategic focus within a college is vested with the president. When he assumes the role of educational leader in the areas of instruction, administration, student services, finance, and community support, he can create an atmosphere conducive to accountability. Rather than becoming polarized into opposite camps, administrators and faculty members should be welded into one team through the leadership of the college president. Junior-college instructors can become effective teachers. Faculty members and administrators must work together to change their institutions into places where learning happens. When a community college does not fulfill its mission, teachers cannot be blamed for (or remedy) failure that may have originated in faulty organization and leadership. Teachers cannot be accountable unless the concept of accountability permeates the entire spectrum of institutional responsibility.

Junior-college leaders must keep abreast of change in an uncertain world and exercise their potential power for dynamic supervision. Change may bring trauma, but change is inevitable. Innovation does not necessarily mean excellence, and we should avoid change for the sake of change. However, the goals and mission of an institution constitute its reason to exist. Consequently, educational leaders must continually ask themselves task-oriented questions. Is the college accomplishing its mission? Are its goals up-to-date? Are its objectives being achieved? If not, what changes are needed to get back on target? Change should be approached with a task-oriented team concept that broadens the base of leadership by involving all members in a common effort to define and meet organizational objectives.

It is people and relationships, not mechanisms and systems, that enable institutions to attain their goals. People generally have a drive toward growth and self-realization that can be fulfilled through work, challenge, and responsibility. They expect recognition as well as satisfaction of personal relationships. They are able to become flexible and responsive when their personal goals closely coincide with their institutional goals; when they feel a common identification; and when they have confidence in their ability to influence their environment. Participation in a team effort to define the school's goals within a concept of accountability and to establish systematic programs to achieve them creates personal commitment through mutually derived objectives. Obstacles, conflicts, and negative attitudes are overcome in a free interchange of ideas at all levels. Members develop mutual rapport and feel a sense of personal involvement in the school's mission. The participation of all members in decisions on common problems integrates the needs and desires of all into an effective system of interaction and mutual influence.

The role of a community-college president should be that of a leader who manages human and material resources through a well-balanced professional team using systematic strategies to achieve specific objectives. The leader is responsible for giving the team direction, coordination, and unity of purpose. He should clarify objectives, stimulate new ideas, reconcile divergent views, and help the team to move ahead. He should offer warm acceptance to individuals but must make clear that all members are accountable for achieving institutional objectives. The junior-college leader should accept the obligation of giving direction instead of merely ministering to organizational equilibrium. Task-oriented, dynamic leadership, coupled with strong team identification and group participation, will enable junior-college educators to change their attitudes, renew their creativity, and become accountable.

The right to control the processes of our schools rests upon a willingness to meet the needs of public clients. Governance is based on responsibility, and responsibility implies accountability. The entire college body, including the board, the president, the administration, the students, and the instructors must become accountable to the community served by the college.

Conclusion

We have already entered what Lessinger calls the age of accountability in education and are obliged to see that the needs of our clients are met by making education answerable to all groups within our society. Rather than respond defensively by considering accountability a threat, we should accept it positively as a professional responsibility and a commonly accepted ethic that we expect from many other professions.

Accountability is a privilege—not a burden. It calls forth the best within us. It challenges us to examine our purposes, to find better ways to make education responsible to the society that pays the bills. In the words of Commissioner Davies, "It holds equal promise for all of education's clients, those who come to school well prepared to share its benefits, and those who have nothing in their backgrounds that would equip them for a successful learning experience." [2]

1. Donald Davies, "The Relevance of Accountability," *The School Administrator* (April 1970): p. 1.
2. Ibid.

Notes

Alker, Hayward R., Jr. "Statistics and Politics: The Need for Causal Data Analysis." Paper presented at the annual meeting of the American Political Science Association, Chicago, September 1967.

———. "Causal Inference and Political Analysis." In *Mathematical Applications in Political Science*, edited by Joseph L. Bernd, vol. 2. Dallas, Tex.: Arnold Foundation, Southern Methodist University, 1968.

Alkin, Marvin C. "Products for Improving Educational Evaluation." *Evaluation Comment* 2 (1970).

Anderson, C. C., and S. M. Hunka. "Teacher Evaluation: Some Problems and a Proposal." *Harvard Educational Review* 33 (1963): 74–96.

Anderson, E. C. "Promoting Career Information–Seeking Through Group Counselor's Cues and Reinforcements." Ph.D. dissertation, University of California, Los Angeles, 1970.

Anderson, John E. "The Auto-Critique Method of Instructional Evaluation." *Proceedings of the Fourth Junior College Administrative Teams Institute*. Pensacola, Fla., July 1964. (ED 013 634)

Apuzzo, M. Pauline. *Summary Report on the Sixth Annual Conference on the Nature and Demands of Two-Year College*. Millbrook, N. Y.: Bennett College, 1968.

Atkinson, Richard C. "Computerized Instruction and the Learning Process." Technical Report No. 122. Stanford, Calif.: Institute for Mathematical Studies in the Social Sciences, 1967.

Ausubel, David P. *Educational Psychology: A Cognitive View*. New York: Holt, Rinehart and Winston, 1968.

Bannister, John et al. "Evaluating College Teaching." *Curriculum Reporter Supplement* (December 1961). (ED 022 450)

Barro, S. M. "An Approach to Developing Accountability Measures for the Public Schools." *Phi Delta Kappan* 52 (1970): 196–205.

Bartlett, W. H. "The Practical Application of Psychological Facts in the Classroom As Demonstrated by Teaching a Specific Study Method to Elementary Algebra Students of the Junior College Level." Master's thesis, University of California, Los Angeles, 1960.

Blalock, Hubert M., Jr. *Causal Inferences in Nonexperimental Research*. Chapel Hill, N. C.: University of North Carolina Press, 1964.

Blocker, Clyde E. et al. *The Two-Year College: A Social Synthesis*. Englewood Cliffs, N. J.: Prentice-Hall, 1965.

Bloom, Benjamin S. *Stability and Change in Human Characteristics*. New York: Wiley & Sons, 1964.

Bloom, Benjamin S., ed. *Taxonomy of Educational Objectives: Handbook I: Cognitive Domain*. New York: David McKay, 1956.

Boudon, Raymond. "Methodes d'analyse causale." *Revue française de sociologie* 6 (1965): 24–43.

Bowman, M. J. "The New Economics of Education." *International Journal of Educational Sciences* 1 (1966): 29–46.

Broadbent, L. A. "The Effects of Two Different Belief Systems on the Perceptions of Two Experimental Modes of Counseling." Ph.D. dissertation, University of California, Los Angeles, 1968.

Bibliography

Bruner, Jerome S. *The Process of Education*. Cambridge, Mass.: Harvard University Press, 1961.

————. *Toward a Theory of Instruction*. Cambridge, Mass.: Harvard University Press, 1966.

Bruner, Jerome S., and A. L. Minturn. "Perceptual Identification and Perceptual Organization." *Journal of Genetic Psychology* 53 (1955): 21–28.

Canavan, Donnah. "Development of Individual Differences in the Perception of Value and Risking-Taking Styles." Ph.D. dissertation, Columbia University, n.d.

Carroll, John. "A Model of School Learning." *Teachers College Record* 64 (1963): 723–733.

Cohen, Arthur M., and Florence Brawer. *Measuring Faculty Performance*, Monograph No. 4. Washington, D.C.: American Association of Junior Colleges, 1969. (ED 031 222)

Conant, J. B. *Education and Liberty*. Cambridge, Mass.: Harvard University Press, 1953.

Congreve, W. J. "Independent Learning." *North Central Association Quarterly* 40 (1965): 222–228.

Coulson, John. "Automation, Electronic Computers, and Education." *Phi Delta Kappan* 47 (March 1966): 310–311.

Cronbach, Lee J. *Essentials of Psychological Testing*. 2d ed. New York: Harper, 1960.

————. "Evaluation for Course Improvement." *Teachers College Record* 64 (1963): 672–683.

————. "The Two Disciplines of Scientific Psychology." *American Psychologist* 12 (1957): 671–684.

Cronbach, Lee J. and G. C. Gleser. *Psychological Tests and Personnel Decisions*. 2d ed. Urbana, Ill.: University of Illinois Press, 1965.

Dave, R. H. "The Identification and Measurement of Environmental Process Variables That Are Related to Educational Achievement." Ph.D. dissertation, University of Chicago, 1963.

Douglass, Paul. *Teaching for Self-Education As a Life Goal*. New York: Harper, 1960.

Duncan, Otis D. "Path Analysis: Sociological Examples." *American Journal of Sociology* 72 (1966): 1–16.

Ebel, R. L. *Measuring Educational Achievement*. Englewood Cliffs, N. J.: Prentice-Hall, 1965.

Fitch, Naomi. *Evaluation of Instructors in California Junior Colleges*. Berkeley, Calif.: University of California, 1965. (ED 014 959)

Frymier, Jack R. *The Nature of Educational Method*. Columbus, Ohio: Charles E. Merrill, 1965.

Gagné, Robert M. *The Conditions of Learning*. New York: Holt, Rinehart and Winston, 1965.

————. "The Analysis of Instructional Objectives for the Design of Instruction." In *Teaching Machines and Programed Learning*, edited by R. Glaser. Washington, D.C.: National Education Association, 1965.

Garrison, Roger H. *Junior College Faculty: Issues and Problems, Preliminary National Appraisal*. Washington, D.C.: American Association of Junior Colleges, 1967. (ED 012 177)

Glaser, Robert. "Adapting the Elementary School Curriculum to Individual Performance." *Proceedings of the 1967 Invitational Conference on Testing Problems*. Princeton, N. J.: Educational Testing Service, 1968.

———. "Instructional Technology and the Measurement of Learning Outcomes." *American Psychology* 18 (1963): 514–521.

Goldberg, A. S. "Discerning a Causal Pattern among Data on Voting Behavior." *American Political Science Review* 60 (1966): 913–922.

Goodlad, John I., and R. H. Anderson. *The Nongraded Elementary School*. New York: Harcourt Brace, 1959.

Guilford, J. P. *The Nature of Human Intelligence*. New York: McGraw-Hill, 1967.

Guttman, L. "A Basis for Scaling Qualitative Ideas." *American Sociological Review* 9 (1944): 139–150.

———. "Structure of Interrelationships among Intelligence Tests." *Proceedings of the 1964 Invitational Conference on Testing Problems*, pp. 25–36. Princeton, N. J.: Educational Testing Service, 1965.

Handbook: Cooperative Primary Tests. Princeton, N. J.: Educational Testing Service, 1967.

Hawkins, R. K. "Comparison of Three Experimental Modes of Counseling." Ph.D. dissertation, University of California, Los Angeles, 1967.

Heinberg, Sylvester. *Procedures for the Supervision and Evaluation of New Part-Time Evening-Division Instructors in California Junior College*. Ed.D. dissertation, University of Southern California, Los Angeles, 1968. (ED 019 958)

Hendrix, Vernon L. "Relationship Between Personnel Policies and Faculty Life-Record Data in Public Junior Colleges." *California Journal of Educational Research* 15 (May 1964). (ED 015 747)

Herrscher, Barton R. *Implementing Individualized Instruction*. Houston, Tex.: ArChem, 1971.

Himmelweit, Hilde, and Judy Wright. "The School System, Social Class, and Attainment after School." Paper presented at the Annual Conference of the British Psychological Society, 1967.

Hughes, Marie M. *A Research Report—Assessment of the Quality of Teaching in Elementary Schools*. Salt Lake City: University of Utah, 1959.

Hunt, Joseph M. *Intelligence and Experience*. New York: Ronald Press, 1961.

Husek, T. R., and K. Sirotnik. *Item Sampling in Educational Research*. Los Angeles: Center for the Study of Evaluation, 1967.

Husén, Torsten, ed. *International Study of Educational Achievement in Mathematics: A Comparison of Twelve Countries*, vols. 1, 2. New York: Wiley & Sons, 1967.

Israel, Jack W. "Innovation in Evaluation: Teacher Assessment by Objectives." Seminar paper, University of California, Los Angeles, 1969. (ED 029 625)

Jacob, Philip R. *Changing Values in College*. New York: Harper, 1957.

Johnson, Lamar. *General Education in Action*. Washington, D.C.: American Council on Education, 1952.

Kapfer, Philip G. "An Instructional Management Strategy for Individualized Learning." *Phi Delta Kappan* 49 (January 1968): 260–263.

Kapfer, Philip G., and Gardner Swenson. "Individualizing Instruction for Self-Paced Learning: A Commitment by the /I/D/E/A/ Materials Dissemination Center." *Clearing House* 42 (March 1968).

Kempthorne, O. et al., eds. *Statistics and Mathematics in Biology*. Ames, Ia.: Iowa State College Press, 1954.

Kilpatrick, Gordon. *Another Look at Teacher Evaluation in American Junior Colleges*. Torrance, Calif.: El Camino College, 1967. (ED 020 760)

Krathwohl, D. A. *Taxonomy of Educational Objectives: The Classification of Educational Goals. Handbook II: Affective Domain*. New York: David McKay, 1964.

Lazarsfeld, Paul F., ed. *Mathematical Thinking in the Social Sciences*. Glencoe, Ill.: Free Press, 1954.

Lessinger, L. "Engineering Accountability for Results in Public Education." *Phi Delta Kappan* 52 (1970): 217–225.

Lieberman, M. "An Overview of Accountability." *Phi Delta Kappan* 52 (1970): 194–195.

Linn, R. L., and D. A. Rock. "An Exploratory Study of Programmed Tests." *Educational and Psychological Measurement* 28 (1968): 345–360.

Lopez, F. M. "Accountability in Education." *Phi Delta Kappan* 52 (1970): 231–235.

Lord, Frederic M., and M. R. Novick. *Statistical Theories of Mental Test Scores*. Reading, Mass.: Addison-Wesley, 1968.

McNeil, Jan, and James E. Smith. "The Multi's at Nova." *Educational Screen and Audiovisual Guide* 47 (January 1968): 16–19, 43.

Mager, Robert F. *Preparing Instructional Objectives*. Belmont, Calif.: Fearon, 1962.

⸻. *Developing Attitudes Toward Learning*. Belmont, Calif.: Fearon, 1968.

Manual for Institutional Self-Study–Community Colleges, Technical Institutes, Industrial Education Centers. Raleigh, N. C.: Department of Community Colleges, State Board of Education, 1965. (ED 021 530)

Morin, Lloyd H. "A Feasible Scheme for the Evaluation of Instructors." Seminar paper, University of California, Los Angeles, 1968. (ED 024 361)

Morrison, Henry C. *The Practice of Teaching in the Secondary School*. Chicago: University of Chicago Press, 1926.

National Education Association, Research Division. *Evaluation of Classroom Teachers*. Research Report 1964–R14. Washington, D.C.: National Education Association, October 1964.

Neisser, U. "On Experimental Distinction Between Perceptual Process and Verbal Response." *Journal of Experimental Psychology* 47 (1954): 399–402.

Nunnaly, J. C. *Psychometric Theory*. New York: McGraw-Hill, 1967.

Overturf, C. L. *Student Rating of Faculty at St. Johns River Junior College, with Addendum for Albany Junior College*. Palatka, Fla.: St. Johns River Junior College, 1966. (ED 013 066)

Piel, Gerard. *Science in the Cause of Man*. New York: Random House, 1961.

Popham, W. James. "Instructional Objectives Exchange, 1960–1970." CSE Reprint No. 19. Los Angeles: Center for the Study of Evaluation, 1970.

⸻. *Modern Measurement Methods*. Filmstrip–tape program. Instructor's Manual. Los Angeles: VIMCET, 1969.

⸻. *The Teacher–Empiricist*. Los Angeles: Tinnon-Brown, 1970.

PROBE. *Instructional Objectives and Items Exchange*. Los Angeles: Center for the Study of Evaluation.

Quinn, J. B. "The Influence of Interpersonal Perception on the Process of Change in Two Experimental Modes of Counseling." Ph.D. dissertation, University of California, Los Angeles, 1970.

Rayder, Nicholas F. *College Student Ratings of Instructors*. Lansing, Mich.: Office of Educational Services, Michigan State University, 1968. (ED 021 527)

Reading Experience and Development Series Test. New York: American Book Company, 1969.

Rosenthal, Robert. *Experimenter Effects in Behavioral Research*. New York: Appleton-Century-Crofts, 1966.

Rosenthal, Robert, and Lenore Jacobson. *Pygmalion in the Classroom: Teacher Expectation and Pupil's Intellectual Ability*. New York: Holt, Rinehart and Winston, 1968.

Roueche, John E., and Allan S. Hurlburt. "Research on Junior College Teachers." *Junior College Research Review* 2 (March 1968). (ERIC Clearinghouse for Junior Colleges, University of California, Los Angeles, ED 021 540)

Roueche, John E., and John C. Pitman. *A Modest Proposal: Students Can Learn*. San Francisco: Jossey-Bass, 1972.

Rudolph, Frederick. *The American College and University*. New York: Vintage Books, 1962.

Ryans, David G. *Characteristics of Teachers*. Washington, D.C.: American Council on Education, 1960.

Schmidt, Rita, ed. *Insight: A View of the Faculty Through the Eyes of Their Students*. San Marcos, Calif.: Palomar College, 1968. (ED 023 405)

Schultz, Theodore W. *The Economic Value of Education*. New York: Columbia University Press, 1963.

Scriven, Michael. "The Methodology of Evaluation." *Perspectives of Curriculum Evaluation*, edited by R. Stake. Chicago: Rand McNally, 1967.

Selected Papers from the Annual Convention of the American Association of Junior Colleges. Washington, D.C.: American Association of Junior Colleges, 1966. (ED 016 448)

Simon, H. A. *Models of Man: Social and Rational*. New York: Wiley and Sons, 1957.

Simon, H. A., and N. Rescher. "Cause and Counterfactual." *Philosophy of Science* 33 (1966).

Sirotnik, K. *An Analysis of Variance Framework for Matrix Sampling*. CSE Report No. 52. Los Angeles: Center for the Study of Evaluation, 1969.

Skinner, B. F. "The Science of Learning and the Art of Teaching." *Harvard Educational Review* 24 (1954): 86–97.

————. "Teaching Machines." *Scientific American* (November 1961).

Smith, Bruce L. R. "Accountability and Independence in the Contract State." In *The Dilemma of Accountability in Modern Government: Independence vs. Control*, edited by Bruce L. R. Smith and D. C. Hague. New York: St. Martin's Press, 1971.

Smith, Robert G. *The Development of Training Objectives*. Washington, D.C.: George Washington University, Human Resources Research Office, 1961.

Stake, R. E. "The Countenance of Educational Evaluation." Mimeographed. Urbana, Ill.: University of Illinois, Center for Instructional Research and Curriculum Evaluation, 1966.

Stolurow, L. M. *Teaching by Machine*. Cooperative Research Monograph No. 6. U.S. Department of Health, Education, and Welfare. Washington, D.C.: U.S. Government Printing Office, 1961.

Strupp, H. H., and L. Luborsky, eds. *Research in Psychotherapy*. Washington, D.C.: American Psychological Association, 1962.

Suppes, Patrick. "The Uses of Computers in Education." *Scientific American* (September 1966): 206–221.

Talbert, Ray L. "A Learning Activity Package—What Is It?" *Educational Screen and Audiovisual Guide* 47 (January 1968): 20–21.

Thibaut, John W., and Harold H. Kelley. *The Social Psychology of Groups*. New York: Wiley and Sons, 1959.

Thomas, C. A. *Programmed Learning in Perspective*. Chicago: Educational Methods, 1961.

Thorndike, R. L. "Helping Teachers Use Tests." *Measurement in Education* 1 (1969).

Tucker, L. "Scales Minimizing the Importance of Reference Groups." In *Proceedings, Invitational Conference on Testing Problems*, pp. 22–28. Princeton, N. J.: Educational Testing Service, 1952.

Tyler, Ralph W. *Basic Principles of Curriculum Instruction*. Chicago: University of Chicago Press, 1950.

———. "The Curriculum: Then and Now." *Proceedings of the 1956 Invitational Conference on Testing Problems*. Princeton, N. J.: Educational Testing Service, 1957.

———. "Modern Aspects of Evaluation." *California Journal of Secondary Education* 29 (1954): 410–412.

Tyler, Ralph W. et al. *Perspectives in Curriculum Evaluation*. Chicago: Rand McNally, 1967.

Webb, Eugene J. et al. *Unobtrusive Measures: Nonreactive Research in the Social Sciences*. Chicago: Rand McNally, 1966.

Wickman, E. K. *Children's Behavior and Teachers' Attitudes*. New York: Commonwealth Fund, Division of Publications, 1928.

Wold, Herman O. "Causal Inference from Observational Data: A Review of Ends and Means." *Journal of the Royal Statistical Society* (London) 119 (1956): 28–50.

———. "La technique des modèles dans les sciences humaines." In *Sciences Humaines*. Rue de Millo, Monaco: Centre International d'Etude des Problèmes Humains, 1966.

Wood, A. D. *Test Construction*. Columbus, Ohio: Charles E. Merrill, 1961.

Wright, Sewall. "The Method of Path Coefficients." *Annals of Mathematical Statistics* 5 (1934): 161–215.

Yee, A. H., and N. L. Gage. "Techniques for Estimating the Source and Direction of Causal Influence in Panel Data." *Psychological Bulletin* 70 (1968): 115–126.